From the desk of
Vicki Escarra
President & CEO
312.641.6601
vescarra@secondharvest.org

America's
Second Harvest
The Nation's
Food Bank Network™

Hunger.

10649784

June 13th

Dear Bo —

Transformation is exciting & challenging —

So glad to have you with us as we continue on our journey—

Thanks for all you do & your leadership. V

Praise for *BIG CHANGE AT BEST BUY*

"Uniquely, *Big Change at Best Buy* views organizational change as a quantifiable business objective, critical to the success of any project. Further, it presents a detailed, systematic methodology for the accomplishment of transformational change and leadership's role in the process. These concepts were integral to Best Buy's success and are important for anyone in a position of leadership to understand."

Thomas C. Healy, President, Best Buy International

"With unvarnished candor and powerful insights that can only come from experience, Gibson and Billings tell a story of change at Best Buy that will strike a chord with most managers. This real-life story is about a straightforward approach tempered in action; it will leave an indelible imprint on the way you manage change."

Hubert Saint-Onge, CEO, Konverge and Know

"*Big Change at Best Buy* goes beyond providing a great case study. It shares lessons that can be applied in any hypergrowth situation."

Marshall Goldsmith, named by *Forbes* as one of five top executive coaches and by *Wall Street Journal* as a "Top 10" executive educator

"The combination of practical and effective change management tools and the Best Buy story makes this book accessible to people with a wide range of business experience. A powerful resource!"

Patricia Woolcock, Executive Director, The California Strategic Human Resource Partnership; Principal, Jackson Hole Group

"This book shows how Best Buy made strategy happen, and how you can as well. Its head, heart, and hands approach to change is powerful and practical, and should be in every change leader's repertoire of skills."

James Bandrowski, author of *Corporate Imagination*; President, Strategic Action Associates

Big Change at Best Buy

BIG
CHANGE AT
BEST BUY

*Working Through Hypergrowth
to Sustained Excellence*

ELIZABETH GIBSON AND ANDY BILLINGS

Davies-Black Publishing
Palo Alto, California

To the Best Buy CIT

Published by Davies-Black Publishing, a division of CPP, Inc., 3803 East Bayshore Road, Palo Alto, CA 94303; 800-624-1765.

Special discounts on bulk quantities of Davies-Black books are available to corporations, professional associations, and other organizations. For details, contact the Director of Marketing and Sales at Davies-Black Publishing; 650-691-9123; fax 650-623-9271.

Visit the Davies-Black Publishing Web site at www.daviesblack.com.

07 06 05 04 03   10 9 8 7 6 5 4 3 2 1
Printed in the United States of America

Library of Congress Cataloging-in-Publication Data
Gibson, Elizabeth
    Big change at Best Buy : working through hypergrowth to sustained excellence / Elizabeth Gibson and Andrew Billings.— 1st ed.
        p. cm.
    Includes index.
    ISBN 0-89106-176-2
    1. Best Buy (Firm)—Management. 2. Electronic industries—United States—Management—Case studies. 3. Retail trade—United States—Management—Case studies. 4. Chain stores—United States—Management—Case studies. 5. Organizational change—United States. 6. Industrial management—United States. 7. Corporate reorganizations—United States. 8. Personnel management—United States. I. Billings, Andrew. II. Title.

HD9696.A3 U554 2003
381'.4568383'0973—dc21

                                                                            2002034973
FIRST EDITION
First printing 2003

CONTENTS

PART 3: LASTING CHANGE
Making It Stick

FOREWORD

This book tells the story of the people and processes that helped turn Best Buy around at a pivotal time in its recent past. Since our beginning in the 1960s as a single store in Minneapolis, we at Best Buy have had a number of "near death" experiences. We are survivors, and we take pride in our ability to change and adapt. But the challenge we faced in 1997 was different. The change was deep and it was wide. In implementing this change, we learned not just business-changing lessons but also life-changing lessons.

As I read this account of what happened when we implemented systematic procedures throughout the retail stores, I was astounded at how far we've come. I'd forgotten how we thought, felt, and acted before the retail SOP (Standard Operating Platform) was implemented as the new foundation for managing all the procedures, processes, and operations in the stores. What surprised me the most was that it worked, and that it worked as quickly as it did. It violated all my notions of what it would take to reach such a scope and depth of change. I was also surprised at how many people were able to change enough to become more effective in their jobs. You *can* connect with them — which is why they were willing to do it.

I had a number of moments of personal reckoning. One was when I feared we couldn't implement the necessary changes and get the beneficial results. The fear was amplified when we got verbal compliance from the stores but no changes in actual behaviors. I visited stores the month after the initial introduction of the SOP. What I saw was that people were already drowning in their jobs while we (management) were asking them to do even more. The next blow fell when one of our change partners from RHR International told me we were lacking the leadership capacity to accomplish what we needed to do to survive, much less thrive. That was tough to hear, but necessary.

Thankfully, we had the humility and strength to hear the message and take action.

This was a make-or-break time for us—absolutely critical to the survival of our stores. And it was our second shot at it. When our change partners told us they thought they could apply the principles of the head, heart, and hands to effect the change, we were willing to take a chance with them. It paid off, big time.

The head, heart, and hands framework has permeated the organization and laid the foundation for our becoming more of a learning organization. The nucleus of the change effort and of the book is that you have to touch all three points—the head, heart, and hands; otherwise, you don't have enough there to be effective. I was amazed that people who'd worked with Best Buy for some time were able to adapt and enhance their skills significantly using this sometimes painful process.

Implementing the SOP gave us consistently high-quality store operations, which has helped us advertise things other than just price and items. We gained a sense of order—not rigidity—so that you could see skills where you couldn't see them before. It allowed people to build careers with wide skill sets and created new opportunities.

I'm a dedicated fan of history because it fascinates me, and I believe in learning from the past. This book describes a crucial part of the history of Best Buy, and I sincerely hope that we remember the lessons we learned and that others can learn from our experience.

Brad Anderson
Vice Chairman and CEO, Best Buy Co., Inc.

PREFACE

This is a book within a book; it tells two simultaneous stories. One is the real-life story about a team of people who gathered together to make major changes in a large company. The other is a recounting of a practical and (now) proven set of methods for implementing change. Rather than separate the two topics, we've woven them together in a tale that you can read in two ways: as a story that shares insights about how members of the team came to think about change, or as a practical study of change management that is richly illustrated by the example of Best Buy. Whatever your approach, each viewpoint complements the other. We believe you will find ideas to help you both cope with and lead change.

PART 1. INTRODUCING CHANGE: SETTING THE STAGE

Part 1 introduces you to Best Buy's history and sets the context for the story that follows.

Changing Times
In Chapter 1, you will see that when hypergrowth occurs, a company must face the possibility of making radical changes to adapt to its new size and needs. To succeed, the company must transform its culture and its processes into those that will be able to face the future successfully. Leaders must be aware of the conflict this creates with the "old" culture that fueled the growth. The shadow side of the old culture is its resistance to the new culture. The greater the company's initial success, the stronger the culture and the darker its shadow. Best Buy learned: never underestimate the power of the shadow.

The Map Is Not the Territory

In Chapter 2, we speak about the approach we took to managing change. A fundamental principle of all natural, living systems applies to organizations: left unchanged, business strategies and organizations inevitably decline. If you are not changing, you are dying. "Jump the curves" from decline to growth. Use a systemic approach that addresses the individual, team, and organizational learning needs of the organization. Though useful for coping with complexity, these frameworks for change leadership are simply maps and not the territory. We learned: don't confuse frameworks (models) with reality.

PART 2. IMPLEMENTING CHANGE: MAKING IT REAL

Part 2 describes methods for change and how the Best Buy change team confronted the massive challenges that were as wide as the company and as deep as the culture. This section focuses on the challenges of the change team as they play out in three human arenas: the head, the heart, and the hands. Chapters 4, 5, and 6 explore these three arenas. Chapters 7 and 8 describe the core skills that Best Buy change agents learned in order to implement change in the three arenas.

Head, Heart, and Hands—Three Arenas for Change

Chapter 3 shows how successful change requires attention to these three arenas. In addition, it describes how change progresses through three stages: (1) coming to grips with the problem, (2) working it through, and (3) making it stick (or maintaining momentum). To successfully implement change, you need to understand all three arenas and work through the three stages.

Using the Head to Change Mind-Set

The message of Chapter 4 is that deep change requires a new mind-set. You need fresh ways of seeing and interpreting your competitive environment and your company to successfully evolve. You must understand the rational-analytic reasons to change in order to dislodge your previously successful mind-set. You must think differently.

Using the Heart for Emotion and Motivation

In Chapter 5 you see that meaningful change engages deep emotions associated with letting go of the old and reaching for the new. To work through these challenging emotions, you must confront the costs of *not* changing and feel the benefits of changing. Answer the question, "What is in it for me?" This is the key to the heart. Though the heart can be mysterious, you can become comfortable working in this arena.

Using the Hands to Make Change Real

Chapter 6 explains why even with a new mind-set and readiness for change, you must yet master the new behaviors required by change. To "know what to do differently on Monday" is to create a powerful learning process. To make new behaviors stick, align them with new priorities for reward and recognition. New behaviors are the paychecks of change. Cash them.

Foundational Skills for Changing Head, Heart, and Hands

Chapter 7 describes these foundational skills: for the head, communicate openly and encouragingly by using active listening. For the heart, create opportunities for emotional venting, assist others to rebalance their gains versus losses, and realign rewards for new behaviors. For the hands, develop behavioral maps—detailed descriptions that show patterns of new behaviors. Follow up with opportunities to practice new behaviors with constructive feedback. An organization is only as durable as its foundation is strong. Attend to these basics.

Changing Yourself

In Chapter 8, you are reminded that there is no place you can hide from the need to change yourself. Only change agents who change themselves are effective. Apply the same tools for changing others to yourself. We learned to look at ourselves and say, "Get going!"

PART 3. LASTING CHANGE: MAKING IT STICK

Part 3 introduces a powerful tool called the Change Scorecard^{SM} that you can use to measure and mobilize change for the long term. And we reach the climax of our story, in which we reveal the results of the change effort at Best Buy.

Tools for Measuring Change

In Chapter 9, you learn that, yes, it's possible—no, it's *required*—to measure what is happening with regard to people's thinking, feelings, and behavior. Behaviorally anchored change scorecards provide the way to measure change. Build them to be reliable and valid—to measure what is important, not just what is easy to measure. People perform according to what gets measured and rewarded. Scorecard carefully selected behaviors that require mastery of critical elements of the change. What you can measure, you can change.

Measuring Change

The point of Chapter 10 is that what you measure is what changes. Measure only those central elements that require the presence of a broader constellation of changes. The construction of Change Scorecards forces everyone to be specific about what "good" looks like. Those who do the rating are under tremendous pressures to make the organization look good. You must build in protections for the rater and the scorecards to minimize the potential for distortion.

Scorecards, though powerful tools to measure progress and create accountability, are even more valuable for giving constructive feedback, increasing learning, and creating further change. Scorecards are powerful; aim them with care.

Sustained Change

In Chapter 11, you see that sustained change is both possible and profitable. Sustained change is demonstrated only over the course of years and is reflected in the business practices and language of the employees. It can be verified through multiple sources. You must learn to lead for sustained change. In this chapter, we look at where Best Buy is now and ask, What changes have been sustained? What now needs to change?

ACKNOWLEDGMENTS

As veterans in the change management arena, we experienced a growing uneasiness with what we and others in the field were accepting as success. We came to realize that it was not enough to implement change that creates an excited buzz, tweaks a few business processes, remodels some organizational architecture, and makes a quick pass at altering the culture—especially when the modifications occur in a time frame measured in months rather than years. Such changes don't stick and they don't pay off.

We are pleased to tell the story of a group of colleagues who, while setting out on what they thought would be a short walk to manage change, discovered the courage and the methods to undertake a multiyear journey in search of deep, sustained change. Ken Weller introduced us to the organization and the organization to us. Mike Keskey was willing to take a chance with us and then kept the journey going. We thank Brad Anderson and our Best Buy friends and partners for their willingness to share this story—both the successes and the setbacks.

We also thank the many other people who helped us tell this story. Our family and friends have coped with the absences and moods that accompany research and writing. RHR International has encouraged us at every step of the way, and we want to thank Al Parchem for his patience and encouragement. Dora Summers-Ewing continued with the change process at Best Buy and has supported us in innumerable ways. And Katie Carson, as editor, coordinator, and project manager, helped us create the book. The genius, wisdom, and humor of Jennifer Joss Bradley is woven into every concept in this book. We are grateful to these people and the many others who have helped us on the journey.

Elizabeth Gibson, Austin, Texas
Andy Billings, San Carlos, California
January 2003

ABOUT THE AUTHORS

As professional change agents and experts in individual and organizational effectiveness, we are uniquely qualified to write this book. Both of us began our careers with advanced academic training in human and organizational change. We both have proven track records in assisting large-scale organizational change. Working with top management support at Best Buy over a number of years, we applied a comprehensive approach to change. We learned as much as did our client. Our learning was less about the concepts of change than about how best to organize and communicate these concepts in ways that capture the hearts and minds of frontline managers.

Elizabeth Gibson, Ph.D.

Elizabeth Gibson is coauthor of *A Practical Guide to Knowledge Acquisition*, a book that focuses on identifying and capturing the tacit knowledge used in building expert systems. After receiving her B.A. degree at Macalester College in St. Paul, Minnesota, She was a steelworker in an iron-mining operation in northern Minnesota. She then went on to earn her M.A. degree at San Francisco State University and her Ph.D. degree in psychology at Stanford University.

Gibson worked in the high-tech world of Silicon Valley, first as a knowledge engineer with Teknowledge, Inc., a firm that builds expert systems, and then as head of the training department at ParcPlace Systems, an object-oriented software company spun off from Xerox Parc Research Center. At ParcPlace, she initiated the development of an object-oriented systems analysis methodology, called Object Behavior Analysis. In both organizations, she contributed to organizational learning, as well as to a positive bottom line.

Gibson joined RHR International in 1991. During her tenure at RHR, she has worked with both public and private sectors in retail, international marketing and trading, advertising, entertainment, manufacturing, financial services, health care, and municipal governments. She has designed and implemented programs for a wide range of individual leadership, team, and organization development initiatives. The July–August 1999 issue of *Fast Company* magazine featured an interview with Gibson that highlighted her work with senior executives. In 2000, Gibson and Dr. Dora Summers-Ewing founded KnoWorks®, a new division of RHR International that specializes in large-scale organizational change, learning, and knowledge management projects.

Beginning in 1997, Gibson led an RHR team in partnering with Best Buy in a highly successful, large-scale change implementation effort. At that time Best Buy had more than 30,000 employees and more than 270 stores nationwide. The company had made only a million dollars in profit on sales of more than five billion, and the stock price had fallen to the single digits. The change implementation effort used a joint team of nine Best Buy managers, who worked as full-time change agents, and their RHR partners. The team developed a set of scorecards for measuring the state and progress of the change effort. The Change Implementation Scorecards were also used to show what kinds of problems were occurring where, and they provided the feedback necessary for learning. Between January 1997 and January 2000, Best Buy's stock price increased by more than 1,000 percent. Executives and industry pundits give credit to the improvement in store operations and leadership practices for a significant portion of Best Buy's recent success.

From that highly successful initiative grew the effort to develop Best Buy as a learning organization. The executive committee of Best Buy engaged Gibson and RHR in a massive, multiyear effort to increase the quality and amount of individual, team, and organizational learning at Best Buy.

Andy Billings, Ph.D.

Andy Billings gained his first change management and retail experience as a high school student working on the floor at an independent grocery store in Connecticut that was fighting for its life against the growing power of large grocery chains. Much later, he once again found himself back in retail as a consultant to several of the country's largest retailers.

Billings earned a Ph.D. degree in psychology and consulting from the University of Vermont. He continued his academic tour at Stanford University and published more than fifty articles on stress, health, and coping with change. While at Stanford, he began consulting in the San Francisco Bay Area. Billings has both academic and applied training in organizational effectiveness that provides a base of knowledge on leading change, which, after all, is the key to behavioral change.

Moving to the business world, Billings joined the well-regarded firm RHR International, a management consulting firm focusing on leadership development and organizational change. In time he became the managing director of the San Francisco Bay Area office. In his fifteen-plus years as a management consultant, Billings worked with a diverse range of clients, including Hughes Electronics, McCormick and Company, Transamerica, Nikon, Steelcase, technology companies in Silicon Valley, and a number of privately held companies. During his management consulting years, he wrote several articles for *Executive Insights* and other business publications.

In the retail sector, Billings consulted with Lucky Stores, the Good Guys, and American Stores (recently acquired by Albertsons), among others. Working with Elizabeth Gibson and Best Buy, he helped structure and manage the multiyear organizational change assignment described in this book. This work grew into overseeing several large client-consultant change teams addressing business process issues, organizational structure, and leadership dimensions.

Billings is vice president of Organizational Development for Electronic Arts, the largest global publisher of interactive software. He continues to apply the concepts of this book to increasing the capacity of Electronic Arts to manage change in the hypergrowth intersection of technology and entertainment. He is on the board of a privately held agribusiness and retailer, the Rod McLellan Company, and is chairman of the board of the California Strategic Human Resources Partnership, an organization for HR executives.

INTRODUCING CHANGE

SETTING THE STAGE

1

Changing Times

ON THE EDGE

Best Buy Co., Inc., in 1996 was an enormous, sprawling company with more than 270 huge stores across the United States. In its quest to be the largest consumer electronics retailer in the country, Best Buy was spreading its name across the states. Consumer electronics, which includes everything from the routine (VCRs, TVs, music CDs, and washing machines) to the complex and sophisticated (cellular phones, PCs, and digital cameras), is a brutal business. To make it into the top three U.S. companies requires a lot of cash, thousands of employees, and the nerve to survive on margins so thin that profits come from peripheral products and services rather than product sales. Best Buy was a "go for broke," brawling, entrepreneurial maverick. It opened stores and took on new product lines with confidence and a sense of fun, but without a lot of thought about whether it could sustain the burst of sales and the quick sense of success that came with the grand openings of new stores every week.

And it nearly sank. The brighter the light, the darker the shadows. The Best Buy culture, with its confidence and swagger, had a dark side—its cockiness, its extreme competitiveness, and its disabling style of letting each part of the company function as independently as possible, with little cross-functional collaboration. Though high on energy and courage, Best Buy lacked the ability to consistently deliver a quality customer experience and the right amounts of merchandise in its hundreds of stores—and to make a profit while expanding at a frenetic pace. Change was needed. New operating procedures, developed at high cost, were introduced as the solution. But the new ways of working didn't work. Best Buy's stock fell to an all-time low of $8.50 a share in February 1997. Senior management, the leaders of the culture—both at its best and its worst—came to a crisis point. Own your shadow or it will own you. These leaders needed to achieve deep, sustained change in the soul of their company. This is the story of their work to transform Best Buy.

THE INTERNAL LIMITS TO HYPERGROWTH

It was a midwestern tornado that triggered the hypergrowth cycle of the company. In 1966 Dick Schulze and a partner founded Sound of Music, a St. Paul, Minnesota, home- and car-stereo store—a single-store company like so many in the industry. Dick began to open new stores and to reach beyond his youthful male clientele by adding appliances and VCRs to his product line to create a wider and more affluent customer base. But in 1981, a tornado struck, severely damaging his most successful store. Trying to make the most of a parking lot "tornado sale" inventory sell-off, Dick put out some precious cash for advertising. The sale was a huge success. The formula seemed to be based on an immense amount of inventory, low prices, and lots of advertising.

The company changed its name to Best Buy and began building and opening "superstores." Dick Schulze became the CEO. By 1985 the company had gone public with eleven stores and in the next four years grew at a phenomenal pace to more than forty superstores. The VCR became a "must have" item that fueled overall growth in the consumer electronics category. Bigger was better—with new Best Buy stores growing both in number and square footage. Concept 1, Concept 2, and Concept 3 store formats were scaled toward a mass merchant "box store" for consumer electronics and appliances. The company, working with consumer feedback and trying to cut costs, began eliminating commissioned sales representatives from the selling floor. This was a major break from Best Buy's competitors. Commissioned salespeople were as much a part of consumer electronics as they were of car retailing. Though a few suppliers pulled their products out of Best Buy, thinking there would not be enough sales staff support for their product, the change stuck. The company added new product lines, information kiosks, and "virtual car" and surround sound showrooms. The stores were big but fun. And the Best Buy culture took a major step up in its confidence and sense that it could make the smartest decisions in the industry.

Best Buy was well into its hypergrowth stage. From 1991 to 1995, Best Buy opened 212 stores—that's an average of more than 42 stores per year! This stage often occurs once the retail concept and store format have been proven locally. Management then pursues expansion nationally. As happens to many companies, Best Buy had handled the initial part of its growth successfully. But with the rapid expansion, Best Buy outran its capacity to manage further growth while remaining profitable. One of the retail executives analyzed the situation and built the case for change. He had seen the problem at close range and had run the spreadsheets on the stores. But perhaps more important, all of the retail executives had spent weeks in the market flying from store to store.

Typically, a new Best Buy store would have a grand opening and initially would be successful (in terms of customer traffic and revenue) until the store management team, now needed elsewhere, moved on to a new store, often within the next six to twelve months. Then the store declined or even went into the red. Why? The customers weren't experiencing consistency in the stores, and operational excellence was not "baked into" the practices of the store. Customer experience seriously deteriorated when the opening team departed for the next town, and with a large number of stores in the post–grand opening stage, divisional profits, naturally, went south. Though expanding, the company was not achieving adequate profitability. The expansion strategy reached a crisis stage.

In fiscal year 1996, Best Buy earned $7.2 billion in revenues and had 251 stores and 33,500 employees. Its net profit was 0.70 percent. Although it was the market leader in revenues, it was weak in profitability. In comparison, Circuit City had $7.0 billion in revenues, 383 stores, and 36,400 employees—and more than twice the net profitability, 2.6 percent. Yes, this retailing category operates with high cash flow and low margins, but it's an unforgiving marketplace in which to begin maneuvering huge corporations. By 1997 Best Buy profitability went nearly to zero.

Each store and its operations reflected the current store manager. Best Buy called them "general managers" (GMs), and for good reason. They commanded mini-empires that generated an average of $30 million in revenues per year as much as a small company. Store GMs had little structure or proven practices to apply. Interestingly, GMs were generally happy with the independence and the do-what-it-takes attitude. The lack of systematic processes, however, made it difficult for people to figure out how to "win." Not everyone loved it. Since there weren't any set processes or procedures, the lack of consistency ate up people's time and energy.

Even the approach to change needed to change. Management practices and culture had been developed for rapid growth but not for sustained profitability. What once worked in a smaller organization was losing more of its effectiveness every day. Organizational and operating changes were usually handled with firm directives from corporate headquarters and the expectation that new procedures would be successfully implemented. The "top down" approach had worked in a simpler organization and in earlier times when major changes came only periodically. Now many changes, major in scope, needed to be implemented more frequently. There was no method to integrate all the directives from above or for the corporate functions, such as visual merchandising, marketing, retail operations, and logistics, to make reality-based decisions for individual stores. As each functional division pushed its changes out to stores, the inevitable collisions between initiatives occurred. It is not surprising that this approach arose out of the maverick, anything goes, improvisational culture that had created such a huge success.

A CALL FOR CHANGE

Best Buy was operating in the dog-eat-dog competitive world of consumer electronics, one of the toughest retail arenas, where survival is the primary goal. Quick fixes and fast change are seductively attractive—but not sustained change. Quick fixes, however, don't last. Best Buy needed to cure its addiction to the fast, nonsystematic, adrenaline-based ways of operating that had helped it grow. It needed to become grounded in deeper, systematic, and integrative changes, which could help the company sustain great results.

The First Rollout of the SOP

As profitability continued to decline, it was clear that trouble was brewing. In October 1996, Best Buy responded by introducing yet another large-scale change—the Retail Simplification Plan. This fix was directed at the store operations that had been diagnosed as key areas for improvement. In late 1995 and early 1996, the company had begun developing a comprehensive yet straightforward set of practices to revise store operations and management to improve customer experience and to return the stores to profitable, effective operations. The plan was called the "SOP." Most thought it meant "standard operating procedures"—new ways of working in hundreds of different ways throughout the organization as the change process was launched. The "P" actually meant "platform," referring to the totality and systemic nature of the change. The platform was the way to manage all the different procedures, processes, and operations in the stores. The platform was the foundation on which they all needed to rely.

Developed by a premier consulting firm, the SOP covered almost every aspect of store operations—from the way merchandise arrived at the receiving docks to the checkout procedures followed by cashiers. Although on paper the SOP looked like a rational solution, there was nothing new in the way the change was being introduced. And the SOP, by its nature, was contrary to the culture of the stores. A "certification checklist" was developed to confirm that store employees were implementing the processes successfully. Another collision was coming—between mavericks and collaborators, between chaos and discipline.

It's Not Working

It soon became clear that the SOP was not taking hold the way it needed to. In November 1996, a GM from Houston described his experiences. "This October was my worst month at Best Buy! Three major initiatives rolled out at the same time, with no consideration of timing—how the initiatives interacted with or affected one another. There was no thought by the guys at corporate about the demands on my store management and staff. There was a total breakdown in implementation!"

One of the problems caused by the SOP solution was that the emphasis on clarifying the specific responsibilities of each function (or discipline) in the stores, such as merchandising (keeping the store well stocked), sales, and so on, was undermining cross-functional teamwork. The Houston GM continued, "This SOP stuff is a mess! Our teams are not working together. Know what bothers me the most? No one in management seems to be trying to think through the big-picture issues." This was the perception in the field, although senior management was trying to pay attention to as many big issues as they could identify.

Sustained change requires that the change reach deeply into the company culture, which controls the current practices and the potential readiness for transformation. The culture of Best Buy was energetic and fast paced, and decisions were often made with little long-term thinking. It needed a systems-oriented culture that could think ahead and encourage collaboration among different parts of the company. Such a culture wasn't nearly as attractive and "cool" as the one that existed.

The quest was for a change in the culture and in the day-to-day practices of the more than 30,000 Best Buy employees working in the retail and operations divisions. And the change needed to be introduced in ways that could be integrated with all the other initiatives taking place in a large, complex national retail organization. To put it into a few words, the contradictory cry was: "Help! Don't slow me down!" But of course, if you're moving in the wrong direction, you'll just reach a dead end faster.

One of the retail executives used this analogy: "It's like driving down the road in your favorite car—say, a VW bug. You're driving fast and you come to a corner in the road and just skid around it. When you come to the next corner, you skid off the road. You get back on the road. At the next corner, you have a team of people waiting for you— you've anticipated that you're going to skid off the road. They get the car back on the road. We had heroics! But we didn't take the time to fix the design of the road or the design of the car."

A fast-growing company will change its culture and its practices only if it can see it will create something that is rewarding and satisfying to its members. There will be resistance to change from those who thrive in the old environment that champions their quick, reactive style and ability to act on their own. Those who propose change will even be seen as wrong-headed at best and, at worst, as having questionable integrity and values. The process requires changes in the way people think, the way they feel and are motivated, and the way they act and run the business.

Getting the Right Answers

When the results of the scoring on the certification checklist came back a few months later, all stores passed! But when retail executives made visits to the stores, it was clear to them that there had been no change at all—no successful changes. Managers and employees had been coached on how to answer the certification checklists to get "the right answers."

On the store floor, a regional operations manager asked an employee a standard question about the SOP and how results were to be obtained. But the question was subtly altered to elicit a different answer, and out came the memorized answer to the expected question—exactly the opposite of the correct answer to the revised question. "Prepped" employees were giving memorized answers to the evaluators. The employees could give "right" answers, but they did not understand the SOP at a deeper level. And certainly they were not engaging in the necessary new behaviors. A district manager said, "We were handed a big book and told to implement it. There was only 44 percent true compliance, even though all the stores passed the certification checklist with a score of at least 90 percent. What was the issue? Each level of management—the retail executives, regional managers (RMs), and district managers (DMs)—thought the plan didn't apply to them. There needed to be real understanding and buy-in from leadership before there could be buy-in in the field."

Rather than reflecting a lack of personal integrity, this difference between "official" vs. real results reflected how strongly the Best Buy culture affected people's thinking. First, it was not clear to managers why the new processes were in place, nor did they see the importance to the company of using similar processes in all the stores. And managers were rewarded for doing whatever it took to get results. Failure to pass a certification checklist was so culturally unacceptable that people felt compelled to look good regardless of the reality. The SOP was therefore "officially" implemented but was clearly not the reality. Even if everyone agreed that the SOP was a great solution, there was no agreement as to how to actually get the SOP to happen.

STEPPING UP TO THE CHANGE

It was a January night in 1997. The retail executives were wrestling with the reality that the solution they had devised to fix the underlying problems in the stores was floundering. They began to perceive that the expansion of stores and the development of the field management team were leading to neither sustainable operating excellence nor profits. The SOP, upon which they had been basing their plans for improvement, was simply not working the way it needed to, despite its promise and performance in several test stores. Store management was not applying the voluminously documented manual of new store operating procedures—the development of which had involved extensive effort and multimillion-dollar resources. People were just not implementing the changes. What management knew was critical to Best Buy's success was stalled. In retrospect, one of the retail executives said, "We didn't fully understand the complexity of behavioral change and how much time it takes to implement."

A consultant was on hand for a meeting with the retail executives on talent selection and development. Clearly, though, the two executives were distracted and not in the mood to talk about those topics. One of them expressed his frustration: "I don't get it. The new SOP just makes sense. Why aren't they [the people in the stores] using it? It's to their advantage—we designed it to make their lives easier; in fact, they designed it. What the hell are they doing?" The retail executives were on the hook for the successful implementation of the SOP in the field.

When the consultant heard this, she remembered hearing alarms go off in November and December, when she was in the field. Store managers had told her that the SOP wasn't working and that they would only superficially support it. They had given several reasons why, and one in particular had stuck in her memory. It was the store GM in Houston who had expressed his concern: "The SOP introduced new roles and teams in the store's structure. The people who landed on the sales team were seen as the 'winners' and the people who landed on the merchandising team were seen as the 'losers.' The teamwork across the store is breaking down, people are taking sides, and the antagonism keeps growing."

The consultant pushed deeper. "How did you introduce the SOP to the stores and help them work through the changes?" After hearing about the rollout of the SOP, which happened at the same time the stores were gearing up for the holiday season and at the same time that marketing had introduced a special promotion in the stores, which was labor intensive, she more fully understood the problem. "Think about it. If this were a cartoon you'd have the drawing but no animation. It's a still life. They can't see how to fit it into their everyday work routines."

"Changing behavior is one of the hardest things for people to do, but it can be done." The consultant then described how successfully changing behavior requires working through how people think about the change (head), how they feel about the change (heart), and how they learn to do things the new way (hands). And, she explained, change is not an event but a process that unfolds over time. First, people have to come to grips with the need to change and what the changes actually mean; then they have to work through the changes, piece by piece; and finally, they have to guard against sliding back to the old ways. "To make the change stick," she said, "to sustain it, takes a lot of skill and hard work."

For a company such as Best Buy, which operated in such a free-form and back-of-the-envelope manner, a simple framework fit. The consultant's words had the ring of authority about what it takes to implement and sustain effective change. The "map" she described would guide the retail executives through these challenges. They acknowledged that they were experts in many things, but not in implementing effective change. These executives were experienced and confident enough to partner with others who had the relevant knowledge and experience that they didn't have. Partnering with people who specialized in changing people's behavior made sense. The meeting ended with an agreement that the consultant would develop a proposal for implementing the SOP in a way that would lead to sustained change.

As you might imagine, there was skepticism about the consultants. "Are they able to push us beyond our own resistances and blind spots?" asked Brad Anderson, Best Buy's vice chairman of the board and chief executive officer (who was president and COO at the time), acutely aware of the need for change. "But what about these consultants?" he asked the retail executives. "Are they tough enough to withstand everything our people and culture will throw at them? We've seen it kill off other outsiders before." One of the executives had worked with the consultants before and gave his honest opinion. "This will be the biggest challenge they have ever taken on. But I know these people; they will do whatever it takes to help us succeed."

"Well," said the other executive, "What are our alternatives?" None of the other options looked viable. So the partnership began.

One of the retail executives was a field-tested veteran of Best Buy with a string of proven successes in the Midwest region where the company began. He was a tough, skeptical pragmatist. The executive for the other half of the retail division was a champion of many controversial ideas who excelled in tough love. He could be hard on people who didn't perform or see the same need to perform that he did, but he was willing to invest in developing those people he did believe in or who proved themselves to him. Both retail executives were bringing ideas of change to a reluctant audience.

THE BRIGHTER THE LIGHT, THE DARKER THE SHADOWS

The stronger the culture, the harder the change. Super-competitive mavericks would have to become collaborative systems thinkers. The Best Buy culture, with its entrepreneurial, can-do attitude, had a dark side: its intense competitiveness and a sense of brash confidence. At its worst, it swaggered and was even arrogant with its success. The competitiveness was directed as much internally, at each other, as it was directed externally, outside the company. The independence granted to each part of the company allowed every department to slip out of cross-functional collaboration. They didn't have to factor in the complexities of cross-boundary integration. The culture also resisted becoming more disciplined and systems oriented. A disciplined and systems-oriented approach was seen as weaker, softer, and less fun.

Comments from the most insightful managers give a flavor of the Best Buy culture at that time.

- "We believe that we have already achieved success. We have an aura of invincibility."
- "We totally disregard 'how' you get results, how you get there. In fact, the 'cowboys' are the heroes."
- "Everyone is happy to work within his own silo. There's no value seen in partnering. We have a 'Superman' perspective that we can do anything in twenty minutes, without putting a lot of effort into thinking about it. We get things done through brute force — pushing things through."
- "Never share a best practice with another store or district. You need to win on your own and not through collaboration."

Looking back, a former store GM described the culture as being like the volume on a stereo: "If it's turned down too soft, you can't hear it. And if it's turned up too loud, it blasts you. Messages like 'win at all costs,' 'drive for results,' 'do whatever it takes,' and 'do it on your own' are not bad, but the volume on those messages was turned up way too high. Parts of the culture got overused; the volume control was out of whack."

An annoyed manager said, "We are running a multibillion-dollar business like it was a music store in Minneapolis."

And there was a corporate vs. retail tension. Each side felt the problems lay with the other. The field was seen as weak because it could not implement the multiple, uncoordinated, often conflicting initiatives. But because the corporate departments didn't have to coordinate among themselves, they sent out directives and initiatives without really understanding the impact of what they were asking for.

Here's an example. The marketing department elected to have specials in the Sunday newspaper inserts that would require extensive reconfiguration of displays in the stores. This seemed like something the stores should easily be able to implement (if they weren't so inept!). Meanwhile, the labor hours gurus in operations had analyzed the staffing of the stores and had cut back on the labor budget. So the store managers didn't have the money to pay people to reset the store to support the advertising campaign unless they paid overtime. But if they paid overtime, they would be criticized for going over their budget.

It was easier to blame the hectic nature of stores' operations than to look at the systemic issues. As the stores and the field started getting their acts together, their improved performance put a lot of pressure on the corporate departments to become more efficient and to coordinate with one another.

At a divisional offsite, the general, district, and regional managers worked on improving themselves in a number of skills, one of which was time management. During a break in the meeting to play golf, one of the GMs said, "I don't know that learning time management is going to help me or any of us GMs. Maybe it will help some who haven't had good time management skills in the past, but I have, and I think that I still do. I think it's out of our hands. The amount of information we get from corporate headquarters on a daily and weekly basis is huge. I'm pretty efficient and I do think that paying attention to that communication is important, so I try to stay up with it, but I simply can't. It's impossible."

The GM was on a roll now. "Our departments just won't talk to each other. They seem to have no clue. They think they have a great idea and just take off without getting us involved. And it bombs out here in the field because we are just not prepared to put it into place. Things like projects in logistics and loss prevention that are critical to this new SOP stuff—we really need them. They just don't seem to realize we should act like we are part of the same company!"

The culture demanded top results, not explanations. It was acceptable to get results even if they were not sustainable. Best Buy measured many, many aspects of the business and was ceaselessly demanding—even though many targets were impossible. Acknowledging imperfection might give room for lower accountability and reduced pressure for results. There seemed to be little interest and even less time to more deeply understand the obstacles to higher performance that were built into the operating environment.

The SOP, at least to the corporate planners and senior executives, was an elegant process that could be easily implemented. Unprepared for the complexities of implementation, the company approached the change from a mechanical mind-set. The solution was designed so that all elements of the store should come together flawlessly, like a perfectly crafted machine. There was no acknowledgment of the dynamic and nonlinear human component involved. The assumption was that employees would simply learn and apply the rationally superior practices, and the process improvements would be quickly put into practice.

LOOKING GOOD MATTERS MOST

Best Buy had climbed to its position in 1996 with an almost hyperactive energy. The sense of urgency that pervaded the company was given much more attention, value, and recognition than planning or design. "Ready, fire, aim," was a phrase used as both praise and concern by many. Best Buy's action orientation was the opposite of "analysis paralysis."

With this brash confidence came a need to look good and to demonstrate that results were, in fact, happening. Best Buy had emphasized checklists and measuring operational activities. A common saying was "Winners keep score." The culture supported a deep belief that the only way to get results was to inspect and reward or punish behavior based on these measurements. If there are winners, there must be losers. The either/or mentality that existed didn't even consider the possibility of both/and. The culture tended to operate blindly, without regard to systems issues such as unintended or delayed consequences or side effects.

One unintended side effect was score inflation. This was seen in many areas but was exemplified by employee performance reviews. Managers seldom gave direct reports less than a perfect score and offered little constructive feedback. People were fired when they didn't produce over a period of time, but they hadn't been coached and counseled about their need to improve. A major example of score inflation was the 90 percent score achieved by all the stores on the Retail Simplification Certification checklist. The high scores weren't due only to people learning the answers by rote; they also occurred because the DMs did the scoring of their own stores. But the scoring was not all intentionally false; people really had no notion of what "good" should look like.

The culture put pressure on its employees and managers to conform as much as perform. To look good on scorecards and other measures was a priority. Many of the operational measures suffered from score inflation—the need to look good was strong enough to affect "objective" indicators of performance. This inflation, of course, came at the cost of sacrificing any reality testing of the company, and the inflation was worst in stores where performance was most in need of improvement. The company was like a smoker with emphysema lying to his doctor about the number of cigarettes he was still smoking each day.

TEAMING UP FOR CHANGE

After numerous discussions and proposals, Best Buy management decided to commit a set of dedicated, internal change agents to a large-scale change process. This group became known as the Change Implementation Team (CIT) and was staffed with nine people from the front lines (seven were store GMs). This was a serious commitment of people. The consultants had asked that the team members have a high potential for creating sustained change (but later discovered that other, hidden criteria had contributed to the selection of some individuals). As one executive later put it, "The CIT members need to be the people the company can't afford to give you." The selection criteria were developed with a process we call a Profile of Success. We wanted the CIT members to be successful at

- Championing the SOP and its benefits
- Leading change within Best Buy
- Operating with a good sense of the big picture
- Influencing others without having direct authority over them
- Being flexible to lead, support, or follow as the situation demanded

The CIT began meeting in April 1997. To establish a shared vision of the future, each team member was given a mock-up of a magazine cover and feature article for **Destiny** (to look as if it were a major business publication) that had been created by one of the consultants (see

Figures 1 and 2). The team had its first dinner together in an Italian restaurant near the Eden Prairie headquarters offices. There was a lot of nervous joking and laughter that evening, perhaps in response to the uncertainty, excitement, and anticipation team members were experiencing as they tried to grasp the enormity of the challenge before them. Some thought the CIT assignment might be a stepping-stone. They had left their jobs for a year and knew they would likely not be returning to their original positions.

One of the CIT members summed up the team's initial reaction: "For the team, the mock-ups of the *Destiny* magazine cover and article were really compelling, and what was said in the article seemed so unachievable. That had a real impact on me and the team." The reality was tough. Another first-year CIT member remembered, "It was our first visit to Eden Prairie. One of the retail executives told us, 'We announced earnings of only $1.7 million in profit for 1996 for $7 billion in revenues.' I was worried that we were going out of business unless we could improve the way we did things."

CIT Members

Nine diverse members made up the CIT. We give a brief profile of four of these people and follow them through the story. Names have been changed for all members.

Melanie

Melanie was a hard-driving, intense woman fueled by a desire to make an impact with her energy and direct influence. She easily mastered the details of the SOP. Though one of the most conceptual thinkers on the team, Melanie learned by personal experience. Given her impatience and fast pace, her best teachers were her mistakes, and she rarely made the same mistake twice. She was gritty in her resolve and demeanor and had a sharp-edged, sometimes cynical sense of humor. She was proud of her pace and could wear out her companions with her very early start in the morning, feeding stops at vending machines, and dozens of conversations with people in the stores before calling it a night after the stores closed, well past most people's bedtime. She was quick to pick a path forward and was direct and bold in her interactions with others. She loved speed, results, and autonomy but could also see the need to become a role model who influenced others through her ideas rather than her intensity.

Figure 1

Cover Story: How Best Buy Navigated the Waters of Change & Landed Its New Operating Platform

DESTINY

May 1998

Volume 26, #8

BEST BUY®

Best Buy: Provides the Best Customer Experience

Figure 2

From Chaos to Discipline: How Best Buy Changed

Best Buy Company has overcome its growing pains to achieve what few large corporations have—the transition from creative chaos driven by recent explosive growth to a systematic and disciplined organization. The complexities of operating a large, growing corporation, coupled with declining profits, prompted Best Buy management to conduct a self-analysis. The outcome was a systematic operating platform, intended to drive efficient, consistent operations across the organization. The result is what some customers have called "The ultimate shopping experience."

How did Best Buy do it? By focusing change on its customers' needs. As one change leader noted, "The customer experience is key! That's where the rubber meets

"The result is what some customers have called "The ultimate shopping experience."

the road." Best Buy implemented its new operating platform on a solid foundation—a corporate culture driven by energy and high performance.

Who made it happen? Everyone involved in store operations was mobilized in the effort. Line managers and employees. Regional and district managers. Senior executives assembled a team of talented managers with line experience to lead the process. They call it their Change Implementation Team (CIT). The CIT guided the transition with the benefit of a side-by-side partnership with RHR International, a consulting firm of management psychologists who are experts in human change technology. By engaging RHR to coach and develop

each member of the CIT, Best Buy invested in its future leadership competency. The CIT is now equipped to help develop the management of Best Buy to lead future change successfully.

Did it work? The project is redefining successful change management in corporate America. With a reaffirmed commitment to their customers, Best Buy appears capable of sustained growth and profitability. One customer remarked, "Best Buy is the only place I shop for electronics, software, and CDs. No other store has such a dedicated team of people serving you. I compare all other retailers with Best Buy."

Best Buy understands, perhaps better than anyone, that today's success can be fleeting in a volatile marketplace. To insure that yesterday's success translates into tomorrow's growth, Best Buy has developed leaders and employees who seek to continuously improve and exceed customer expectations. The Best Buy of tomorrow pro-

"Best Buy is the only place I shop for electronics, software, and CDs."

mises to have the next generation of service leaders, as the corporate culture shifts from chaotic to disciplined. So when you visit a Best Buy store, you will find employees committed to ensuring you walk away delighted. Now that Best Buy has landed its new operating platform, it will apply the lesson learned to create continuous improvement. This story is only the beginning. Continuing growth and profitability is imminent as disciplined, customer-centered efforts, and newly equipped leaders, now drive Best Buy's success.

Chad

Chad was the analyst and the deepest into details of anyone on the team. He always wanted to know, How are we going to do this? and insisted on developing a well-thought-out plan. Melanie and Chad were very different and had little appreciation for each other, at least at first. Chad put a premium on being accurate, complete, and delivering on his commitments. In another life, he was probably a Swiss watchmaker. He had extremely high standards for himself and high expectations of the senior leaders of Best Buy. He was focused on the concrete steps of how to implement the SOP. Thinking in broader, conceptual terms about the underlying processes and culture seemed to him to have little payoff. Chad appeared tentative and felt nervous and awkward when dealing with those more senior than he who wanted ideas and plans without the analysis he depended on. Confronting others took a huge amount of energy for him. To convince others of his value, Chad used his energy and drive to work hard and get things accomplished.

Tom

Tom was different and enjoyed letting you know it. He was lively and offbeat. Many of those in consumer electronics first went to work in music stores because they were musicians trying to make a living close to what they loved. Tom had been a rock-and-roll musician and writer before getting into retail management. He was ambitious and looking to step up in his career. He had an infectious level of enthusiasm and appreciated recognition. His ideas came out in declarative, colorful riffs performed at turned-up volume. He was charming and intense. Underneath, he was much more sensitive than most people realized. He also had a strategic mind-set not often seen in Best Buy in those days, and he naturally thought in terms of systems. He was always engaging and sometimes irreverent and challenging, but he was certainly more than show, with a strong will and consistent delivery of results as a store GM. Most of his leadership skills were based on being a manager where the GM was king. The CIT world of influencing without formal authority was new territory for him.

Charles

Charles wanted to be number one. He was a competitor 100 percent of the time. He was a great salesperson and always pushed his stores to have the highest sales revenues. He drew energy from being in front of audiences and promoting the company and his stores—and himself. He had natural talent as a retailer and a manager. He was a smooth talker and an accomplished persuader. He was decisive and did not put much emphasis on coordination with other elements of the organization. If he could have finessed more collaboration with his peers, he would have been rated as most charismatic on the team. The other members did not know whether to feel disrespected, because he did not see them as candidates for the position of leader of the group, or to take bets on the outcome.

Real Versus Ideal

The CIT was not everything it needed to be. The participants requested by the consultants were not all put on the program. Members were nominated by the RM from each region and were interviewed by the consultants. During the interview cycle, a few of the nominees turned out to be low performers that RMs were looking to park somewhere. The retail executives turned these nominees back. Others turned out to be simply average performers who had been championed through the "old boy" network. Part of the deal for committing this group of people for a year was not only implementing the SOP but also accelerating the development of the team members themselves. Fortunately, mixed into the team were some true rising stars. A successful executive who was a regional manager at the time said, "I was a fairly new RM. When I first heard about the SOP change initiative, I thought that it was just another thing being thrown against the wall. I was raised in the Best Buy environment, where you were rewarded for being a cowboy. I thought, 'It sounds like a neat thing they could do, but it has nothing to do with me.' The first CIT member I appointed was not an ace. I didn't understand how powerful the position could be. For the second generation of CIT members, I appointed someone very different and very talented."

STARTING OUT

The team began with little sophistication or experience in managing large-scale change. And members lacked confidence in asserting themselves with upper management. The team lurched off to a start with misgivings on the part of the consultants, and the members were certainly skeptical of the consultants. But everyone was also enthusiastic about helping the company change—and ready to make the sacrifices of extended overnight travel, long hours, and lack of appreciation (sometimes even skepticism and rejection) from their colleagues.

The CIT needed to learn some complex and delicate skills. For instance, the CIT would need to evaluate and give candid feedback to members of regional management—their superiors. They had never been in positions of such authority. Outside the team, they would not have acted in such a candid yet "insubordinate" manner. And they wanted to become individual heroes, which came as no surprise, given the culture. Teamwork, collaboration, and recognition were new and unsettling ways of working.

Many, perhaps most, of the team members had not been tested on a highly challenging assignment. The initial sessions of the team were trying. The members didn't work well together. Many of the members had previously succeeded based on asserting their personalities and by "chest thumping." The initial meetings involved a lot more talking than listening. What one CIT member remembers most is going through stages of team formation: "Forming, storming, and norming. We didn't even know how to meet at first. We had no idea what we were up against. We were good retail people, but there was lots of debating and positioning."

The team lacked the substance, professionalism, and direction to directly report to the retail executives. Questions from these executives triggered fear reactions on the team's part or energetic soapbox performances and grandstanding. As an interim solution, the CIT members received their day-to-day direction from the lead consultants, who acted as a buffer. This bought some time for the CIT members to develop. Quickly, the CIT improved to the point that they became direct spokespeople to senior management. Teamwork improved to the point that the group became a self-managing team.

Members of the team hit a turning point when they recognized that they must first change themselves before they could become fully effective as change agents. As a team, they could maintain their credibility and effectiveness. If they operated as individuals (in the Best Buy way) they would be picked off and neutralized. This turning point was different for each individual, and some learned the lesson more deeply than others did.

Learning to work together as a team also required dealing with the tensions that developed between individuals. For example, Melanie grappled with new challenges by trying to see the big picture and how things fit together. It was her way of becoming comfortable with something new. Her thinking was conceptual and broad. She found anything with too much detail exasperating. Her term for delving into great (and in her opinion, unnecessary) detail was "shaving eyeballs" (what others might call "splitting hairs").

On the other hand, Chad was the team's most ardent eyeball shaver. Chad, who thought about and learned new things by focusing on concrete examples, insisted on working through all possible details. Melanie and Chad were giving each other fits—until they both realized that they could utilize their differences to make the team more effective. This was a big breakthrough and a beautiful example of team learning.

A team meeting in Denver about three months into the process was pivotal. Chad recalls, "I remember that we took the Myers-Briggs® [*Myers-Briggs Type Indicator*®, or MBTI®] instrument. I'd already found people on the team who were similar to me. When we looked at all of our Myers-Briggs results and discussed how and why people were different, I found out why some didn't speak up and so on. I learned to tolerate, even appreciate, someone being a devil's advocate. I was (and am) very different from Melanie. She is very much a visionary—a great thinker—who comes up with brilliant stuff. Me—I'm the pragmatist. I always ask, 'How are we going to do that? How are we going to implement it?' We drove each other nuts. After that meeting in Denver, Melanie told the group, including me, 'Chad brings incredible value to the team.' We moved past the frustration into appreciating and using our differences."

The CIT members, struggling to turn themselves into a team, faced the challenge of understanding the SOP well enough to become its champions.

The Map Is Not the Territory

KNOWING CHANGE

Why are some changes relatively simple to carry out and others extremely difficult? Why do some change efforts succeed and some fail? Knowing which changes are going to be simple and which more difficult is not always easy. The retail leaders of Best Buy thought they were introducing a broad but straightforward change by putting new store procedures into place. They discovered, however, that they were actually introducing a deeper, massive change—moving from entrepreneurial chaos to systemic discipline. They weren't just changing some things in the company system; they were changing the system itself. This kind of change goes by many names, but the one that best describes the process at Best Buy is *transformational*.

Best Buy was changing how it saw and thought about itself, as well as its way of understanding and doing work. Here's how one regional manager described his shift in perspective: "Early on, we thought that the SOP would be implemented in sixty days—just like we did everything else. We would roll out plans and strategies. We didn't recognize it as a culture change—a complete face change of the organization. This turned out to be more than just another task to

25

implement." And, from a district manager: "When the SOP rolled out, I saw this as simply taking the best practices and trying to make them standard in all the stores. I was wrong."

In this book, we describe how to make the difficult changes— what levers to pull to successfully implement transformational change. People don't like to change what has made them successful and comfortable. This story is about integrating human nature and the requirements of business and organizational change. At Best Buy, we created and communicated a new vision based on the company's strategy, but we didn't stop there—we also communicated the *specific behaviors* that had to change at multiple organizational levels. We identified people who could implement change and brought them together in a powerful team to do so, and we ensured that the changes became part of the institutional culture that has led to long-term transformation and growth.

THE NATURE OF CHANGE

Some fundamental principles of growth and change apply to all natural, living systems, from human lives to ecosystems to business organizations. Knowing some of these principles (or systems dynamics) helps in understanding the growth and change that occurred at Best Buy.

Growth may appear as a steadily increasing, linear process. Think of a growing child whose height increases as you measure it by marks on a yardstick year after year. But seen from a different perspective, growth is an irregular process that involves jumping from one state to a qualitatively different state, resulting in a transformation. Think of your growth from childhood to adolescence. Changes in your body and brain chemistry made you a fundamentally different being as an adolescent. The same is true in organizations. To reach the next level of effectiveness, start-up companies have to grow up, or move from a chaotic, entrepreneurial company—whose people break the rules and do things differently every time, but who get the job done—to a more mature organization that runs efficiently, effectively, and with minimal reworking. This type of growth is not likely to evolve naturally from repeated patterns of behavior. It requires a significant jump into new territory and the learning of new behaviors.

As you start on a new path, inevitably there is an initial drop in effectiveness. (If you don't believe this, try changing your forehand tennis grip or your golf swing!) After some practice, though, you change your old habit and begin to improve and develop. Then at some point, your effectiveness begins to fall off, because the demands of the environment have changed, and you reach your capacity to improve in your present form or method. At Best Buy, the fast and furious, "cowboying it" way of growing and operating was useful in the beginning and got the company a long way—up to a point. Over time, however, the demands of the business environment changed and the company needed to change, too. The old way of operating was no longer effective, so working harder in that mode didn't help.

To thrive, Best Buy needed to move from an entrepreneurial organization characterized by chaos to a more mature organization characterized by systematic and disciplined ways of operating. Best Buy's people needed support from a system that would increase their effectiveness by allowing them to work better, rather than simply working more. And the system that could help people work better and smarter had to be implemented by the very people who would benefit from it.

A PARADOX IS THE TRUTH STANDING ON ITS HEAD TO GET ATTENTION

Should the company go with quick, dramatic, and highly visible results, without emphasizing longer-term outcomes? Or should the company go for deeper growth that could lead to slower, less dramatic but sustained change and long-lasting results? Best Buy began to realize that what got the company where it was in the first place was not going to get it to the next stage of success. Management and the CIT struggled with the choices. Should we keep doing what we've been doing, but do more of it faster? Do we really need to change some things about our culture and practices? If we do change some things, will we still be "us"? Can we be fast moving, fun, innovative, and spirited, yet more disciplined, more coordinated, and less competitive internally?

The answer to the question about whether the company should go after fast, dramatic results or slower, sustainable change with long-lasting results would turn out to be "both." And, as one Best Buy executive described the process, "It's like trying to change a tire on your car while it's still moving down the road."

THE WHOLE AND ITS PARTS

Change in complex, large-scale, and multifaceted environments has to be addressed on several fronts simultaneously. To convey the totality of the Best Buy SOP change implementation process, the story of five blind men trying to describe an elephant seems to fit. One man touches the elephant's leg and says, "Ah, the elephant is like a tree." Another touches the elephant's ear and says, "No, the elephant is like a leaf." A third blind man touches the elephant's tail and says, "You're both wrong; the elephant is like a snake." And so on. They are all right and they are all wrong, since none of them can grasp the whole elephant.

Best Buy was and is big. In fact, it's massive. Implementing change on such a large scale required an approach that could encompass individual, group, and organization-wide development and learning. When we describe Best Buy's success in implementing large-scale change, the overall picture often seems too broad or too abstract for people to understand. But when we describe specific components, people tend to attribute the overall success of the Best Buy SOP change implementation to that particular aspect of the change program: "So it was successful because you developed a scorecard to measure the progress of change?" Or, "because you worked side by side with an internal Change Implementation Team?" Or, "because you put a lot of effort into individual leadership development?" Or, "because you had the support of top management?" And so on. The Best Buy change effort was successful because of all these factors. Knowing that you can't "unscramble the egg," we used a systems-wide and systems-deep approach that recognized the individual human needs, the team needs, and the overall learning needs of the organization (see Figure 3).

Many elements of the Best Buy change process are well-known methods for successfully changing organizations—for example, build-

Figure 3

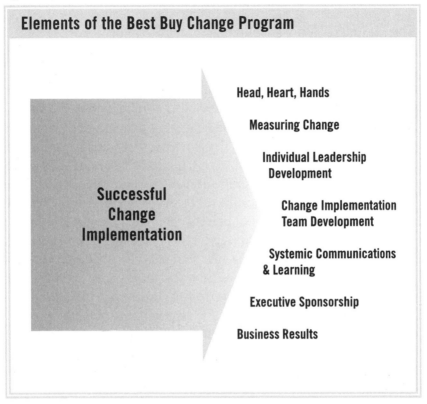

Elements of the Best Buy Change Program

Head, Heart, Hands

Measuring Change

Individual Leadership
Development

**Successful
Change
Implementation**

Change Implementation
Team Development

Systemic Communications
& Learning

Executive Sponsorship

Business Results

ing a team of change agents to lead the change effort, developing a shared vision for the team and ultimately the organization, communicating frequently and in multiple directions and modalities, and so on. Two of the processes we used in implementing change, however, are unique. These are

- Skillfully working in the three arenas of human change: the head, the heart, and the hands
- Building tools, such as the Change Scorecard[SM], and developing a methodology to measure the progress of the change effort

In this book, we focus on these two distinctive components of the successful Best Buy change effort. We look at: (1) working the change through the head, the heart, and the hands, and (2) measuring the state and progress of the change to give people feedback so they can better learn the new ways of thinking and behaving necessary for the change to be successful.

Introducing the Head, Heart, and Hands

The core dilemma facing the CIT was the conflict between the need to produce fast results that would pay off and the need to pursue deeper, longer-lasting change. To get results that would improve the profitability of Best Buy rather than just produce high scores, it seemed that the team needed to opt for the deeper, longer-lasting change. The company had run out of quick fixes. The deeper change would require a systems approach and a culture change. And the culture change would require changing employees' ways of thinking (the head), feeling (the heart), and behaving (the hands). These deeper changes would have to happen at the same time that the company and the CIT would be under immense pressure to show immediate improvement. The shift in perspective, from thinking of change as something that is done quickly and superficially to thinking of change as something that requires personal commitment, time, and learning would be a test of the CIT members' perseverance, integrity, and objectivity. Their personal and team success would be measured by company progress, as evaluated by the new, dynamic Change Scorecard.

Measuring Change

The CIT, with the guidance of the consultants, would embark on the creation of a new approach to evaluation called *scorecarding*, and more specifically, behavioral scorecarding. This approach was to be very different from the usual Best Buy checklists. Behavioral scorecarding involves asking questions and making observations that are anchored in descriptions of actual behavior. The measuring tool, the Change Scorecard, would be designed as a dynamic scorecard; it would change over time, as the change process evolved.

Introducing a new scorecard was certain to be a risky venture, because although the old culture endorsed measuring and scorecarding as many business results as possible, everyone also knew that the credibility of scorecard results was suspect. Use of such a tool, though critical to measuring implementation, could undermine the credibility of the whole change effort. On the other hand, the Change Scorecard potentially could do a lot more than simply measure the progress of the change effort. It could be designed to give people feedback on how they were doing and to let them know if they were on or off course. Since accurate, timely feedback is essential for learning, the Change Scorecard could be designed to help people both learn and change.

Individual Leadership Development

Prior to the SOP change implementation, Best Buy had not put many resources into the selection and development of talent. One of the retail SVPs had quietly brought in some consultants who were experts in developing human talent, as well as in understanding and changing human behavior in individuals, teams, and organizations, to assist him and his division in selecting and developing leaders. When he put money, expertise, and effort into selecting and developing the leadership talent in his division, he was going against the company norm.

A key incentive dangled in front of candidates for the Change Implementation Team was the individual leadership development that each team member would receive. The experts in human behavior who would be working with the individual members of the CIT usually worked with top management. That the company was ready to allocate such resources to developing the CIT members clearly sent them the message "You're worth investing in."

In addition to an early screening interview before joining the team, each CIT member was to have a complete executive assessment, a leadership development plan, and regular coaching from one of the consultants. For several of the team members, the experiences would prove to be intense and personal. As one member explains, "I would learn so much about myself—as much from being coached as from my team experiences. I would 'grow into my own skin.' I would learn what I'm good at and not so good at. I would develop the language to describe and frame things that I'd perceived."

Each CIT member would have her own consultant partner, who, in addition to the assessment and coaching, would shadow (accompany) the CIT member for several days a month while the CIT member visited the stores in her region. Actually, the partners were to do more than simply shadow the CIT members. They were to transfer as much know-how to their CIT partners as possible. The know-how was to include such skills as good behavioral interviewing, giving feedback effectively, and influencing others without having direct authority over them. The coaching and transfer of know-how was intended to be purposeful and intensive. As the story unfolds, you will see that it also paid off.

The CIT members would also need to learn how to interact effectively with senior management. One of the team members recounts that a key aspect of what he took away from the experience was "learning to deal with the executive level; briefing them—talking about wins and opportunities; learning that upper management was going to be involved. We had DMs up as a roadblock. The retail executives really reacted and wanted to remove any of the problem DMs. Execs only get snapshots. We, the CIT, learned that we needed to choose our words carefully. We went from dealing with line-level product specialists to executives at the top. Learning to speak the language appropriately was important. We made lots of mistakes in the beginning, but we learned a lot."

Change Implementation Team Development

Most of the members of the CIT had grown up in Best Buy with the "leader as hero" model. And although there was a strong sense of camaraderie within Best Buy retail, the members of the newly formed CIT were not used to playing on a team, nor were they knowledgeable about what it takes for a team to be effective. The development of the team would happen in monthly group meetings, during informal group outings, on weekly phone conferences, via e-mail, and in everyday encounters. The members of the team were widely dispersed, but they met together for two to three days each month, and each time in a different region, so every team member could host the team in his home territory. Part of each monthly meeting was to be dedicated explicitly to team process and development. Investing meeting time and effort in asking and answering questions such as, How are we doing as a team? and, How are we treating one another as team members? would be a new concept to the CIT. They were more accustomed to spending group time in discussing tactics, wrestling through decisions, and trying to impress one another.

Fortunately, the Change Implementation Team did have the key ingredient necessary to become an effective team—a clearly defined goal. Agreeing on how to achieve that goal and what objectives to reach for during the process was another story. The consultants would need to teach the CIT about team development and teamwork, including the stages of team development (forming, storming, norming, and performing), the different roles that people typically assume on a team, what it means to engage in dialogue rather than debate, and so on. The consultants would also need to teach the team about situational leadership, how to influence others over whom they did not have authority, and good facilitation skills.

The team was to discover that its success would depend on working as a team rather than as individuals. As a team, they could succeed and maintain their credibility and effectiveness. If they continued to operate as individuals (in the old Best Buy way) they would be "picked off and neutralized." As Jason, a member of the CIT, said, "At the D.C. meeting, the team felt that the RMs had sent in a mole. There was a point at which the team had two or three consultants in the room, plus two retail executives and the RM, and they were all watching us. We felt like we were in a fishbowl, and we asked all of the non–team members to leave. And they did. This was the point at which I felt that the team was really coming together as a unit."

A good deal of the development of the team was to happen in less formal settings. Again, as Jason commented, "Also at the meeting in Washington, D.C., I felt that we came together as more of a self-directed work group. We [the team, minus consultants and executives] went on a walking, historical tour of D.C. We went to the National Holocaust Museum. One of us on the team is Jewish, and we all felt that the experience was incredibly moving and emotional."

The team's ability to engage in dialogue, both with each other and with others outside the team, would become one of its main strengths. The team would come to exemplify Peter Senge's informal definition of team learning: "You know it's team learning when the team has a great idea and you can't remember specifically whose idea it was."

Systemic Communications and Learning

When you are trying to change the behavior of tens of thousands of people, using only a few change agents and consultants, you need to choose your words very carefully. In the SOP change implementation, the executives, CIT members, and consultants would have to work together to ensure that they were using the same words to describe the same things. All of them needed to put a premium on using a consistent vocabulary, as well as on thoroughly checking out how people interpreted what they said. The protocol they would need to follow was

1. Message sent?

2. Message received?

3. Message interpreted (how)?

One of the SVPs emphasizes the importance of paying special attention to communications: "The way we communicate is very, very important. Our communications must present a united front and a consistent message. Also, it needs to be 'in the right direction.' We don't have much time to communicate upward and to our peers. We need a mandate so that we can focus our energy and communication toward our constituency."

Retail people, especially at Best Buy, move fast and are incredibly busy. Instead of calling for new, additional meetings to focus on the SOP, the CIT would look for opportunities to attend and participate in regularly scheduled retail meetings. Over time, hearing from the regional CIT member would become part of the regular agenda of district, regional, and divisional meetings.

The team was to communicate with the sponsoring executives on a monthly basis, to be supplemented by joint store visits, phone calls, and one-on-one meetings. Quarterly, the retail executives and the CIT would update all the officers of Best Buy. Special color-coded charts were designed to display the results of the SOP Change Scorecard. (See the examples of these charts in Chapter 11.)

At approximately the same time that the CIT was forming, a new retail group, the "Gatekeepers," was also being formed to monitor the retail calendar and to prevent the uncoordinated scheduling of directives and events that had overwhelmed the stores in the past. Among other things, the Gatekeepers would consolidate all information flowing to the stores in a weekly newsletter. The CIT was asked to contribute a monthly column to the weekly newsletter that would provide information about best practices related to the SOP.

Over the course of the SOP change implementation, the CIT would become aware of larger, systemic issues affecting the stores (issues originating outside of the retail stores' function) and would have to consider how to best deal with these issues. For the first year, the CIT would decide to not address these issues, unless an issue's impact had the potential to be catastrophic, and to stay focused on getting retail disciplined and using the SOP. After the first year, the CIT would form liaisons with various corporate functions and together work on ways to convey how the stores could be or were affected by decisions and directions stemming from these functions.

The "Managing Change" Workshop

Know-how would need to be transferred not just from the consultants, who were experts in human behavior, to the CIT, but also from the CIT to the people in the field. For the organization to increase its synchronicity and its flexibility, all the employees would need to know more about how change affected them and others, how to collaboratively work through issues, and how to learn more effectively. Fortunately, the consultants had already developed materials, including a framework and a workshop, on managing the human side of change. To meet the challenge of transferring change know-how throughout the company, the consultants would tailor the change management workshop for Best Buy and, even more specifically, for the SOP implementation. The workshop contained much of the material in this book, with the addition of role-playing, exercises, and examples taken from real-life episodes that occurred in the stores while the SOP was being implemented.

To maximize learning, appropriate timing is important. The CIT was not given the formal training on how to manage change until after the team had made its first extended foray into the field. One of the CIT members remembers that the timing was critical: "I thought it was key that the consultants didn't teach us change implementation/change management right away. Instead, they just sent us out to do a baseline. Then, once we had real examples from our own experience, they taught us about the head, heart, and hands, using actual examples from what we'd just been through. We all thought that we had the answers, since we'd been successful GMs. Things started to click, and the rhythm started to change. Also, they started to teach us about facilitation—how to facilitate a meeting. I saw that we used a sequence of having an experience from which to draw real-life examples, going into a meeting and discussing it, really learning the how-to's, and then applying it right away."

After the consultants and the CIT jointly taught the workshop to each regional team, the CIT took parts of the workshop into the field to use on a daily basis.

The SOP *Field Guide*

Another challenge presented by the SOP change implementation was how to help people understand the deeper change and the incredible opportunities inherent in it. The consultants worked with the executives and the CIT to develop descriptions of the change in ways that would resonate within the Best Buy culture. As a result, the consultants created A *Field Guide to Implementing the SOP*. The *Field Guide* contains the "whys" of the need for the SOP in everyday language. The explanation of "why" and "what" in the *Field Guide* ranges from the broad (the entire company) to the specific ("why" and "what" for each of the store functions). The guide explains why it is important for each individual to learn her part thoroughly, as well as to put it together with her fellow employees. See excerpts from A *Field Guide to Implementing the SOP*, on pages 37–38.

For each discipline at Best Buy (inventory, operations, merchandising and media, and sales), the *Field Guide* also discusses

1. Why we have the operating platform
2. What's important about it
3. What it can do for me, the employee

See Appendix A for further details on how points 1, 2, and 3 are explained under each of the five disciplines to help employees truly understand operations at Best Buy.

📓 EXCERPTS FROM *A FIELD GUIDE TO IMPLEMENTING THE SOP*

At Best Buy, we are committed to building a thriving organization for the future. This is why we introduced retail simplification last year. Retail simplification, as our new "Standard Operating Platform," fundamentally changes the way we do business. This is not an issue or objective to manage, such as preventing merchandise from being lost or stolen or increasing warranty sales. *It is the way of working and understanding work that underlies all you do.* If lost or stolen merchandise and warranties represent the walls of the house, the operating platform is the foundation on which those things stand. And, as such, it is vital in helping you achieve your other objectives.

The operating platform is designed to organize and streamline practices and processes throughout the store. It systematizes operations across the company. It allows us to learn from each other and apply best practices across the company. It limits rework and costly mistakes by using proven methods. When it is really humming and everyone knows his or her part (why it's important and how it fits into the whole), the Standard Operating Platform runs the store, freeing up managers to coach and develop people and manage their objectives.

We introduced the Standard Operating Platform as retail simplification last year. We gave it to you all at once so you could see the whole puzzle. It's very hard to build a puzzle when you don't have the whole picture in mind. Today, some months later, we are partway toward reaching our goal. We have successfully implemented the Standard Operating Platform in some areas. A majority of employees can answer questions about the Standard Operating Platform correctly. But we all know that we are still some steps away from our goal of making the Standard Operating Platform our new foundation, of really *living it* day to day.

Growth and change take time. In the early stages, you will naturally be more focused on your own areas, learning to perform effectively in your individual disciplines. You have to learn to play your own instrument well before you can play with others, melding the individual sounds into a coherent piece of music. As we have worked to get our act together in the separate disciplines—sales, merchandising and media, operations, and inventory—we have at times lost track of our common purpose. At this point, we need to refocus on the whole to be effective. We have to work on "the spaces between"—on the interconnections and handoffs from discipline to discipline. We have to raise our level of support for the entire store and learn to play music together if we want to make the charts.

One principle of change/growth in natural systems is a bonus for all of us. Those of you who have had positive experiences working with teams have experienced this firsthand. A group of diverse individuals with diverse skills, working together collectively toward a common goal, will make decisions and perform better than the individuals would if you added up all of their separate efforts. When the members of the group have learned to respect and draw upon each other's differences, the result is a higher-level synthesis of the diversity.

A simple way of saying this is that the *collective* intellect is better than a *collection* of intellects. People in a collection will run in different directions and waste the system's energy. A collective, on the other hand, channels all the energy and experience of the separate parts into a high-functioning whole.

At the same time, it takes work to become a collective. Without developing common agreement and common goals and working on how we work together, we are destined to remain as a mere collection of people pulling in different directions, leaking energy from the system. As a leader, your job is to help people see the advantage of becoming a collective intellect. You need to guide them in shaping common goals and ways of working together that every member can support.

We have tried to tease out the essence of the platform for each of the disciplines, to give you conceptually the "whys" and "benefits" at the next level of implementation. This should help you in your efforts to communicate and lead your teams through change. At this point, we know that some of you could write these lists. So feel free to add your own benefits and reasons as you discuss this with your team.

Shared Vision, or What Does "Good" Look Like?

One of the most important things that the CIT and the organization would learn was a relearning of something great organizational thinkers have described as "developing a shared vision." In down-to-earth, Best Buy terms, this notion would be translated into, Do we know what "good" looks like? The team started with the goal of implementing the SOP so that it would be used consistently in every store, every day. That sounds like a pretty clear goal, but no one had ever witnessed what the retail stores would look and feel like with the SOP fully implemented. It hadn't happened yet. So, people in line positions, in management positions, and on the CIT would need to fill in the picture of "what 'good' looks like" over time.

Executive Sponsorship

The retail executives knew that they had the mandate to implement the SOP. One of them clearly remembers that Brad Anderson, then Best Buy's president and COO, gave his support but made it clear that they were in charge: "His hands-off approach would prove to be essential."

The CIT was to be given the full backing of the three retail executives. Initially, there were some rough spots while both the executives and the team were learning what full backing really meant. For example, before the team was formed, the executives gave their word that for a full year the CIT members could not be recruited off the team to go into another job. They let the rest of retail management know that people could not leave the team during the first year—that they shouldn't even try to lure them away. (This practice of moving people around and promoting them rapidly, without determining whether the individual had been in the job long enough to become competent, was part of the old Best Buy culture, and it happened frequently.) In spite of the retail executives' apparent commitment, just after the very first CIT meeting, the only one of the CIT members who had been a district manager was offered another DM position. He was pulled from the team. Two of the executives challenged the third executive who had sanctioned this move, and then all three of them reconfirmed their commitment to leaving people in place on the team for a year. This time their agreement held. As one retail executive puts it, "We all had the same goal."

One of the CIT members states explicitly, "Having the executive sponsorship gave us necessary momentum. The turnaround was led by a few visionaries and the willingness of executive leadership to change in order to save our company. That was the reason we were willing to follow them up the hill."

The executives took turns helping and supporting the CIT, sometimes by running interference with each other. Often they would use their influence and sometimes their authority. They gave the consultants and the CIT one silver bullet to use during the change process. The consultants could make the case that one person in retail management be removed if that person was resisting the progress of the change effort. The executives wanted to send a clear message that resistance would not be tolerated. This silver bullet was never used, at least not due to the recommendations of the consultants. Later in the process, those managers and leaders who would not or could not change went into different roles or left the company. Often they had not originally been cast in the right roles or they wanted to work in a different kind of company than the one that Best Buy was becoming.

Business Results

All of this change and learning was brought to the bottom line. None of the executives, CIT members, or consultants ever lost sight of the importance of getting the desired business results, although some were more explicit about it than others. The credibility of the SOP Change Scorecard, as well as the credibility of the CIT, increased over time as the business results started coming in. The face validity of the SOP Change Scorecard grew, along with the stores' and the company's profitability, and so did the stock price. Official statistical correlations between the results of the SOP Change Scorecard and the business measures were analyzed, and the results are presented in Chapter 11. Not incidentally, the stores started to look and feel different when the executives visited them. It didn't happen overnight, but it did happen and it did stick.

AN EXERCISE IN CONSTANT AWARENESS

Every attempted organizational change is unique, but if there are human beings involved in it, there will be some common underlying patterns of behavior. In this book, we provide a map and a framework for traversing the change process. However, since successfully implementing change requires constant awareness and adjustment, the map is definitely not the territory. Successfully implementing and sustaining change requires a flexible plan, a plan with a map for action that keeps the change on course while adjusting to emerging needs, crises, dilemmas, and learning. The potential payoff is huge—and not just in terms of implementing the specific change. The larger payoff can come in increasing the organization's capacity for incorporating transformational change and learning, which in turn can provide a lasting competitive advantage for the organization. The transformation at Best Buy revolutionized how the company sees and changes itself, and it made learning a part of the culture.

Imagine what it might be like to set sail to a place you've never been before, on a ship powered only by the wind. What and who would you want to have on board? You'd need maps and instruments to help you chart your course, other necessary equipment, provisions, and a skillful crew, each of whom could do multiple jobs well and can think on her feet.

You have a destination (a goal) but you've never actually been there. You would plot a course and, to some degree, know what to expect along the way. However, you would want to be on the lookout for potential danger. You might encounter all kinds of obstacles: massive storms, other ships with unfriendly crews, dead calm, the Sargasso Sea, tainted water, and so on. The ship could be destroyed; some or all of the crew could be lost. Given all the hazards and uncertainty, what could possibly give someone the confidence to set forth? Who would take such a risk?

How is this voyage to a new destination similar to implementing change? Most change initiatives—whether mergers/acquisitions, rapid growth or downsizing, changes in business practices/processes or reengineering, introduction of new technologies, or shifts in strategy— have a goal. Someone in a leadership role has a notion, or vision, of the goal of the change process but has never seen it in place in the targeted organization. The course can be charted, but the crew needs to be experienced and skilled enough to read the changing situations accurately and respond appropriately. There is no single approach that will fit all situations. For instance, you wouldn't want a navigator who can only see the earth as flat. The crew has to be constantly aware of changing conditions and adapt what they're doing to fit the emerging challenges while staying on course.

IMPLEMENTING CHANGE

MAKING IT REAL

Head, Heart, and Hands—Three Arenas for Change

WHERE TO BEGIN?

It was time for the consultants to get a firsthand experience of the Best Buy stores and a street-level sense of what implementing a new way of operating in the stores really meant. Exiting a Colorado freeway in midsummer and driving into the scorching-hot parking lot of a Best Buy store, we are overwhelmed by the immensity of this "box" store. Although such enormous stores are the face of today's retail operations, entering one still feels like walking into an arena. Stepping inside, we take a deep breath as the size and complexity of the store hit us.

Making a change here is going to be a challenge. The interior of the store is measured in multiples of football fields. The ceiling is more than thirty feet high. Gigantic signs, hanging from the ceiling, call out the location of each department. Merchandise is stacked on racks above and below the product displays. In the home office/PC area an impressive array of items grabs our attention. What are all these products? The quantities, colors, and packaging are enough to overload our minds. But there are only two people working the department, and both of them are busy. Some of these products need a good deal of informational support, and there are dozens of customers in every department. People are wandering through without receiving any assistance. Something seems out of whack. Is the lack of sales support hindering Best Buy's expansion strategy?

Some areas of the shelves are completely bare—not enough to make you feel the store is going out of business, but enough to let you know there are substantial holes in product offerings. If retail stores are not finely tuned, they lose essential points of profit margin from missed sales on key items. In a high-volume, razor-thin-margin business this means serious trouble. The situation is a bit like a ship that leaves port not quite on course—perhaps only a tenth of a degree off—and then, a thousand miles into the voyage, finds itself nowhere near its destination. Clearly, poor merchandising of the shelves is a sign of certain upstream points of operations breaking down.

We walk a couple of miles, just moving around and up and down the aisles of the store. Swinging by the service counter, we take time to watch what's going on. A few harried people are staffing the counter. They are faced with frustrated customers with purchases that are apparently defective. Often, simply educating the customer with basic product information (sometimes as basic as how to turn it on) helps the customer discover that the device he thought was defective works perfectly well. Whenever service people can "save" a customer, the company benefits in significant ways. The staff looks stressed. Some of them frown, none of them smile, and probably all of them feel pressured. The cool sense of competence of people who know what they are doing is missing. Unanswered phones are ringing behind them. A customer standing near the middle of the queue slips out of line and begins to walk toward the exit doors. Service wasn't fast enough for him?

The TV department is always an eyeful. A football game is playing on twenty-five sets simultaneously, and we feel like we're in an electronic theme park. Plenty of merchandise and customers are here. The department appears to be well staffed, but most salespeople are either talking with each other in clusters of two or three or just standing by themselves. In the radio and personal electronics department, some areas are staffed and others are not. What's going on here? Best Buy has been justifiably applauded for being the only noncommissioned retailer of consumer electronics, but this is going too far. The sales staff seems tentative. Do they have floor territories to cover? Do they have enough training? They look youthful and fresh in their blue Best Buy shirts. They *look* ready to work, but somehow they're not. What is going on in their minds?

The music section has dozens of aisles, each filled with hundreds of CD cases with different titles. Customers are browsing intently. In some aisles are empty or partly empty product boxes. Here and there some two-person teams are pushing wheeled metal carts filled with boxes of new CDs. The department feels active and busy but unfinished. The customers don't complain but walk around the clutter. What would it take to get the product out before the customers enter the store? Maybe the merchandising team whose job it is to restock product is behind schedule?

An uneasy, tight feeling is developing in our stomachs. This store is huge. There are many staff members and even more customers. How does one begin to create change at this level? To add to the task, each of the 272 stores operates differently depending on its regional and store management teams. We have only a small team of people: nine full-time Best Buy change agents and what now feels like a very small band of consultants. We need some time to take all this in!

Nearly every organization experiences major change a few times in its life. The changes at Best Buy fall into that "major" category. As one of the retail executives puts it, the company is moving from a style best visualized as a free-form blob to a disciplined and more orderly circle or network. It's time for Best Buy to make the transition from an exciting, entrepreneurial organization to a more disciplined, mature organization, but no one at Best Buy wants to work for a bureaucracy. The heart of the company is in its people's can-do spirit and openness to experimentation and innovation. The executive asks, "How do we get a new culture to increase our effectiveness by allowing us to work *better*, rather than simply working *harder*? We can't run any faster than we are running. We have to learn to work smarter. How do we find a way to change to remain profitable, continue to grow, and develop into a world-class organization?" These questions are ringing in our ears.

A week later, in Eden Prairie, Minnesota, just outside of Minneapolis, the Change Implementation Team gathers for the first time.

Though young in age, the CIT members are experienced retailers fresh from the front lines of store management. They know how to keep these huge stores running with their personal effort, charm, and intensity. These are vigorous people who are at home in the cavernous "big box" stores. But as they cluster around a conference table, their shoulders are rounded forward and their mood is solemn. Tom raises his hands in a question and puts it into words for all of us: "Where do we begin? There are a million things we need to work on and everything is connected to everything else. We need to figure out where to get started."

CHANGE CREATES AMBIGUITY

Like the organization, the CIT needed a place to begin its thinking and work. The team was energized, but where to start? Best Buy was operating in 32 states with 272 stores and 36,000 employees, and, with the exception of the physical locations, just about everything needed to change—and change in an orchestrated manner.

Earlier, the company had chartered a team of retail specialists to redesign store operations. The specialists had come up with a set of ideas, tested them in several stores, and documented the new procedures in an immense notebook the size of the Manhattan phone book. The CIT needed to generate a vision of what the stores would look like when the company successfully implemented these changes, and they needed to develop a strategy to make this vision real. The team had to translate the new procedures into something that the fresh-faced staff in blue shirts and khakis could understand and actually put into practice—something they could dance to.

A change as large as this does not come in an easy or straightforward manner. Growth occurs not in a straight line but in a series of jumps from one state to a qualitatively different state. Just as changes in your body and brain chemistry took you from childhood to adolescence, making you a different person, evolving organizations must make fundamental shifts to move to higher levels of effectiveness. Just as free-form jazz dancers may come together to form a dance troupe that works with choreographed material, Best Buy needed to move from its solo improvisational style to collaboration and coordination.

Figure 4

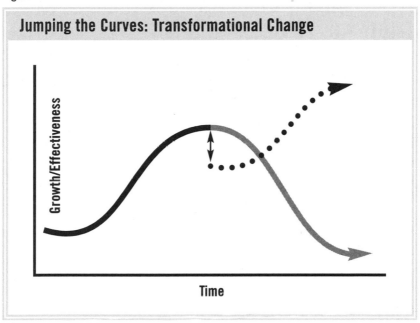

Jumping the Curves: Transformational Change

Growth/Effectiveness (vertical axis)

Time (horizontal axis)

Best Buy had grown successfully and dramatically in a steep, accelerating, upward motion that was beginning to slow, especially in terms of profitability. CEO Brad Anderson had voiced his concerns about hitting a wall. Profitability had not just stalled but appeared ready to decline sharply. The culture change facing Best Buy, toward a more systematic and orderly way of operating stores and training people, was a revolutionary, nonlinear, discontinuous change—unlike reorganizing a division or changing a customer service method, which would be a relatively simple change.

All business strategies eventually fail. All organizations that try to survive without implementing new approaches and methods go into decline. Innovative competitors replace them. This is the way of all living systems. In nature we see growth, maturity, and decline. Often after a period of rapid growth, business organizations hit a "stall point." The key to sustained success is to jump from the old approach that has reached its zenith to the growth curve of a radically new approach. As you can see in Figure 4, this kind of change—transformational change—means moving to a completely different approach, pattern, culture, and rhythm.

IF YOU AREN'T CHANGING AND GROWING, YOU'RE DYING

A number of large retailers filed for bankruptcy in the past ten years, all with assets of $2 billion or more: Federated Department Stores, Montgomery Ward, Macy & Company, Allied Stores, Southland, Ames Department Stores, Circle K, Carter Hawley Hale. A more recent example is Kmart. In 1990 it held a 30 percent market share among discount stores and supercenters. Over the next ten years, its market share would plummet by more than half, and Kmart would file for Chapter 11 bankruptcy. Meanwhile, Wal-Mart would double from 30 percent to almost 60 percent of the market share and become one of the largest companies in the United States. What happened to those other companies that were once dramatically successful?

Looking at past generations of retailers, one can see the trends. The supermarkets that first appeared in the 1920s and 1930s with their price discounting and wider product offerings eventually overtook conventional grocery stores. Variety and general merchandise stores of the 1950s such as Kresge, Woolworth's, and Ben Franklin thrived and then declined as Sam Walton and others introduced the discount department store in the 1960s and 1970s. In the 1980s there were more growth curves and more decline curves. "Big box" stores such as Costco and Home Depot emerged. Their competitors declined. Superchains such as Albertsons and American Stores (recently acquired by Albertsons) surged in the 1990s as they acquired other chains to build huge national purchasing and distribution machines (each with a market positioning and character localized to a geographic area). Remarkably, some companies found ways to refresh and remain viable: Macy's, Wal-Mart, and Sears (after a scare). They seem to have learned how to jump the curve, at least so far. As markets continue to evolve, it may be necessary to jump more often, but by jumping you create your own future.

As you see in Figure 4, growth and effectiveness fall off after inherent limits to growth come into play. The next curve represents qualitative growth (working differently) because quantitative growth (working more) is no longer getting you where you need to go. This curve represents a fundamentally different way of being in and seeing the world. If you persist in your old mode, your destruction is assured. We've all seen entrepreneurial companies fail to make it to their next level of growth. They are like people who want to remain adolescents forever, but it isn't possible to do so and survive in society.

Like hearing the stall alarm that goes off in the cockpit when a plane loses lift, Best Buy was sensing it had reached its stall point. The new Standard Operating Platform had to fundamentally change the way the company and its stores did business. Moving to the SOP would be jumping to the next curve. This was not an issue or an objective to manage, such as stopping the loss of merchandise due to mistakes or theft. This was a matter of changing people's way of working and understanding work. When a company is at the stall point, making the jump to the next "new thing" needs to be done quickly. If a company can make the change deeply, widely, and faster than others in the industry, it can leap to a competitive advantage.

CIT member Alex explained it this way: "I went to every single store to personally tell them the SOP story and where we were and where we were going. I always used a simple flip chart when I talked about how your body adapts to any change and how your body normally resists it, but it is important to go through with it. It is the same with the SOP. We must make this change. I often put an unexpected twist on a familiar metaphor: 'Our ship is sinking! But it's stupid to go down with the ship. You must jump off this ship and get on a better one. It's not a wise captain who goes down with a ship. Get aboard the new ship!'"

During this difficult time, the company bought back shares and offered them as options to first-line managers. Even first-level supervisors got some options. To recognize the potential of the CIT, each member also received additional options. This show of commitment helped get buy-in to the changes the company needed to make.

CONSISTENT FEATURES OF CHANGE

Jumping the curves is like jumping from the top of one tall building to another—letting go of one secure place to try to get to another. The one thing certain about change is the uncertainty it creates. Table 1 lists some of the feelings that invariably accompany change. Being able to anticipate them, yet not be overly distracted by them, can bring you back to a sense of control and confidence.

Table 1

What to Expect During Change

- Sense of loss; control is a major issue
- Confusion and high uncertainty
- Mistrust and a "me" focus
- Fear of letting go of what led to success in the past
- Low stability
- High emotional stress
- High energy, often undirected
- Increased conflict, especially between groups

For Best Buy, the new operating procedures in the telephone directory–sized SOP book were tangible signs of change. Getting merchandise out on the shelves at the right time, staffing the service counter with the right number of people and within the labor budgets—these are the "hard" or concrete issues, and they are the easiest to assess and change. By contrast, the "soft" issues are more difficult—issues such as how to capture people's awareness of the need for change, especially when the people range from a newly hired stocking clerk to a regional manager who is responsible for more than a billion dollars in revenue per year. Such soft, or intangible issues are difficult *and* they are the heart of transformational change. The tangible features may represent the face of the change, but the human factors—dealing with uncertainty, motivating and energizing people, and creating behavioral change—are critical to success. When soft issues are not addressed, the organization and its people appear resistant to change. As with any large system, organizations have their own inertia. Resistance, though an inevitable feature of change, becomes the convenient term for failure to address the soft side of change.

Knowing what will be easy and what will be difficult is critical for successful change management. And what do you do with the difficult issues? Pull the right levers and change goes smoothly; pull the wrong ones and change derails. There are two important points to keep in mind. First, there is no "one size fits all" approach. People at different levels and in different parts of the organization differ in their readiness for change. Second, there are different phases of change. Understanding the optimal approach in each stage can make a big difference in the success or failure of the change effort. The CIT's distress was understandable. The group had some awareness of the issues but lacked a framework to organize their concerns and ideas. These people needed to find some answers right away.

BEST BUY ADOPTS A FRAMEWORK

As the CIT continued its early, unsettling work sessions, the team adopted a framework that provided a sense of confidence and clarity. It's called the "head, heart, and hands" framework, and we'll take a look at it in this chapter.

Although most of the SOP changes seemed sensible, every member of the CIT was ambivalent about one or another specific process dictated by the platform. It took a while for the members of the team to voice their concerns, but as we dug into the nitty-gritty of the operations, their opinions spilled out. For example, several of the team members took issue with one of the sales procedures, in which the supervisor was to define a "zone" or part of the floor that each member of sales staff was restricted to. These zones were to be updated when someone came on or went off a shift. In reality, people didn't stay in their zones, because it didn't seem to make sense. What if a customer outside your zone needed help? What if one of your friends was working another, nonadjacent zone? In our discussions, the bigger issue emerged: Could zoning increase the store's sales and profitability, and if so, how? As the problem topics emerged, we learned how to use the head, heart, and hands framework to understand why some changes might be difficult to implement and how to overcome the obstacles.

Best Buy people moved fast. They were comfortable with "Ready, fire, aim." Analyzing a process, generating theories and testing them, and questioning the results from multiple angles—these were not the team's competencies. However, after venting their fears, uncertainties, and doubts (we call that the FUD factor), CIT members started challenging one another's thinking and learned to engage in dialogue and joint problem solving rather than haranguing one another. Clearly, we needed to start with the business case and the reasoning behind the SOP, both in general and in regard to specific processes. Then we needed to understand it in detail. We needed to understand the entire SOP well enough to be able to teach it to others and to problem-solve using the fundamental concepts underlying the specific directives.

In other words, CIT members needed to understand the business case and what the SOP was before they could believe in it. The notion of understanding why and what, as well as believing in the benefits of some aspects of the SOP, started taking hold when a few team members began to get results. The others wanted to get results, too, and the team started learning as a team, rather than as a group of individuals. The CIT team itself needed to work through the process of change.

Is there a methodology for implementing change? Yes, there is a framework and a set of tools and practices that flow from it. The framework explains what to do and when, and it builds confidence in your belief that change can actually be managed. The framework points out the challenges and obstacles to implementing major changes. When you understand the challenges and obstacles, you begin to see the best solutions. The change framework also gives a team a common vocabulary—an invaluable asset in sharing experiences and helping one another learn.

A regional manager explained, "The 'head, heart, and hands' framework is the best way to help people understand what we are doing. It gives us an easy way to assess the organization. We ask, 'On a 1 to 10 scale for head, where are we?' It can be used as a scorecard and then as a tool to see what to do with each area. Before we had this framework, we didn't know how to define what was going on in these areas. Using them increases awareness and understanding of where we are going and provides alignment."

HEAD, HEART, AND HANDS: A SIMPLE BUT POWERFUL FRAMEWORK TO MANAGE CHANGE

Human change takes place in three arenas: the head, the heart, and the hands. Successfully managing changes requires attention to the challenges and questions that arise in each arena. Just as the CIT did, let's get familiar with the three arenas.

 HEAD. *Directional challenges, rational-analytic questions and mind-set.* What leads to the need for change? Where are we headed? Why change? What's the business case or rationale?

 HEART. *Motivational and emotional needs.* Why must I change? What's in it for me? What are the rewards or the consequences of changing? What are the consequences of not changing? Am I capable of making the changes I'll need to make?

 HANDS. *Behavioral requirements and operational issues.* What do I do differently as an individual? What are our new processes? How do I learn the new things I'm going to have to do? Who's going to teach me? When do I get a chance to practice and get feedback on how I'm doing?

Now look at Figure 5, Change Takes Place in Three Arenas, on the following page, for a visual representation of where changes must occur simultaneously.

The term *arena*, like the three arenas at the circus, captures the simultaneous, nonhierarchical, nonlinear aspects of change. Something is usually going on in each arena at any given time, although what's happening in one of the three arenas may grab most of our attention. In using the word *arena*, we are careful to steer clear of linear, time-based words like *stages* or *phases*. Later we'll talk about stages that describe different time periods in the change process.

Perhaps paradoxically, while it is easier to think about three separate and unique arenas, they are most effectively handled by dealing with their interrelations. Successful change means accomplishing integrated change in these three arenas.

Head: Altering Mind-Set

The *head* arena includes the rational-analytic side of change and addresses the mental sets that people have about change. This arena

Figure 5

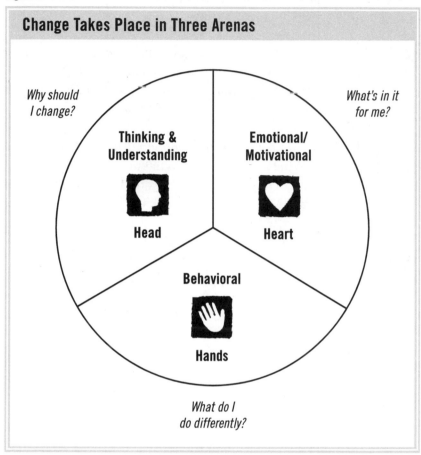

includes the thinking about business strategies that gives rise to the change imperative. And it speaks to the specific, definable reasons that the company must change. Best Buy was moving from free-form, maverick-style management and processes to consistent, carefully organized store operations through implementation of the SOP. The Globetrotters were getting ready to play in the NBA.

The challenge of the head arena is that people at all levels of the company must understand the reasons for change and its benefits to the business. See Table 2 for ways the head can meet challenges. The way you think about the world has a fundamental effect on your readiness for change. At one time, people believed the earth was flat and

Table 2

Head: Key Actions to Meet Challenges

- Change mind-set. Educate with facts and information.
- Provide compelling examples of what the change means to them—positives about the future and concerns about failing to change.
- Forget about telling people what to think—it doesn't work.
- To best help people learn, you must first understand their perspective.

would not sail too far from land to avoid falling off the edge of the world. When Columbus and his astronomers shifted their thinking to "the world is round," they became ready to sail around the globe to new lands. Ditto for Queen Isabella's mind-set shift as she decided to fund the expedition.

Although the senior retail executives had studied the issues and worked with experts to analyze the business case and develop the SOP to turn things around, their knowledge had not been communicated to the people in the retail organization in ways that they could understand. Generally, the SOP was seen as something that top management said to do without saying why. People simply wanted to know why the SOP had been introduced, and then they needed the time and space to work through the details and understand how everything fit together.

Heart: Harnessing Motivation

Heart is the motivational and emotional arena. Here live feelings. How do people feel about the changes that they've identified in their heads? What is their sense of readiness and their confidence in their ability to learn the new behaviors that will be needed? The "me" focus so often seen in change situations is an adaptive survival reaction: "Where do I fit in? Where am I headed? What do I have to contribute? What's in it for me? What do I have to give up? Do I want to be part of this?"

The key challenge in the heart arena is to increase the readiness and emotional commitment of individuals and teams to engage in change. Engaging the heart requires opportunities to confront and work through the loss of the old and familiar ways of doing things and grapple with the new. Before people can shift their motivations (heart), they typically ask three very important questions (often unconsciously).

- Why is this important?
- What's in it for me?
- Can I be successful?

To be ready to change, people must develop a compelling conviction that there are positive answers to these questions.

One of the SVPs of retail saw the need to motivate change when he said, "Companies do their best when their backs are against the wall. We have $300 million in inventory we cannot pay for. We have to change toward something very different. When you fire a rocket at the moon, you don't fire it where the moon is right now, but you fire at where it's going to be."

Learning something new often involves struggle, and resistance is a natural part of growth. This is, for some, a difficult principle to understand; it seems like a paradox. But remember the initial dip in effectiveness when you jump curves? This dip represents the time when people are wrestling with the change, arguing against it, but actually trying to learn it. This period of resistance is essential to the change process because it allows people to voice their objections and work through them with others. Often people can change a little faster when someone listens to what is on their minds, or they may hear positive and convincing reports from others in the group. Learning about change is a struggle. The energy engaged in resistance can be leveraged to help people work through the change. The silent resisters are the most difficult to change, because they are not even investing enough energy into the new way to fight it.

Deep organizational change requires that change take place at the core of the company culture, which controls the unofficial daily processes and practices for conducting business. It seemed that Best Buy's change to a thoughtful, systems-oriented culture would not be as fun, individualistic, and emotionally satisfying as the present culture, and people needed the opportunity to talk about this change.

The chaotic "old" Best Buy culture had made the company successful, but the company had outgrown it. At its worst, the company's

Table 3

Heart: Key Actions to Meet Challenges
■ Provide opportunities to talk, express, and emote. Promote expression of concerns and fears about letting go of the past and taking on the future.
■ Provide answers to What's in it for me? (WIIFM?) What if I don't change?
■ Provide experiences that give a deeply personal feeling for the benefits of change and how success will feel when it comes.
■ Overall, create the will to succeed.

culture was arrogant and did not tolerate self-reflection or criticism. The pre-SOP Best Buy honored results but put little emphasis on how the business got those results. It measured many things (but not always the right things) and ceaselessly demanded near-perfect results, while knowing that such results were impossible. There was very little reflection on the issues and obstacles that kept individuals from meeting their objectives. Table 3 lists ways the heart meets challenges to change.

A few months after the initial introduction of the SOP to the stores, each store was required to pass an audit, or test, that had been designed to assess the degree to which the store was following the SOP guidelines. The audit consisted of closed-ended questions, such as "How much of your time is spent on non-selling activities?" Each district manager audited the stores under his leadership, and all of the stores passed the audit with scores of at least 90 percent compliance, which had been the preset requirement. People could answer the questions accurately because they had memorized the right answers, but they hadn't changed how they did their jobs.

People's energy and efforts had been directed at fulfilling the letter, but not the spirit, of the SOP. This routine of complying but not accepting and changing, extended all the way from the front lines of hourly employees to some of the RMs. The "just do what I say, not what I do" brand of leadership prevented people from voicing and working through their concerns about the SOP, so the resistance had gone underground.

Hands: Shaping New Behavior

The behavioral-operational arena is about acquiring the specific skills and capabilities to execute the new practices or processes. This came to be known as "What do I do differently on Monday?" What are the new skills and practices that I must apply on the floors of the store? At Best Buy, new behaviors were required across the entire store, from the receiving dock and merchandise staging areas in the back of the store to the selling zones and up through the cashier and service desks. You know that you are in the *hands* arena when you hear questions such as, "What do I do differently? How do I do it? How am I doing?"

The challenges of the hands arena include understanding, in obsessive explicitness, the behaviors needed to implement a new operational or management strategy, then finding ways to teach, nurture, and reinforce the new behaviors—as well as finding those older behaviors, which are incompatible with the new, and acting to block, suppress, or unlearn them. In nature, nothing can grow unless something declines or even dies. So in planning for change we like to ask, "What must die before the new can live?"

There was a major emphasis in Best Buy on *process* (the ways of doing things) but much less on *behaviors* (the skills of the employees). A vice president in a retail-related function helped develop an equation that caught on:

$$B + P = R^3$$

It means *behavior* plus *process* will get us *results* exponentially raised by three. The notion of focusing on behaviors as much as process at Best Buy was revolutionary.

Early in a change process, people naturally focus on their own behavior, learning to perform effectively in their individual disciplines. To be a good dancer, you have to learn your own moves before you can dance well as a member of a troupe. Similarly, people have to learn the individual behaviors that the change requires of them. Then they can focus on the team behaviors—or team learning. Sales, merchandising and media, operations, inventory—all the different parts of a store needed to work together. Thus, in the hands arena, behavioral

Table 4

Hands: Key Actions to Meet Challenges
■ Create detailed maps or descriptions of the new behaviors.
■ Provide intensive feedback, often using behavioral measurements (scorecarding) to show levels of progress.
■ Reward, coach, and reinforce new, emerging behavior patterns.
■ Align all consequences (rewards, promotions, money, recognition) to systematically reinforce the behaviors.
■ Unlearn, extinguish, even (though rarely) punish old, incompatible forms of behavior.

change is required both for individuals and for teams. And, although it may be less visible at the larger level, change must also occur at the cultural or organizational level. Table 4 shows actions the hands must take to meet the change challenges.

A RECAP OF THREE ARENAS: HEAD, HEART, HANDS

Tables 5 and 6, on the following page, contain summaries of the three arenas, their unique challenges, and symptoms indicating when the challenges have not been adequately addressed.

NO WAY AROUND BUT THROUGH

All change requires energy and time. Without adjustments in the way people think, feel, and act, nothing really changes. And these changes don't happen all at once. As a successful change process unfolds, it passes through three consistent stages. These are shown in Table 7.

Table 5

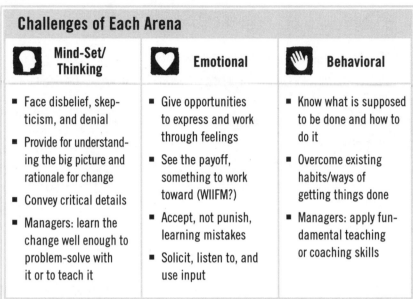

Challenges of Each Arena		
Mind-Set/ Thinking	**Emotional**	**Behavioral**
<ul><li>Face disbelief, skepticism, and denial</li><li>Provide for understanding the big picture and rationale for change</li><li>Convey critical details</li><li>Managers: learn the change well enough to problem-solve with it or to teach it</li></ul>	<ul><li>Give opportunities to express and work through feelings</li><li>See the payoff, something to work toward (WIIFM?)</li><li>Accept, not punish, learning mistakes</li><li>Solicit, listen to, and use input</li></ul>	<ul><li>Know what is supposed to be done and how to do it</li><li>Overcome existing habits/ways of getting things done</li><li>Managers: apply fundamental teaching or coaching skills</li></ul>

Table 6

Symptoms Indicating Arena Needs More Attention		
Mind-Set/ Thinking	**Emotional**	**Behavioral**
<ul><li>Failure to understand the rationale for change</li><li>Failure to understand the new model</li><li>Confusion about what is expected of them as leaders in the future</li></ul>	<ul><li>Still too comfortable with the status quo</li><li>Not realizing the benefits; unable to identify the costs of not changing</li><li>Feeling left behind, stuck, when the rest of the team or organization has moved ahead</li></ul>	<ul><li>Giving rote, preprogrammed answers to questions about the change</li><li>Understanding the need for change, but continuing to do things the same old way</li><li>Thinking/acting like the change is over and complete</li><li>Not knowing what to "do differently on Monday"</li></ul>

Table 7

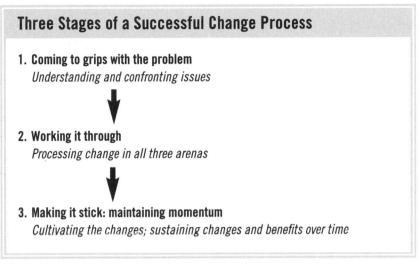

Three Stages of a Successful Change Process

1. Coming to grips with the problem
Understanding and confronting issues

2. Working it through
Processing change in all three arenas

3. Making it stick: maintaining momentum
Cultivating the changes; sustaining changes and benefits over time

Equipped with insights about each arena, an organization can accelerate to warp speed through these three stages. Given the required critical skills, acceleration can be exponential. However, you must accurately assess the stage of change for each group in the organization and for major issues. If you apply the change methods that go with a later stage than a group is in, progress stalls. Similarly, different individuals can be in different stages with different issues.

There is plenty at stake around these timing issues—the success of the company, profitability, and the risk of stalling out on growth. With Best Buy, some would even say the survival of the company was at stake. The company was in something of a Catch-22 situation. It needed to drive for and get results at the same time that it needed to embed deep principles of change and learning into the culture. When is the best time to drive for results? One of the retail executives emphasized the need to work fast because of the urgency of the situation. He continually emphasized the need to keep an eye on the business results and to produce results quickly while changing deeply. This created tensions with the consultants, the other retail executives, and the CIT over how much time to invest in the first couple of stages. Everyone wanted results and deep, lasting change. But each stage needs its own approach and time to unfold.

CAN ANYONE TELL ME WHAT STAGE IT IS?

Since stages are so important, we need an accurate way to determine what stage a company is in. We need to look for indicators that the challenges of that stage have been mastered. The main indicators are as follows.

1. **Coming to grips with the problem.** Look to see if people are getting it—that they intellectually recognize a need for change and have a sense of how the new organization must respond. The dominant mind-set or filters through which people see the world must change.

2. **Working it through.** People do the difficult, intense work of accepting and internalizing the needs to change. People are adopting a whole new economy of personal motivations.

3. **Making it stick: maintaining momentum.** The organization is finding ways to bake the changes into operational and management practices and, most important, into the culture of the organization.

These stages, and the questions to ask, are shown in Table 8, What Stage Am I In?

A MAP FOR CHANGE

Putting together the three arenas of the head, heart, and hands and the three stages provides a map and a related, complete technology for managing change. (A technology is an organized body of knowledge along with a set of tools and the skills necessary to use them.) The map or framework defines what needs to change at each stage, wrapped into a simple matrix. The CIT now had some answers; it knew where to begin and had a plan for what to do. See Table 9, Technology for Managing Change, and Table 10, Overcoming Challenges of Each Stage.

Table 8

What Stage Am I In?	
Stage	**Questions**
1. Coming to grips with the problem	▪ Do they see a need for change? ▪ How uncomfortable are they with the status quo? ▪ Do they have any sense of urgency about changing?
2. Working it through	▪ Are they struggling with making the change work? ▪ Are they looking for ways to make it work?
3. Making it stick: maintaining momentum	▪ Are they communicating with others involved in the change to get solutions to problems, share best practices, etc.? ▪ Are they looking for ways to leverage the change? To enhance it?

Table 9

Technology for Managing Change			
Stage	**Mind-Set/ Thinking**	**Emotional**	**Behavioral**
1. Coming to grips with the problem			
2. Working it through	*Breaking the conventional mind-set and generating a picture of the future*	*Dealing with reactions to loss and creating the will to succeed*	*Changing behavior and developing competency and capability*
3. Making it stick: maintaining momentum			

Table 10

Overcoming Challenges of Each Stage			
Stage	Mind-Set/ Thinking	Emotional	Behavioral
1. Coming to grips with the problem	▪ Gather data to convince you/ others that old way no longer works ▪ Confront myths, assumptions, and beliefs that prevent seeing problem and changing	▪ Increase dis-satisfaction with old way ▪ Increase confi-dence that change is achievable ▪ Outline costs of old way and benefits of new way	▪ Form team to gather data ▪ Have manage-ment talk about data and need for change ▪ Assess individ-ual readiness to change ▪ Identify spe-cific behaviors to change
2. Working it through	▪ Create a vision of future and articulate new mind-set ▪ Help people understand both the big picture and the details ▪ Broadly com-municate the purpose and benefits ▪ Help people make link be-tween solving today's issues and the change	▪ Hold reality check meet-ings to work through threats, losses, and re-sistance (dis-cussed in Ch. 7) ▪ Work through the leaders' own emotion/ resistance first ▪ Use individual gain vs. loss analysis as tool ▪ Discuss how to manage stress and be sup-portive of one another	▪ Develop a pro-file of success-ful leadership behavior ▪ Evaluate top levels of management ▪ Involve employees in building change plans ▪ Provide oppor-tunities for practice; reward successes; ex-pect and learn from mistakes ▪ Drive individ-ual behavior change

Table 10 (cont'd)

Overcoming Challenges of Each Stage			
Stage	**Mind-Set/ Thinking**	**Emotional**	**Behavioral**
3. Making it stick: maintaining momentum	▪ Continually update vision of desired future and teamwork ▪ Create forum for feedback and continuous learning ▪ Continue to articulate reasons and benefits	▪ Celebrate and reward successes ▪ Establish two-way communication ▪ Involve people for buy-in ▪ Deal with people who will not change ▪ Continue to support each other in managing stress and change	▪ Make sure systems and rewards reinforce desired behaviors ▪ Train incoming people in the new behaviors ▪ Coach, give feedback, and reinforce new behavior ▪ Deal with people who cannot change

In later chapters, we put the muscle and flesh onto this skeleton of a framework. We give you more insights into what will challenge and change people's existing mind-sets, shift them to a higher degree of readiness for change, and create and sustain new behaviors. But first, here's a brief example that illustrates this cross-referencing of arenas and stages.

Part of the design of the SOP required that the stores break into different functional teams or disciplines: sales, merchandising and media, operations, and inventory. One of the rumblings we'd heard was that the teamwork in the store had really broken down under the SOP. As we investigated, it became clear that some of the teams, mainly merchandising teams, felt they had been shortchanged, while other teams, mainly sales teams, felt they had achieved an elevated status. To make the SOP work, there needed to be effective hand-offs between the sales and merchandising teams, and these hand-offs weren't happening. Clearly there were emotionally charged issues for both types of teams—they were struggling in the arena of the heart—as they tried to work through the change (stage 2).

SCORECARDS MAKE IT REAL: OBSERVE, MEASURE, AND GIVE FEEDBACK TO DRIVE CHANGE

Have you ever watched a group listening to a new topic but knowing that they would not have to actually apply the content or be evaluated on what they learned? It's a bit like a tour bus loaded with tourists listening to the guide as the scenery rolls by—entertaining but not behavior changing. The unengaged tourist is simply visiting and never plans to live in that new region. But the person moving into town is paying attention, taking notes, and getting ready to apply her knowledge of the roads, locations of stores, and the ways people speak and interact. She knows her knowledge, motivation, and skills will be challenged and tested.

Measuring change is itself a change management technique. In the change management business, providing this measurement turns tourists into intense students of the new territory. We call this *scorecarding*—measuring important dimensions of people, teams, and organizations that are learning something new. Scorecards are measures of performance (like the amount of merchandise on the shelves, numbers of technical saves by the customer service desk) and the status of the change process—how people are thinking, feeling, and behaving in a particular area. Without keeping score on the change process, you can find yourself in two bad situations, the second one being worse than the first. First, with no score, you don't know when you are not winning. Second, and even worse, you don't even know *how* to keep score.

Deciding what to measure defines what must change. To be efficient and avoid measuring everything, you must define what is at the core of what is to be changed in each arena: the head, heart, and

Table 11

Scorecarding Drives Change

1. **What gets measured is what will get changed.**
   Are we changing the right things?

2. **Evaluate progress in each arena.**
   How are we doing?

3. **Provide the feedback necessary for new learning and development of skills.**
   How can we do an even better job?

4. **Assign the accountability necessary to make the changes a priority.**
   Does it matter?

hands. Scorecarding, often accomplished by behavioral interviewing and observational methods (rather than self-reports), evaluates the thoughts, emotions, and behaviors of people and teams on critical dimensions of change. This measuring is not just something "nice to have" done at the end of the change process to help create an interesting conclusion to a case study; it must be threaded throughout the process. Table 11, Scorecarding Drives Change, is the first of several tables in a similar format outlining change measures for head, heart, and hands that you will see in Chapters 4, 5, and 6.

Additionally, a scorecard must be designed to answer several questions in the three arenas.

 HEAD. Are the changes and the rationale for them well understood? Have the things that must change been well communicated? Have people's mind-sets changed?

 HEART. How do people feel about the changes? What is their level of motivation regarding the change, and are they adequately ready for the change? If not, then where and why not?

 HANDS. Are people using the new behaviors and practices? How well? What results are being obtained?

The CIT, in the early days of its formation, politely listened to the discussions about change scorecards. But like students at the beginning of the semester, the "tests" were too far in the future to be real. And, in truth, they had only a hazy understanding of how to measure these "squishy" concepts about organizational change. These were people who were skilled at getting live, human customers to walk out of the stores carrying boxes and bags of merchandise; they were not skilled in figuring out what must go on inside the minds and hearts of their employees. And let's be candid. The consultants did not yet know exactly what would go on these scorecards and how well they might work. They knew only that those scorecards must somehow be designed. We will talk much more about scorecards in Chapters 9 and 10.

HEAD, HEART, AND HANDS: SIMPLE BUT POWERFUL

As we've said, change always requires energy and focus. Nothing changes without sweat and emotion. We assert that successful change requires overcoming the challenges and obstacles unique to each of the three arenas—head, heart, and hands—across three stages of change. Though the framework is simple, it requires thoughtful application to achieve lasting results. As the CIT and consultants stepped up to their assignment, they established a set of tools and practices to assess and manage the obstacles of each arena.

In following chapters, we go deeper into the Best Buy experience and each of the arenas and stages. We describe the critical foundational skills necessary to master the challenges and obstacles of change in each arena.

YOU HAVE TO THINK IT TO LEAD IT

First and foremost, you have to understand and believe in the change yourself so you can provide a living example of it day to day. People learn by watching what you do as a manager rather than listening to what you say. So next we turn to the head arena and look at how to change the dominant mind-set of an organization.

Using the Head to Change Mind-Set

TO CHANGE AN ORGANIZATION, FIRST CHANGE MINDS

The success of an organization rests more with how it thinks about the world than many business strategists acknowledge. Where America Online saw a mass audience ready to have an Internet portal and services, other media companies saw nerds, PCs, and a hopelessly tiny market. Similarly, Woolworth's saw the retailing world as small-town main streets and familiar customers—and failed to change its thinking as the retail world drove past main street on its way to malls and big discount stores. To change an organization—its people and processes, even its values and strategies—you must change the organization's mind-set about the world first.

Figure 6

What Do You See?

What do you see in Figure 6? A man's face? Or a woman holding a baby? What is more remarkable than the fact that there are two figures is that your first mind-set predominates, and it requires conscious effort to keep the alternate image in mind. This is the power of mindset. We get in a groove (and sometimes a rut) in the ways we see our world. Our habits of thought, how we perceive and interpret a situation, and what we see as its implications are automatic. It is difficult to be aware of these filters without something jarring our perceptions and changing our worldview. This is the arena of the head: how we think about our business models and our images of the organization. To change in the arena of the head is to alter our minds.

Business people, especially retailers, are often hypercompetitive. In Best Buy, the hypercompetition between stores, districts, regions, and divisions drove people to succeed. The prevailing mind-set was "either you're winning or you're losing." The either/or thinking went deep. Although the true competition was and is other electronics retailers, the perception was that the competition was your Best Buy co-worker. People were ranked against each other every month on a number of business outcomes, or scorecards. When someone proposed sharing best practices and learning from one another, the audience looked puzzled—sharing ideas for the benefit of all just didn't happen.

Most Best Buy managers had stock in the company but hadn't made any money on it in a long time. One of the necessary shifts in mind-set involved being able to focus on the "big win," the overall success of the company, which would pay off in the stock. It needed to become acceptable to ask questions and learn from successful co-workers and to balance competitive spirit with collaboration.

There was an unwillingness to confront the reality that mind-set and behaviors do not automatically change. For example, in October 1995, before the CIT was formed, the retail leadership agreed that everyone would consistently hold morning and evening meetings in the stores. These meetings were meant to reinforce best practices and to give people feedback. They would at least let store personnel review the store's business performance in the areas of product, peripheral, and services sales, as well as discuss loss prevention issues. A few months after the meetings were supposedly institutionalized, a senior manager attended a meeting at which the RMs and other retail leaders stated, "All of our stores are on the program and are holding the daily meetings. We nailed it!" The senior manager then spent two days conducting phone surveys and discovered that only 35 percent of the stores were actually holding the meetings.

At first, the CIT thought that changing another person's mind-set might involve manipulation—influencing others without their awareness or consent. And they found that simply *telling* other people what to do, when you're trying to get them to look at things in a new way, doesn't work. The CIT came to realize that we all seek to influence one another all the time—usually not consciously or well. Helping someone become aware of automatic patterns of thought (filters) or mind-set is not about manipulation. It is about learning to understand another person's perspective so that you can speak to her in ways that allow her to hear your message. Then you can resolve differences and collaborate to achieve common goals. Knowing this was important, as the CIT needed to influence thousands of people over whom they had no direct authority.

CHALLENGES IN CHANGING MINDS

As outlined in the framework, effective change requires successful change in all three arenas: *head*, by altering mind-set; *heart*, by harnessing motivation, and *hands*, by shaping behavior. Each of these arenas gives us a primary challenge.

The key objective in the head arena is to help people realize what no longer works with the old way of seeing things and what must change. And change to what? The change is to the new mind-set and includes a new vision and a rationale for its success. How is such a basic part of us as our mind-set changed? Simply telling people they need to change won't accomplish deep results. To change minds, you must create an environment in which people ask their own questions, find their own answers, and make their own changes in the arena of the head.

As we have said, Best Buy was peopled with entrepreneurs, and success meant doing whatever it took to get new stores up and running, then moving on to the next emerging market. Alex summed it up, "Do anything you want, any way you want. No structure. And no sharing or collaboration." Decisions were made on the fly, and people did not ask, What might be some unintended consequences of this decision? or, Who else in the company does this decision impact? or, Have we been down this road before, and if so, what did we learn? These mind-sets worked until the needs of the organization shifted.

Implementing the SOP required seeing the entire store as a system of interdependent, interacting parts. Initially, the lack of teamwork was especially evident between merchandising and sales, and the rationalization "It's not in my job description" was causing costly breakdowns. A key challenge for the CIT in the head arena was to get the stores to see themselves as one team. And, of course, CIT needed to see the stores as part of a larger system called Best Buy. The team had to understand how all parts of the system/company worked. This was a whole new ball game. As the CIT changed its mind-set, it began to pay attention to complaints such as "Logistics changed the delivery schedule, which means that we can't follow parts of the SOP" and "The decreased labor budget means that key areas of the store can't be covered the way they're supposed to be." Out of necessity the CIT was developing a more systemic view of the organization.

IT'S ALL IN YOUR HEAD

If telling people to change doesn't work, what does work? Looking back at the many tacks we took, we see three methods that helped us successfully create change in the arena of the head.

1. **New eyes.** This means helping people and teams see with a fresh, new perspective. It involves gathering data and asking questions to explore gaps between the "as is" and "should be" models of the world (or company). This approach can range from gentle questioning and assessment to an all-out assault on the prevailing mental models and old views. It means bringing to the surface and looking at hidden or automatic assumptions.

2. **Visioning.** This is creating a picture of the organization in the future, seeing its strategies, processes, and values. What it will feel like to work in the future organization. "What does 'good' look like?"

3. **Dialogue.** By this we mean specialized forms of communication with the power to unfreeze and change thinking. Dialogue creates an environment in which individuals can look with new eyes, and see for themselves the new vision.

Table 12, Creating Change in the Head Arena, charts three levers for change, with their challenges and techniques. Each will be discussed in greater detail.

Table 12

Creating Change in the Head Arena: Three Levers		
Levers to Change	**Challenge Addressed**	**Techniques**
1. New eyes	▪ How do we get people to move beyond the fixed, old ways of seeing the world? ▪ How do we get people to see the liabilities of the old methods? ▪ What if people fail to see the benefits of new approaches?	▪ Analysis of pros and cons of current business models and methods of operation ▪ Business rationale for change ▪ Surveys and observational ratings of employee behavior ▪ Data that show the need to jump to a new curve
2. Visioning	▪ How do we present a picture of what we are changing to become? ▪ How do we communicate the business case for a new approach? ▪ How do we develop guidelines for decisions and new behaviors?	▪ Vision formation sessions ▪ Getting the word out on the new vision ▪ Forums and small-group discussions to understand implications
3. Dialogue	▪ How do we unlock frozen or resistant thinking? ▪ How do we deal with alienation, apathy, or cynicism about change initiatives? ▪ How do we build understanding and commitment?	▪ Employee forums ▪ Employee feedback and survey tools ▪ Small-group and one-on-one meetings with key individuals ▪ Asking "Why?" five times

Lever 1. New Eyes: How Does the World Look Now?

The CIT saw building rapport and establishing credibility with their internal client base as their first priority. And they saw the need to communicate a new way of looking at the world that emphasized consistency, discipline, and all changes related to the vision. What everyone underestimated was the depth of disbelief, skepticism, and even denial about the need to change, let alone the specific details of the change. The team realized it must confront myths, assumptions, and beliefs about "the way we've always done it around here" that were preventing their colleagues from seeing how bad things had gotten. They were often frustrated—on a personal level—with their internal clients. They soon realized it was more constructive to confront the old mind-set than to take any approach that could be interpreted as a personal critique. They needed solid, compelling information to help people see, with new eyes, the problems and the need for change.

In this early phase, the CIT members were not trusted. As one CIT, Tom, noticed, "Our peers in the stores look at us with suspicion. We are in their stores doing assessments with some outside consultant. We are like the political officers on a Soviet submarine. Nobody knows what we are there for, but they know that having one of us here is a requirement."

Remember the figure of the man or the woman and the baby? You probably needed a jolt of information to enlarge your view to get the second image. For a brief moment, you could see the second image before your first view quickly regained control. The challenge of the head is to provide the information, facts, and logic needed to bring a new image into view. This is analytic and strategic work that helps the organization see the need to abandon an approach or strategy that is plateauing or declining and to jump to a new strategy with an upward growth curve. It helps people see why jumping the curve is imperative. In the arena of the head, such information is logical, rational, and fact-based.

One approach is to collect information about the status quo, identifying both its strengths (how it got us this far) and its liabilities (why it's now time to change). This information can be quantitative information about the marketplace, competitors, and changing consumers. It may involve mapping internal operational processes and key decision points. The processes of an organization—its methods to cope with risks and areas of unpredictability—reflect the mind-set of its leaders. In the Best Buy culture, each store operated with considerable independence, and thus each store's operations reflected the one-store mind-set of each general manager. If the GM changed his mind or moved on, the processes would change. Improvements to process, in the form of the SOP, thus could not be implemented with a simple "find and replace" keystroke. Even the assumption that GMs set their own store processes needed to change.

In the Best Buy "as is" model, a good manager was good at fighting fires. It did not mean he was good at taking a step back, assessing and analyzing the situation, and dealing with the combustibles that had started the fires. No time for that! And where's the glory, the heroics? But as the business grew in size and complexity—from 73 stores in 1989 to 270+ in 1996—so did the problems. With no underlying, coordinated processes, many problems had mushroomed out of control. The wasted effort and misdirected energy were devouring the profit margin. Now that the CIT was seeing the entire fleet of stores, they could see how destructive the old ways of thinking were. But how could they help their internal clients see the same things? As Chad put it, "We have a mentality of doing rather than thinking. The really young, inexperienced people, who are just going out and doing things, have a very singular point of view based on the one company they've worked for—Best Buy."

The most powerful information to change mind-sets usually comes from face-to-face interactions. These interactions can be exploratory interviews that convey an appreciation of the people's current worldview and then proceed to constructively and respectfully challenge their thinking. Framing and reframing work well for this purpose. Framing is making the underlying assumptions and implications specific. Reframing means changing and replacing the assumptions and rethinking their implications. For a concrete example, think about one of your favorite paintings. Picture it in an elaborate, old-fashioned, gilt-edged frame. Now think about it in a sleek, black, minimalist frame. Does the painting itself look different, depending on what frame you put it in?

Often it takes a compelling personal experience to change a person's thinking. These experiences sometimes can be orchestrated. For instance, store visits by the retail store executives always helped them get a read on the status of the stores. By personally walking the aisles and talking with employees, managers could get a firsthand view of both successes and problems. The CIT asked regional and district managers to work in other regions and districts for a week to get immersed in a different way of operating. Managers also made visits to competitors and even retailers from other industries. Sometimes we asked RMs to make presentations for and against the SOP implementation. We had department heads become general managers for a day. All these experiences prompted new thinking and created enough emotional charge to unfreeze locked-in patterns of thinking.

And finally, scorecarding—the use of structured questions-and-answers and observations about behaviors—can also help evaluate mind-set. In our Change Scorecard developed for Best Buy (described in Chapters 9 and 10), we asked store managers and employees to describe their reasons for using various processes and procedures. When an employee can say only that she was told to do it this way, you quickly see that there is no understanding. Showing "head" data scorecarding results to managers provides them with a real picture of the thinking of their employees and whether or not employees are looking at the organization with new eyes.

Somewhere in Michigan, a store manager boxed Melanie in: "Okay, so by defining certain sales zones and keeping people in their zones, I'm supposed to sell more computer accessories. Show me how that would work." Melanie thought about it a minute, then said, "I've got a proposal for you. Let's run an experiment and do three things. First, follow the zoning guidelines to the letter. Second, observe what happens, looking for opportunities to coach the salespeople on making the most of zoning. Third, compare the results to times when you weren't using zoning, like yesterday." Both Melanie and the manager were surprised by the results. Using zoning, and coaching people on how to make the most of it, worked. They both had to see, with new eyes, that the SOP was a solution, not just another task at hand.

This profound shift in mind-set was evident when Chris, one of the RMs, broadcast a personal revelation: "The SOP is the way you get all the other scores. It's not just another score to manage. It's the way to manage the whole process to get the results we need. I'd been thinking of it as another plate to keep spinning, but now I see that it's the platform that all the plates are sitting and spinning on."

Lever 2. Visioning: A Picture of What We Will Become

Crews in rowing shells are jockeying for position as they strain to pull upstream against the current and head-on wind blowing down the Charles River. It's the head of the Charles Regatta, the Boston marathon of rowing, on a cool, crisp, blustery October day. The sleek shells charge up the river and around bridges with boat-destroying abutments, surrounded by snarling currents and the traffic of other competitors. Even some of the best teams are tripped up as they make course changes to avoid abutments as they approach the bridges. In each crew are individuals, each with unique capabilities, and each of whom must constantly discern, "Are we working together? Do we agree on what direction we want to go? Are we consistent and in sync with our execution?"

So, too, does an organization need alignment on direction and approach. Lack of common direction can run a boat into an abutment. Yet to go in a safe direction without consistent and synchronized rowing will cause the team to lose power and fall behind. Vision provides the picture of where an organization wants to go and how it will get there.

Consider the power of alignment around a shared direction or vision. It's like a magnetic force that pulls a team together. Alignment to a vision can pull an entire organization together. But beware: at times alignment may appear to exist only because disagreements lie unspoken, under the surface. Alignment should not be confused with compliance. At Best Buy, the CIT saw four ways to build alignment both within the change team and across the organization.

- Create a climate of open communication.
- Take the stigma out of identifying and discussing problems. Avoid finger pointing and blaming.
- Maintain spirited debate among members of the team.
- Develop emerging ideas rather than kill them with instant critiques. Look for possibilities rather than holes in the logic of others.

We also rediscovered some fundamentals of creating alignment around a vision. First, coach the key leaders on the vision and how to communicate it. So much has been said and written about this process that we won't go into it here except to say that it is critical. Get the entire leadership team aligned through meetings, discussions, and forums that provide opportunities for spirited debate and the developing of a complete and effective vision. Express the vision in simple, understandable terms, and begin communicating it to early adopters and change agents first. And of course, commit to a process of broad, multichannel communication to the organization.

We often grinned when we used the phrase "What does 'good' look like?" because it always got us thinking in tangible and constructive terms. It takes vision out of the stratosphere and brings it to where the rubber meets the road. Table 13, Effective Visioning, summarizes the elements of an effective vision and the process of implementing it.

To create a shared vision is to create a picture of the future and appropriate terms to describe it. Involving people in the envisioning process and incorporating their mental images and descriptions not only increases people's understanding of and commitment to the vision, but also creates a fuller, "better" vision than any individual could create alone. Even if you are handed an aspect of a change to implement or are designing a vision yourself, you will need to co-create a shared vision of the future with a wide audience.

At Best Buy, different pieces of the vision came from different employees. A new slogan that appeared about eight months into the Best Buy change implementation reflected a fresh way of defining success"(or, What does "good" look like? The slogan was "Stores, not scores." Another slogan that appeared was "Work the plan; the plan works," which defined a new, coordinated way of getting things done.

In a hotel conference room in a city now forgotten, we created a simple list of questions to evaluate our progress on creating and communicating vision.

- How clear and compelling is our vision of where we want to be? How well is it understood throughout the organization?

- Do we believe there is a threat to our success if we continue with our business-as-usual mind-set? Are the liabilities clear? Do we have an appropriate sense of urgency about change?

- Do we discuss this vision in a climate of openness and with constructive communication?

Table 13

Effective Visioning

Functions of Vision	Focus Questions	Ways to Go Wrong
Pictures future	▪ Where are we going? ▪ What does the future look like for us?	▪ Either too specific to be long lasting and valid or too vague to have meaning
Energizes change	▪ What motivates us to achieve the vision? ▪ What is meaningful to people and teams?	▪ Either too rational and "pure business" to engage emotions and imagination or all emotional with no substance
Honors and closes past	▪ What were the wins of the past? ▪ Why must we move on? ▪ What are the costs of not moving forward? ▪ What must die so the new vision can grow?	▪ Hypercritical of the past and disrespectful of heroes and their efforts or leaves the door open for continued adherents of the old vision to survive
Explains future	▪ What is the business rationale? ▪ How will this help us succeed?	▪ Too linear and quantitative about possible outcomes or fails to specify a viable, sustainable business model
Affirms values	▪ What will not be changing? ▪ What will be valued and rewarded in the future?	▪ So much emphasis on change that core values are lost or so much emphasis on continuity that necessary culture change gets lost

- Are we getting input from the right audiences? Will we get full acceptance and the smartest solutions?

- Are we providing positive incentives for achieving our vision?

To influence people's perspectives on the changes, the team found it essential to create a shared vision of the future and to articulate the new mind-set. The team involved many sets of people in the envisioning process and incorporated their mental images and descriptions.

The CIT's job description expanded to include creating forums for people to explore, practice, and get accurate feedback while learning new ways of thinking and behaving. The excitement of learning and getting results sustained the momentum for the change and continuing improvements. At the same time, the CIT continued to supply information supporting the reasons for the change and the benefits it was bringing.

Lever 3. Dialogue Shifts Mind-Set

The third method to use in shifting mind-set is dialogue—two-way communication that creates a sense of connection and shared purpose among the participants. All the dynamics of the head arena require dialogue: making the case for change, communicating the vision, and fostering understanding and buy-in of the new mind-set. Dialogue helps assess the current state of the change process: "How much has really changed? What are people really thinking?" Frequent, consistent communications help paint a picture of the successful outcomes and benefits that will come with change.

Dialogue (some might use the more sophisticated term *appreciative inquiry*) can unfreeze and change thinking. It begins with questions, using questions both to understand a person's mind-set and to influence it. It involves suspending immediate judgment about a situation. Instead of focusing on problems analytically, this approach looks for the positive energy that fuels the growth and creativity of the organization. Today's problems can be seen as the results of yesterday's efforts to deal with the organization's challenges and problems. This leads to questions about what the organization can become if it addresses these challenges.

To test the statement that "organization is an artifact of the mind that views it," run an experiment. Ask two people who attended the same meeting to describe to you what happened in the meeting. You will probably hear different accounts of the meeting. Your truth is not another's truth because your mind-sets, or mental models, are different. To be able to influence the other person, you first have to understand how he views the world. We all fall into the trap of assuming the world is as we see it, and therefore our way is the right way. Usually there is no one right way. We first must uncover each of our assumptions to come to an understanding of what we do see in common. With this sense of rapport and acceptance, we are then in the right climate for changes in the head arena.

Using questions skillfully is a powerful way to draw out and understand another person's mind-set. If you mentally frame your questioning as mutual problem solving with the person, rather than confronting or interrogating her, questions can be used to collaborate with and influence her, as well as to understand how she sees the world. "Guided discovery" is another name for this process. The skillful use of questions is a subtle art and requires a good deal of practice. It should be used with caution. The danger is that you might be—or might seem to be—coercive, attempting to maneuver the person into a corner. Or you may be seen as condescending ("I have the answers"). To guide yourself, keep in mind that you always have something to learn from the person, as well as something to teach. People and teams can accept a healthy level of challenge and confrontation if they feel listened to, accepted, and trusted. Successful change involves both support and challenge. Getting the right balance is a skill, and like any other skill, it requires practice to become good at it.

One of the members of the CIT liked being at center stage, in a starring role. Early in the change implementation, he was antagonizing a lot of people, both on the team and in the region he was assigned to. He came across as the "expert" who knew what was right and who knew that it was his job to tell you what you were doing wrong (or that his way was better). He was telling, not asking. Here's a portion of a mind-altering dialogue between this CIT member and his consultant-coach.

Coach: How do you react when someone tries to tell you what's what—when he comes across as the expert, or a know-it-all?

CIT member: I resent the guy and want to compete with him and show him I'm better. I want to outdo him or at least outtalk him.

Coach: Do you listen to what he's saying? Do you take it in?

CIT member: No.

Coach: When do you listen?

CIT member: When someone seems interested in how I do something or how I think about it.

Coach: How does that feel?

CIT member: Like the person respects me and is interested in what I've learned—that there's something in it worth paying attention to.

CIT member: Okay, I've got it. You've made your point. Now, the question is, can I remember it?

The coach's part seems simple, but if we could hear their voices, we'd know when and where the coach introduced this topic, and we'd have a sense of how much these two people trusted each other. Asking questions skillfully to help someone think through something (that he or she usually already knows but hasn't paid attention to) means having a good sense of the appropriate time and place, mutual respect and trust, and a genuine interest in working through something with the person for his or her growth.

Dialogue needs to occur across multiple channels of communication. These channels vary in their power. The following list is ranked with the most powerful channels presented first.

1. Verbal, face-to-face communications with two-way exchanges. These are personalized interchanges. They create the climate in which minds will be ready to change.

2. Presentations and briefings by respected and well-known individuals. These provide information and can help increase the readiness for change.

3. Written or video or electronic communications. These are closer to mass media and typically provide information rather than change minds in an organization. They are the least expensive on a per-person basis—and the least effective. Can you really change minds with just an e-mail message? No.

SO EXACTLY WHAT DO WE TALK ABOUT?

So far we have discussed the "how" of dialogue and its benefits but not the content of such communications. What is important to cover? Dialogue must include the key challenges and topics of the arena of the head. Table 14, Dialogue Changes the Head, describes the rational, logical elements of the head arena, including mission, vision, strategies, goals and objectives, and cultures and values.

Distinguishing between conceptual elements of mission and vision often results in confusion. Here's our way of clarifying it. Mission is the overarching reason the organization exists—its fundamental purpose for being. The mission of an organization rarely changes. When it does, it often means the most radical of redirections. For instance the March of Dimes organization created a new mission, focusing on birth defects, when polio, the original focus, was almost completely eradicated. More precisely, this was a change in *vision*, as the organization's highest purpose as a charity was to improve health. Vision is the basic approach to accomplishing the mission. Our vision will need to be updated as our mission changes or as our world in which we accomplish our mission changes. Vision, our desired future state, is often described as a picture or story of the future. It changes infrequently and usually requires a transformational change.

Now look at Table 15, Dialogue Topics at Best Buy. It follows the same format as Table 14 but gives definitions and dialogue topics for the five dimensions, from mission to culture and values, that are specific to Best Buy.

Table 14

Dialogue Changes the Head		
Elements of the Head	**Definition**	**Dialogue Topics**
Mission	■ Overarching reason for existing ■ Aim or highest purpose ■ Mission changes infrequently	■ Are we clear on our mission? ■ How does our mission make these changes necessary and urgent?
Vision	■ A picture or story of our future ■ What we are going to become	■ What is our old vision? ■ What are the implications of our new vision for strategies, goals, and values?
Strategies	■ Identifies the key approaches in which we will implement the vision ■ Defines the competitive advantages that will lead to winning in the marketplace	■ Where are we positioned in the marketplace relative to competitors? ■ What can we do that will give us some unique advantage?
Goals and objectives	■ **Goals** are long-term outcomes to be achieved by the strategies ■ **Objectives** are time-defined, tactical outcomes that guide implementation of strategy ■ Often objectives are set for financial results, processes, operations, people, and customer retention	■ What is the fit between our goals and objectives and our organizational competencies? ■ What are our strengths and limitations in accomplishing our goals? ■ What changes are required for us to successfully accomplish them?

Table 14 (cont'd)

Dialogue Changes the Head		
Elements of the Head	**Definition**	**Dialogue Topics**
Culture and values	■ The personality and soul of the organization ■ Often unstated (even un-conscious) principles and practices about how to treat people, competitors, and customers	■ What is our style of doing business? ■ What principles do we value so much that we would forgo an opportunity that required us to go against them? ■ What changes do we need to make in our culture and values to help our new vision succeed?

Table 15

Dialogue Topics at Best Buy*		
Dimension	**Best Buy's Definition**	**Dialogue Topics**
Mission	■ We improve people's lives by making technology and entertainment products affordable and easy to use	■ What's the purpose of Best Buy for customers? ■ What do we want to be known for by our cus-tomers?
Vision	■ To be at the intersection of technology and life	■ What will make us special in our retail category? ■ How can we sum up our ideal customer experience in one sentence?

Table 15 (cont'd)

Dialogue Topics at Best Buy*

Dimension	Best Buy's Definition	Dialogue Topics
Strategies	■ SOP ■ Store openings ■ Customer experience	■ What does the SOP mean to you? ■ What do we need to do differently to get new stores to operate with sustained excellence? With sustained profitability? ■ What is it like for the customer to shop in your store?
Goals and objectives	■ SOP implementation ■ Customer-based scheduling (CBS) ■ Market share ■ Merchandise mix ■ Workforce objectives	■ How do we measure success? ■ What are the most important milestones in our journey?
Culture and values	■ Honesty and integrity ■ Respect for our customers, communities, and fellow employees ■ Respect for our company and shareholders ■ Encouraging discovery and learning ■ Embracing speed and change ■ Having fun while being the best	■ What does Best Buy stand for? ■ How do we want to treat our customers? ■ Why did you join Best Buy? What would make you leave? ■ How do we want it to feel to work at Best Buy? ■ What can we do to help you have fun and grow?

*Best Buy's dialogue topics listed here apply to 1996–2002.

For Melanie, a turning point in the use of dialogue happened when she was in the field trying to get the attention of a DM. "For me, it was when Bill was arguing with me. He had about nine other people clamoring to see him. He told me that he had to start delivering warranty sales and some other key numbers or he would lose his job. He told me, 'I don't have time for you unless you can help me figure out how to sell warranties and accessories.' I realized that I had to figure out how the SOP process really could help him sell warranties and accessories. At that point I became very aware of the connection between people being willing to change and adopt new practices and then starting to get results." Melanie describes being impressed by the people who could find ways of letting go of the familiar. Part of her job, as she saw it, was giving them the language and pictures they needed to understand what they were doing and to understand how adopting new practices could benefit them.

FIVE WAYS TO FAIL AT CHANGING THE HEAD

It's late, and people are tired and getting punchy. It's our third city in a week. At times like this, we might stop to have some fun and to look at things from a cynical mind-set. We would laugh, share some gallows-style humor, and through some paradoxical process feel refreshed. Summarized in Table 16, Five Ways to Fail at Changing the Head, are some ways to go wrong that we wrote down during our conversations.

Table 16

Five Ways to Fail at Changing the Head

1. Be surprised when the old mind-set resurfaces under stress.
2. Assume the rationality of the new vision will ensure its acceptance.
3. Go slowly. Strike no chords of urgency.
4. Act like achieving acceptance of a new mind-set comes without work and sweat.
5. Underestimate the power of mind-set on the heart and hands arenas.

JUST WHEN YOU THOUGHT IT WAS SAFE TO COME OUT

Not only is it easy to make mistakes, but also the organization often seems to defend its old, familiar ways of thinking. A defensive system spiral, which we call the "vision-killer spiral," often occurs. This vision killer can cause teams that are designing and implementing the vision to come up short—if not fail outright.

Vision-Killer Spiral

Key elements of the spiral are listed here, along with a visual that shows what can happen (see Figure 7).

1. The team or committee is charged with developing a vision, but full executive support might not be given. There is a lack of political support. Less than the best people are put on the team. And finally, not enough time seems available to do a thorough job.

2. There is a rush to deliver results and conclusions. Quality of the work processes suffers; not enough groups are involved to ensure adequate buy-in. Senior leadership is not fully engaged. The team is not able to confront its sponsors on the issues with time and resources.

3. The deliverables lack needed levels of depth and quality. The vision and supporting deliverables are not simple, crisp, and compelling. The momentum for change falters.

4. The new vision and its benefits are seen as lacking adequate promise and power. The old mind-set and vision are either re-affirmed or remain alive to compete with the new vision.

Stopping the Vision-Killer Spiral at Best Buy

This is the way the potentially vision-killing spiral was halted at Best Buy before it gained too much momentum (see Figure 8).

1. The CIT charged with implementing the SOP nationwide for all Best Buy stores found a lack of full support and a mixed degree of buy-in among regional managers. Some CIT

Figure 7

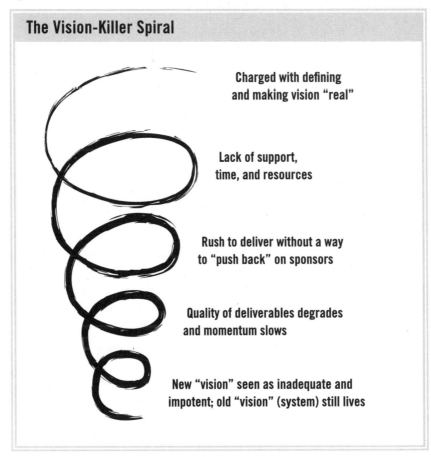

The Vision-Killer Spiral

Charged with defining
and making vision "real"

Lack of support,
time, and resources

Rush to deliver without a way
to "push back" on sponsors

Quality of deliverables degrades
and momentum slows

New "vision" seen as inadequate and
impotent; old "vision" (system) still lives

nominees were people "left over" after structural reorganization of district and regional staffs. Some nominees were sent home, while others were accepted.

2. The team had to actively resist the company mind-set that required scores to be high (e.g., a four-out-of-five score was barely acceptable on performance reviews) quickly and consistently.

3. The team really had to work on delivering its message and showcasing results. They used a mix of visual cues to effectively illustrate the patterns of results across the nation.

4. The team had to work with managers at all levels, up to and including the most senior retail leaders, to get them to look at the

Figure 8

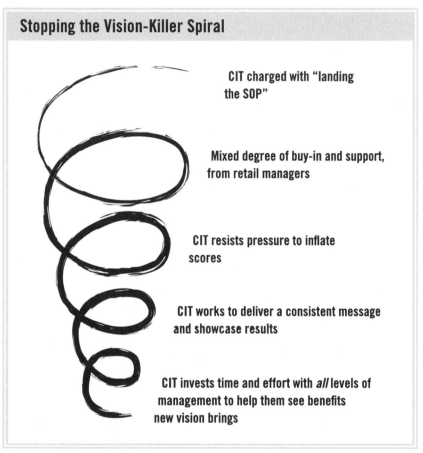

Stopping the Vision-Killer Spiral

CIT charged with "landing the SOP"

Mixed degree of buy-in and support, from retail managers

CIT resists pressure to inflate scores

CIT works to deliver a consistent message and showcase results

CIT invests time and effort with *all* levels of management to help them see benefits new vision brings

store results differently and to reinforce using the SOP as a system that enabled the stores to achieve the desired results on other piecemeal measures.

CHANGE, CHANGE, CHANGE: MIND-SET CHANGES ACROSS THREE STAGES

As we discussed in previous chapters, a successful change process unfolds in three stages.

1. Coming to grips with the problem
2. Working it through
3. Making it stick: maintaining momentum

Matching the optimal change method to each stage will often increase the value of that activity. If you are a systems thinker, you are right to object that all change processes are nonlinear, but it's a bit easier to approach the change with these stages in mind, even if there are complex interactions and loops of influence underlying the change process. Table 17, Changing the Head in Three Stages, shows each of the levers—new eyes, visioning, and dialogue—with three stages of change.

The best approach to creating change in the head arena varies in each of these three stages. In the first stage—coming to grips with the problem—the "new eyes" method is used most. This provides fact-based information that shows the liabilities of the current mind-set and the benefits of a new approach. During the next stage—working it through—visioning gets the biggest workout. In this stage, a new worldview needs consensus, and specific strategies must be confirmed. In the final stage—making it stick: maintaining momentum—dialogue needs the most emphasis. Two-way communication creates the necessary mind changing and buy-in to shift the organization into a new groove. It also is the best way to bring to the surface concerns and obstacles that will slow the adoption of change. Through dialogue, the reasons for change and the benefits to all parties become internalized.

HEADACHES TO BRAINSTORMS: SCORECARDS FOR THE HEAD

How do you measure the way people are thinking? Does it seem impossible? Are people perceiving the benefits of change, or are they stuck in the old ways? Are they getting the power of new mind-sets? The way to measure thinking is to ask people questions that require answers that reveal their underlying thinking. Or even better, watch them in action. In short, you do not directly ask; rather, you get samples and evidence. We are what we do.

Table 17

Changing the Head in Three Stages

Stage	Coming to Grips with the Problem	Working It Through	Making It Stick: Maintaining Momentum
1. New eyes	■ Ask questions that get others to test beliefs and assumptions ■ Gather data to convince others that the old way does not work ■ Create the business case for change: the change imperative ■ See things in a new way and help others to do so	■ Test people's understanding of both big picture and details ■ Explore gaps between where we need to be and where we are today	■ Build interview-based scorecards to assess understanding of change and what it consists of (see Chs. 9, 10) ■ Use scorecard to track changes in mind-set ■ Give feedback on progress in a form suitable for the audience
2. Visioning	■ Articulate the old vision and why it used to work ■ Identify why the old vision must change	■ Create a livable vision of the future ■ Articulate the new mind-set	■ Test people's understanding of both the big picture and details ■ Explore gaps between where we need to be and where we are today

Table 17 (cont'd)

Changing the Head in Three Stages

Stage	Coming to Grips with the Problem	Working It Through	Making It Stick: Maintaining Momentum
3. Dialogue	▪ Confront myths, assumptions, and old beliefs that prevent seeing reasons for change	▪ Create forums for interactive communications on purpose and benefits of change ▪ Help create link in people's minds between the vision and solving today's problems	▪ Create forums for feedback and problem solving on issues of implementation ▪ Continue to articulate the reasons and benefits ▪ Uncover frustrations and concerns

Scorecard Example 1

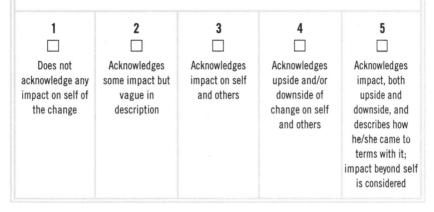

Describe the upside and downside of how the change has had an impact on you.

The CIT members were to look/listen for the following: Can this person (a) deal honestly with the impact of change on him/herself first, and then (b) use his/her experiences to help others through the change process?

1	2	3	4	5
☐	☐	☐	☐	☐
Does not acknowledge any impact on self of the change	Acknowledges some impact but vague in description	Acknowledges impact on self and others	Acknowledges upside and/or downside of change on self and others	Acknowledges impact, both upside and downside, and describes how he/she came to terms with it; impact beyond self is considered

All of the retail managers needed to be aware of how they were reacting to and working through the changes. Scorecard example 1 is one of the items on the SOP Change Scorecard. In the scorecarding process, CIT members check the scorecard boxes after interviewing and observing employees. Scorecarding is explained in further detail in Part 3.

Measuring the head creates change. Scorecarding measures learning and readiness to apply these new concepts. Chapters 9 and 10 go into greater detail about presenting the scorecard and change management. Because it's so important, we give you a brief preview in Table 18 of how scorecards help change mind-set and measure the progress of change in the head arena.

Scorecarding allows us to leverage the three methods of change for the head. Scorecard data can present a picture of the "as is" status of the organization. In working with "new eyes," this information provides undeniable evidence as to what people think and their perceptions of the current vision, strategies, and processes. And scorecard information is invaluable in helping you determine what stage of change you are in—coming to grips, working it through, or making it stick. In visioning, scorecarding can measure progress and describe

Table 18

Scorecarding Changes Mind-Set
1. **What gets measured is what will get changed.**   *Do we have a clear vision and a mind-set that can be measured?*
2. **Where are we making progress?**   *How well do people understand the reasons for change?*
3. **Provide the feedback necessary for new learning about old and new mind-sets.**   *How can we make clear the gap between the "as is" and "should be" models?*
4. **Give a focus point for accountability and recognition.**   *Shows that underlying beliefs and thought patterns must change and that simple external compliance is not enough.*

what people do and do not understand about the new vision. The process of scorecarding raises awareness of the need to change and opens the doors for dialogue to bridge the gap between the "as is" and "should be" models.

WHEN HEAD, HEART, AND HANDS ARE NOT IN THE SAME HOUSE

We have focused on the head as a single arena, but it is inextricably linked to the other arenas. The best approaches to changing mind-set simultaneously consider the heart and hands. A team or an individual may have successfully accomplished change in one arena but not another. Tailoring approaches to different situations and different audiences gives the best results. In Figure 9, Change Readiness Map, we look at the connection between the head and heart arenas and how this analysis helps you tailor your change methods. In later chapters, we consider the hands in more detail.

As you can imagine, each quadrant is best addressed with a different message and change strategy. Those who understand the changes (head is okay) but lack the motivation to implement (heart is not okay) need help to understand why it's important to them and what obstacles

Figure 9

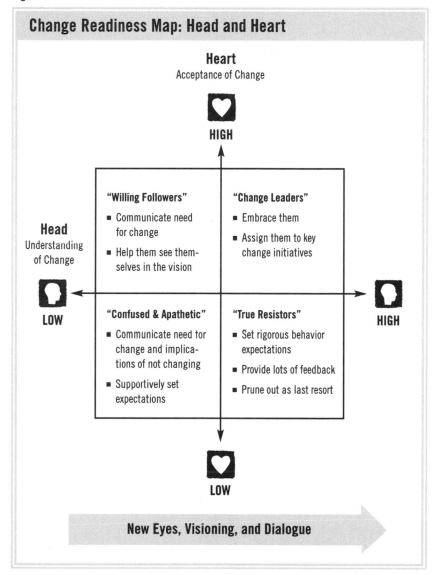

Change Readiness Map: Head and Heart

Heart
Acceptance of Change

HIGH

Head
Understanding of Change

LOW ← → HIGH

"Willing Followers"
- Communicate need for change
- Help them see themselves in the vision

"Change Leaders"
- Embrace them
- Assign them to key change initiatives

"Confused & Apathetic"
- Communicate need for change and implications of not changing
- Supportively set expectations

"True Resistors"
- Set rigorous behavior expectations
- Provide lots of feedback
- Prune out as last resort

LOW

New Eyes, Visioning, and Dialogue

they may feel are in the way. To continue to bombard this group with more communications about vision is a waste of time, if not counter-productive. Chad captured the CIT's role in changing mind-set one night while sitting in a hotel lobby: "I was thinking our charge was to implement the SOP. But I realized today that what we are really doing," and he paused a moment, "is about leadership."

Using the Heart for Emotion and Motivation

ALL SUCCESSFUL CHANGE IS EMOTIONAL

Emotion is always a factor in changing human behavior. Emotion, in its various guises, can either power or derail change. One reason for this is that all change involves loss. As we enter a change, we move out of our familiar comfort zone. We lose some of our sense of control, which triggers fear and anxiety. Like hunger pangs on an empty stomach, anxiety is the companion of change. Such emotions, if not extreme, can lead to constructive rather than destructive behaviors. Establishing successful change always involves helping participants understand and cope with their emotional reactions in an adaptive manner.

How do you know when you are dealing with an emotional reaction to change? Sometimes the emotion is obvious. You see it in a person's actions, expressions, or voice. But sometimes it is disguised as apparently rational arguments. Whether emotions are expressed overtly or not, you need to look "under" whatever is happening and ask *why*. In Chapter 4, we discussed the importance of a clear vision and a strong business rationale for change. This sense of direction is essential, but it leads to change only if it engages the emotions that can power such a change.

Those who created the SOP developed their design primarily in several "experimental" stores. The logic of the SOP and the elegance of its process improvements perhaps were thought to be enough to ensure their implementation. If you look at an organization from a mechanistic mind-set, you might assume that a well-designed platform will put the pieces of the machine (or store or company) together flawlessly. This viewpoint doesn't take into account the complexities of implementation—the messy, dicey, human element. The designers of the SOP sometimes appeared aggravated with store employees who, they thought, should be faster and brighter about learning and applying what the designers believed were rationally superior practices.

Within the stores, people were upset and unsure about the change effort. They hadn't had opportunities to express and work through their feelings, and they didn't see any payoff in changing. Some thought the bar was rising, and they were worried they couldn't learn the skills needed to be successful in the new environment. In the past, mistakes had been punished. Many people felt their input was either not solicited or, if listened to, not used. They hadn't had the opportunity to come to grips with what the change meant to them as individuals or as teams. Of course, emotions are not just an issue for those on the front lines—from the store floor to the executive suite in Eden Prairie, change needed to take place in the arena of the heart.

CIT AND THE HEART

Dealing with people's emotional reactions to the change forced the CIT to grapple with tough questions, such as

- What benefits are people currently getting from the status quo?
- What are the costs of the status quo and the resulting missed opportunities?
- What might be better after the change is implemented? What are the benefits of changing?

- What are the threats and losses for the individuals—from clerks through senior managers?
- How do these benefits and losses balance out? How will people show their emotions, either actively or passively?
- How do we manage something as apparently ambiguous and difficult to discuss as the emotional side of change?

Melanie was wrangling with one of the retail executives over the viability of a particular innovation. She kept coming up with logical arguments in favor of the innovation, but the executive wasn't buying into it. The discussion was going nowhere because the retail executive was reacting from the heart. He saw the proposed innovation as potentially undermining the core of traditional, but proven, retailing. When Melanie realized that she was trying to make her case in the head arena, she realized why she wasn't getting through. Once she moved to the arena of the heart, the conversation moved forward.

In the arena of the heart live our feelings and motivations about business models and our images of the organization. Since work is such an important part of our lives and our identity, changes in our work deeply affect how we see ourselves. This complex realignment of emotions and motivations is what people cope with in the arena of the heart.

CHALLENGES IN CHANGING HEARTS

As you will recall, effective change requires action in all three arenas—head (altering mind-set), heart (harnessing motivation), and hands (shaping behavior). The heart has its unique challenges. To work through the heart requires you to balance patience with the complexities of emotional change while still responding with the urgency needed to accomplish the change.

The key challenge of the heart arena is to increase the readiness of individuals and teams for change. This often involves overcoming resistance in the pursuit of commitment to a new mind-set, a vision, and specific behaviors of implementation. To accomplish this challenge, one must deal with the central question in everyone's mind: What's in it for me? (or WIIFM?). The challenges can be visceral. As Tom put it, "We think we can convert the masses, but people are accepting us like the Pharisees accepted the Christians!"

READINESS FOR CHANGE

Every organization, team, and individual is ambivalent about change. There is almost never either complete openness or total opposition to change. Successful change involves moving individuals and teams into the "more ready than not" category. As eminent organizational psychologist Henry Levinson said, "All change involves loss. And all loss requires mourning." Even positive changes and achievements involve loss. When your teenager leaves home for college, he loses some of the close parental support (as well as the laundry service!) that has been so familiar to him, even though the increased freedom and self-direction he gains may far outweigh the losses. In the corporate world, change means the loss of familiar and comfortable patterns—usually successful ones, up until now. You can see this when a person is promoted to a managerial position for the first time or when the restructuring of business processes affects the roles and responsibilities of those involved.

Resistance to change occurs when you perceive your losses to outweigh your gains. Conversely, readiness to change increases when your gains appear to outweigh your losses. Gains and losses are evaluated in the arena of the heart; they are the central determinants of our emotions and motivations. Gains are motivating in a positive way. Losses are uncomfortable, even fear producing, and the motivation is to avoid them. A key dynamic in the heart arena is that you must help individuals change their perceptions of the loss-versus-gain ratio. In Figure 10, we see how individuals' change readiness adds up to an organization's collective change readiness. Some proportion of people will actively resist change. For them, losses appear to outweigh gains. For most people, gains and losses are balanced, and thus they feel ambivalent. They sit on the fence, watching to see what happens.

As Figure 10 illustrates, there is usually a small proportion of the people who recognize that the potential gains of change outweigh the

Figure 10

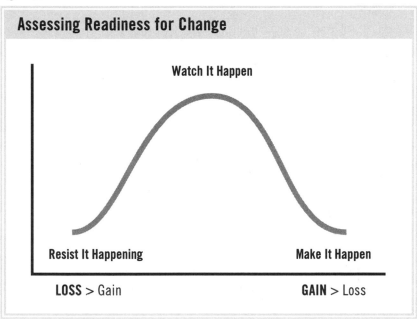

Figure 11

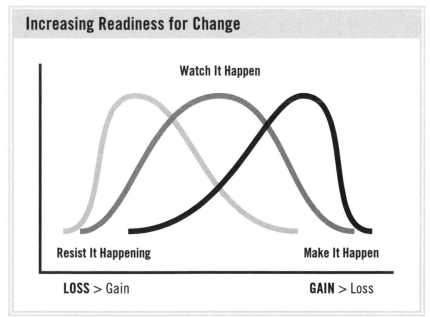

losses and costs of inaction. They are ready, even committed, to change. But an organization cannot change with most people either resisting or watching from the sidelines. As illustrated in Figure 11, successful change requires moving an organization toward the distribution pattern on the far right—where a large proportion of people are ready to change. Note that even in a change-ready organization, there will still be a significant number of people either resisting or just watching the changes. Shifting the motivational state—capturing the positive emotions and motivations of people—is the work of the heart arena.

WHAT DETERMINES READINESS FOR CHANGE?

The organization's readiness to change is determined by its overall perception of gains versus losses. The ratio will vary throughout the organization. For instance, at Best Buy the impact of SOP changes on the district managers involved issues about decision making and scope of authority, how DMs spent their time, and how their operational effectiveness was to be evaluated. Their sense of gains versus losses was quite different from that of sales associates, who were also affected by the change. When salespeople were assigned selling zones, they weren't able to spend as much time with friends. Also, they needed to work with the merchandising staff, whom they didn't think of as part of their team. Identifying how different individuals and teams see the gains and the losses is the first step in determining the organization's readiness for change.

How do you assess these factors that are essentially hidden from view? In brief, you look for external behaviors that are indicators of these internal motivational states.

Determine Current Emotional States of Individuals and Teams

To understand people's emotional states, apply these three steps: observe, sense, and ask.

1. **Observe.** How do they look, sound, and act? You can often infer readiness for change by listening to what people say. Are

they talking mainly about the benefits of the change and the future? Or are they talking more about the past, losses, and what they will be missing?

2. **Sense.** How do you feel when you interact with them? Use yourself as a sensor. Do you feel energized and enthusiastic when you meet and interact with them? Or do you feel discouraged, demoralized, or even apathetic?

3. **Ask.** Ask the difficult questions: "How are you really feeling about these changes? What are you having most difficulty with? What are you most looking forward to?"

Understand Resistances to Change

Apply these same steps—observe, sense, and ask—to resistance.

1. **Observe.** Resistance is the inevitable tendency to stick with the familiar and the proven and to move away from what is unfamiliar and uncomfortable. Where do you see disruptive people and behavior? Who is complaining or criticizing and about what? Who is withdrawing, being passive, or not communicating? About what?

2. **Sense.** Where do you feel frustrated or blocked? Where do you feel challenged or even attacked? Where do you sense anxiety and fear?

3. **Ask.** Where are you feeling stuck? Blocked? When you are being critical, what is going on inside of you? What is leading you to disengage? How do you feel?

Determine Motivations to Change

Again, apply these steps—observe, sense, and ask—to get a clear picture of people's motivations to change.

1. **Observe.** What seems to be moving forward smoothly? What are people struggling with? What benefits seem to attract their interest? To what extent do they see something in it for themselves?

2. **Sense.** What issues seem to be at the core of their resistances? Where is the fear? What are the antidotes to fear? Where do you feel encouraged? And by whom? What seems to be energizing to you?

3. **Ask.** What seems clear and positive about the changes? What are your concerns? What do you think needs adjustment? What would give you deeper reasons and desire to change?

CREATING COMMITMENT TO CHANGE: THREE MAJOR LEVERS

You cannot directly or forcibly make people want to do anything. So how do you influence their motivations and emotions? There are three important ways to help individuals and organizations address the challenges of the heart.

1. **Rebalance the gains-versus-losses equation.** Provide opportunities and experiences that help individuals rebalance their gains-versus-losses equation by helping people see what's in it for them under the new scenario. Understanding personal benefits is a necessary and natural need, not a selfish or self-centered one.

2. **Surface and release fears.** All change involves loss and thus negative emotions. Underneath anger, frustration, skepticism, and uncertainty lies fear. Too much fear is an obstacle to learning and change. To release fears you first have to acknowledge them and then examine them. We use the slogan "name it and frame it." Give the fear a name and a description, and then look at it from different perspectives.

3. **Realign rewards.** To be learned and applied, new behaviors and ways of thinking must have clear rewards. Old behaviors, once heavily rewarded, are now in conflict with the new vision. These old behaviors, which up to now were encouraged by the company culture, must no longer be rewarded. This takes some major realignments.

Table 19

Creating Change in the Heart Arena: Three Levers		
Levers to Change	Challenge Addressed	Techniques
1. Rebalance gains-versus-losses equation	▪ How do we deal with people who are too comfortable with the status quo? ▪ What do we do if there is a low readiness for change? ▪ What if people are stuck on the losses associated with change? ▪ How do we keep people from overrating negative impacts of change? ▪ What if people underestimate the liabilities of failing to change? ▪ What can we do if the payoffs are not seen—if there is a failure to see benefits of change? (WIIFM?)	▪ Chart gains versus losses ▪ Enumerate benefits ▪ Use feedback from surveys and observational ratings of employee behaviors and perceptions ▪ Have reality check sessions (described in Ch. 7)

Table 19, Creating Change in the Heart Arena, provides an overview of these three levers. Then we describe each of the three levers in more depth.

Lever 1. Rebalance Gains-Versus-Losses Equation

To commit to change, individuals must see that their potential gains exceed their losses. The balance of positives versus negatives is a personalized equation for each person and team. Early on, it's far easier to

Table 19 (cont'd)

Creating Change in the Heart Arena: Three Levers		
Levers to Change	**Challenge Addressed**	**Techniques**
2. Surface and release fears	■ How do we manage fear, which is an inevitable element in change? ■ How do we deal with reluctance to learn and experiment with new behaviors due to fear of failure or not being good enough? ■ What if collaboration and teamwork seem too risky? ■ How do we provide time and place to practice and learn new behaviors?	■ Make visits to "Pity City" (described in Ch. 7), to surface and ventilate concerns and fears ■ Have forums and small groups to talk through personal impacts ■ Avoid punishing mistakes ■ Build relationships ■ Develop forums for practicing new behaviors and getting feedback and coaching to accelerate learning
3. Realign rewards	■ What if old patterns of behavior remain unchanged? ■ How do we provide external rewards to help jump start learning of new behaviors? ■ How do we increase sense of engagement or commitment?	■ Ensure alignment between desired behaviors and rewards ■ Celebrate and reward even small successes ■ Involve people in planning and adjusting new changes ■ Have "early adopters" teach others

see what is being lost than what is being gained, especially because the losses often occur before the gains can be received. When negatives predominate, the change feels unrewarding and people seek to avoid it. Conversely, when positives predominate, there is energy for change. What is most challenging for the change agents is that each person puts his own weight on the benefits and the liabilities. No objective calculation applies uniformly to people or teams. In addition, the weighting of each item shifts over time. As you will see, facing up to the losses and allowing the negative emotions to be acknowledged and worked through often reduces their weight, which swings the equation toward change.

Rich resources for the CIT were their personal experiences in working through their own emotional reactions to the operational changes and the drastic alterations in their roles. The team brought to the surface and started to work through their resistances and emotions first, before they started working with others. Then they began to talk about their own experiences in ways that made it okay for people to discuss their feelings about change.

The members of the CIT had been successful store managers and had coached their employees on how to "beat" the original SOP certification checklist. Each of them talked about why and how they had instructed people to give the right answers instead of actually implementing the required processes. They talked about how circumventing the change achieved some short-term payoffs. They even admired and joked about each other's expertise in "beating the scorecard." Acknowledging what they had done, why, and how they did it helped them to empathize with the people they were now about to "score."

Lever 2. Surface and Release Fears

Have you ever seen the tall, narrow, flaming torches that sit high above petroleum refineries burning off the by-products of the process? Fears and negative emotions triggered by change are like the highly volatile—and if blocked, potentially dangerous—fumes that get burned off on these torches. Fears obstruct the change process. They intimidate the change agents and can paralyze the organization. The best way to change negative emotions is to allow them out to expand, be understood, and worked through. First, fears need to be acknowledged. Individuals will remain focused on their sense of loss, fear, and uncertainty until they perceive that they have been listened to, that the issues have been addressed, and that their pain has been recognized. Only then will they be ready to grapple with their fears and move forward.

As we worked with the people at Best Buy, we perceived that the company had a macho culture. Typically, the leaders had been heroes who seemed to show no doubt or uncertainty. They didn't admit to weaknesses or acknowledge that they didn't have all the answers. So when people worried about being good enough under the new SOP, which contained some pretty stringent guidelines, they just squelched their fears. At first, it didn't seem safe to admit to uncertainty, fear, or doubt. Then a few brave, mature, and understanding executives started owning up to what they didn't know or understand. And their uncertainty didn't diminish them. Instead, they came across as being honest, unapologetic, and open to learning.

The CIT carried the notion of learning forward. They worked with the store management to develop everyday forums in which people could practice the needed new behaviors and get feedback and coaching to accelerate their learning. A community of learning started to emerge.

Lever 3. Realign Rewards

Changing a reward system is both an obvious step to take and an extremely difficult task to accomplish. Most rewards, or reinforcement for behavior, come in the form of recognition and encouragement from other people who are still operating under the old rewards structure. For new behaviors and systems to grow, something must die. The structures and dynamics of the company that continue to support the old patterns must now die.

A sure way to undermine change and breed resentment is to reward people for behaviors other than those required by the new vision and practices. This can occur inadvertently, because the old culture is deeply rooted. Best Buy had succeeded with its cowboy culture, but now the company needed to make a change from the "run and gun" days of rapid expansion—when the criteria of success was an exuberant store opening and sales, sales, sales—to a culture that measured success by sustained store results, sustained profits, and customer retention. Making this shift called for dramatically different incentives for Best Buy managers and employees.

The CIT looked at existing reward systems, both formal and informal, and asked, What behaviors are being rewarded? and, What message does that send? The Best Buy retail rewards systems favored competition—between groups within the store, between stores, between regions, and between divisions. There were no incentives to engage in team behaviors, collaboration, or sharing best practices among groups. When the CIT started bumping into these disconnects between required new behaviors and old reward systems, they alerted executive-level decision makers to the problem. An observation of author and futurist Marilyn Ferguson applies here: "It's not so much that we're afraid of change, or so in love with the old ways, but it's the place in between that we fear . . . it's like being between trapezes. It's Linus when his blanket is in the dryer. There's nothing to hold on to."

MISTAKES ALONG THE WAY

The heart is an arena of great power, but it is difficult for leaders to address. It feels like climbing down into a very deep and very dark well. Yet you must go down, despite the darkness and threat, to find, illuminate, and bring to the surface what has been hidden. Naturally, we made mistakes going into this well and got demoralized at times in the darkness. We found a number of ways to go wrong in this arena. For a summary of them, see Table 20, Five Ways to Fail at Changing the Heart. And we found that laughing at oneself is a great antidote for terminal cynicism and self-doubt.

Effective change teams allow room for its members to periodically play the role of trickster. Tricksters embody the energy of both mischief and change. Tricksters cut big egos down to size. They are irreverent, but relevant. They have a sense of humor. They modulate the intensity level of the story. There were tricksters in the Best Buy story. As a team, the CIT often played this role, and their focus was often senior management and consultants.

For example, at each CIT meeting, members selected a phrase of the day (also known as "the phrase that pays"). These phrases were usually off-color one-liners that had nothing to do with business language. The CIT kept the phrase of the day a secret from the consultants. The team members would each put some money into a pool, and whoever could insert the phrase of the day into a plausible

Table 20

Five Ways to Fail at Changing the Heart
1. Try to change others before you have first changed yourself.
2. Hope commitment to change will automatically come when people understand the new vision.
3. Expect that people will see that gains outweigh losses. It's only rational.
4. Manage the change process without acknowledging negative emotions. Be surprised as fear, uncertainty, and doubt surface.
5. Let reward systems take care of themselves. Change should be its own reward.

question or comment to the consultants collected a small pool of money and lots of laughs. The team used such cleverness to test the boundaries and show their growing confidence by making fun of complicated concepts and keeping everyone humble.

CHANGING HEART ACROSS THREE STAGES

As noted in previous chapters, a successful change process unfolds in three stages.

1. Coming to grips with the problem
2. Working it through
3. Making it stick: maintaining momentum

Each arena has its distinctive signature, as shown in Table 21, and in different stages one arena may be more active than another. The head arena is most active in stage 1. The hands arena is most active in stage 3, when the focus is on implementation and behavioral change. For the heart arena, there is most activity in stage 2, when people are trying to work it through. In this stage, the internalization of change and the realignment of motivations and rewards—all functions of the heart arena—are critical.

Table 21

Stages of Change and the Three Arenas			
Stage	Arena		
1. Coming to grips with the problem	**Head**	Heart	Hands
2. Working it through	Head	**Heart**	Hands
3. Making it stick: maintaining momentum	Head	Heart	**Hands**

COMMITMENT TO CHANGE ACROSS THE THREE STAGES

The focus of change in the heart arena varies in each of these three stages. In stage 1, coming to grips with the problem, the rebalance-gains-versus-losses lever gets the heaviest use. At this first stage, the benefits of the old ways are most familiar, and the coming changes appear primarily as losses and liabilities. In this first stage, leaders must begin to rebalance the equation by illuminating the negatives associated with the old ways and identifying new benefits and gains that will come with the changes. Again, people will not be receptive to change until they understand there is a favorable WIIFM? that lies ahead.

In stage 2, working it through, "surfacing and releasing fears" comes to the forefront. Losses and fears must be recognized and discussed so that their power to obstruct change is decompressed and released. In stage 3, making it stick: maintaining momentum, "realign rewards" becomes an important lever. At this stage a new culture and system of rewards must form to provide the continued motivation and commitment that are required for long-lasting change. A summary and some additional texture for these points are shown in Table 22, Changing the Heart in Three Stages.

Table 22

Changing the Heart in Three Stages

Stage	Coming to Grips with the Problem	Working It Through	Making It Stick: Maintaining Momentum
1. Rebalance gains-versus-losses equation	■ Ask questions to uncover the liabilities and dissatisfaction with the old ways ■ Help individuals see how costs and liabilities personally affect them and their futures	■ Hold reality check meetings (see Ch. 7) to list gains and losses ■ Chart individual gains-versus-losses equations ■ Acknowledge losses and distress ■ Help individuals discover personal benefits of change ■ Reframe descriptions of losses into gains where appropriate	■ Confirm that gains are being realized ■ Use testimonials of early changers ■ Compare "then" and "now" to bring home how far individuals, teams, and the organization have come

Table 22 (cont'd)

Changing the Heart in Three Stages

Stage	Coming to Grips with the Problem	Working It Through	Making It Stick: Maintaining Momentum
2. Surface and release fears	■ Confront myths and taboo topics about the old culture and its heroes ■ Make it okay to give voice to fears, doubts, and concerns ■ Increase confidence that change is achievable	■ Foster direct discussion of losses and concerns ■ Explore resistances, since fear lies below them ■ Provide support and encouragement ■ Promote a climate and culture of discovery and learning	■ Surface frustrations and concerns; keep communications flowing ■ Firmly but fairly address those who remain uncommitted to change; the whole organization is watching how they are handled ■ Encourage rather than punish failures that reflect well-motivated efforts toward change ■ Find and remove obstacles to learning

Table 22 (cont'd)

Changing the Heart in Three Stages

Stage	Coming to Grips with the Problem	Working It Through	Making It Stick: Maintaining Momentum
3. Realign rewards	▪ Determine how old culture exercises influence through recognition, awards, compensation, etc. ▪ Begin to define the new payoffs that come with change ▪ Determine "old" vs. "new" WIIFM?	▪ Recognize and reward early adopters of change ▪ Celebrate early successes ▪ Help create link in people's minds between the vision and solving today's problems ▪ Eliminate organizational roadblocks to learning ▪ Scorecard changes in motivations and provide feedback on results	▪ Formalize rewards and recognition to align with new motivations and behaviors ▪ Examine and shape the culture to lock in new values, beliefs, and behaviors ▪ Keep asking, What behaviors are we rewarding?

A regional manager had this additional thought on staging change: "First, winning the heart is 80 percent of success. To win the heart, sometimes you need a role model. We had a victory with a store that put almost exclusive focus on the SOP. It became a testimonial to . intensity, drive, and having a singular focus. This store went through the resistance and pain. Later, the other stores saw its success and how it related to focusing on a smaller set of objectives. And then the change process spread to all of the stores in our region."

MEASURING THE MYSTERIOUS

How do you measure the way people are feeling? What is their readiness to change? Scorecarding can measure these dimensions of change. Though we delve more deeply into the mechanics of scorecarding in Chapter 9, Tools for Measuring Change, a couple of comments will be useful here. First, scorecarding the dimension of the heart provides key feedback to those managing change. And second, measuring the heart creates change.

Scorecards can be designed to measure the key levers that change the heart: (1) rebalancing gains versus losses, (2) releasing fears, and (3) shifting rewards. Since these are emotional issues and thus are not always visible, the people who are scorecarding change readiness are trained to listen and make inferences about the emotional status of those they are rating. This may sound subjective, but with detailed scoring instructions and examples, one can achieve consistency (reliability) in determining if people are putting more weight on gains or losses. In the early stages of change, it's a matter of determining whether individuals recognize any potential gains in the coming changes. Publishing the results of scorecarding in the heart arena (for instance, posting results on bulletin boards) tends to "normalize" the emotions. People can be asked what they see being rewarded and what they see being discouraged, even punished. And scorecarding provides data for assessing the extent to which compensation and recognition processes are aligned with the changes.

In developing scorecards for the heart arena, Table 23, Scorecarding Changes Heart, offers guidance on questions to address in this process.

Table 23

Scorecarding Changes Heart

1. **Measure the right things.**
   Are we measuring the critical dynamics capable of creating deep commitment to change?

2. **Measure change readiness.**
   What is the readiness for change in all areas of the vision and new set of behaviors?

3. **Feedback acknowledges concerns and releases fear.**
   How can we use feedback to make people feel their concerns and fears have been acknowledged?

4. **Measurement of commitment puts responsibility on management.**
   Are we assessing emotions, resistance, and commitment so that these factors can be changed, rather than blamed on the participants?

WHEN HEART AND HANDS ARE NOT CONNECTED

We have focused on the heart as a single arena, but its links to the other arenas, head and hands, are critical to effective change. If the heart arena is the motivational engine of the vehicle, then the links to the other arenas are the transmission that translates emotion into motion. Figure 12, Change Readiness Map, shows some potential links between the heart and the hands and their implications for accelerating the change process.

For instance, when individuals or teams are showing movement in both the arenas of heart (acceptance of change) and hands (behavioral capability to execute), they become powerful instruments of change. And when there is a disconnect between two arenas, distinct patterns of dysfunction appear. Figure 12 reminds us that when change needs to occur in the heart arena, it is accomplished by rebalancing gains versus losses, releasing fears, and realigning rewards.

People at Best Buy got an additional nudge to change when they saw a number of the old-school regional managers who were not

Figure 12

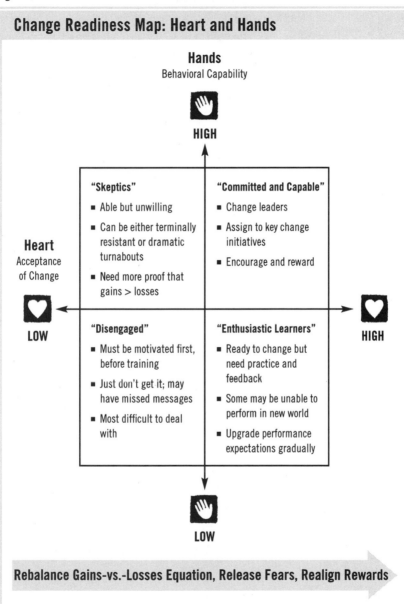

Change Readiness Map: Heart and Hands

Hands
Behavioral Capability

HIGH

Heart
Acceptance
of Change

LOW

HIGH

"Skeptics"
- Able but unwilling
- Can be either terminally resistant or dramatic turnabouts
- Need more proof that gains > losses

"Committed and Capable"
- Change leaders
- Assign to key change initiatives
- Encourage and reward

"Disengaged"
- Must be motivated first, before training
- Just don't get it; may have missed messages
- Most difficult to deal with

"Enthusiastic Learners"
- Ready to change but need practice and feedback
- Some may be unable to perform in new world
- Upgrade performance expectations gradually

LOW

Rebalance Gains-vs.-Losses Equation, Release Fears, Realign Rewards

adopting the cultural and operational changes being moved into other positions—out of the line of store leadership. The moves took place in a low-profile manner, but the CIT knew what was occurring in each case. Though the moves were not labeled as successes, they did give the CIT a sense of support and alignment that helped keep them going.

A regional manager summed up this arena, "Don't underestimate the heart. You need evangelistic leaders to win over the heart. You need people's buy-in. The head is easier; you can get trainers and writers. To win in the arena of the heart, you need local leaders to motivate the hearts of the people."

6

Using the Hands to Make Change Real

SO WHAT DO I DO DIFFERENTLY ON MONDAY?

Change efforts often do not lead to sustained change because a link is missing between vision, strategies, and incentives and the actual, on-the-job behavior of employees. Sustained change occurs in an organization only when each person is applying new ways of behaving on the job and is enjoying the rewards of these new practices.

Best Buy was not only changing its store operations; it was introducing a systematic, consistent way of operating in the stores for the first time. But how could Best Buy's leaders guide people into making tangible behavioral changes while preserving the company's soul of creativity and innovation? The answer lay in learning to introduce innovations in ways that could be translated into explicit behavioral guidelines without turning people into mindless, rule-bound robots. To transform Best Buy, or any large organization, you must change thousands of behaviors for thousands of employees—and have those changes cumulatively result in realizing a new vision and creating a new culture.

The changes at Best Buy ranged from very specific store employee behaviors to broad shifts in leadership style. These changes needed to be introduced in ways that would be integrated with all the other corporate initiatives taking place in this large, complex retail organization. And there was backsliding after the changes were introduced. For example, early in the SOP implementation, a CIT member who had visited a particular store would revisit that store a month later to find that the manager and employees had reverted to their former patterns of behavior. Why?

One important reason for this regression was that often leaders were not modeling the necessary new values and behaviors. Looking deeper, the CIT began to watch store employees in action, ask questions, and join managers and retail executives as they toured and inspected the stores. These leaders, starting with the executives, were paying attention to the same things they'd paid attention to before the SOP was introduced. They were not looking at things differently, evaluating operations differently, or giving feedback that emphasized how people in the stores needed to behave in the new environment. Instead, they were emphasizing the same need for people to strive for piecemeal results that they had in the past.

This leadership behavior had enormous influence on the forward (or backward) movement of the change. In response, members of the CIT broadened their client group to include all of retail leadership to help them define, learn, and practice new ways of paying attention to the people reporting to them. The impact of this shift in day-to-day leadership behavior was amazing. The change effort surged forward. Best Buy was learning a new way of behaving. It was answering the question, What do I do differently on Monday?

WHAT DOES "GOOD" LOOK LIKE?

The CIT worked to define the new behaviors needed at every level of the store and in every job. In this change implementation, "the hands" referred to changes in store processes—for instance, how inventory is put onto the right shelves at the right time or how a salesperson walks the floors and interacts with customers (zoning). The team repeated the process of watching what was actually happening, asking questions, and working through what was and wasn't being effective. The CIT realized that people needed to understand the new behaviors and skills and have a place, a forum, in which to practice them while getting feedback and coaching. We used the phrase 'What does 'good' look like?" to remind us of the need to define the desired behaviors. This phrase was the trigger for managers to paint very explicit pictures of specific people doing specific things in specific situations to be successful. This is the core of the hands arena.

CHALLENGES IN CHANGING HANDS

By now the change framework is embedded in your thinking. Effective change requires success in all three arenas: head (altering mind-set), heart (harnessing motivation), and hands (shaping behavior). The hands arena is critical, as it channels all the changes of the head and heart into tangible behavioral change that produces outcomes. If there were a balance sheet for the change process, "hands" would be the bottom line—where it all pays off in better business results.

The key challenge of the hands arena is to help people answer two questions: What exactly am I supposed to do differently? How do I learn and master these new skills and practices? Answering these questions involves helping work through a learning cycle that requires goals, practice, feedback, and room for mistakes. And it involves aligning the underlying culture, assumptions, structures, and systems that shape and sustain these new behaviors.

LEARNING KNOW-HOW: TURNING NEWBORN BEHAVIORS INTO MATURE PRACTICES

Have you ever watched the genesis of a new behavior? You get an idea to try something. Or maybe you decide to imitate a practice of a colleague. Or maybe someone suggested that you change your behavior. You initiate the new behavior—it's born. The behavior is weak, wobbly, and tentative. If it gets a positive response—you like the consequences or someone signals that the behavior is desirable—the newborn behavior gets stronger. And with practice, feedback, and some (even inconsistent) positive reward, the behavior grows sturdy and bold. It's now self-sustaining. The behavior has become habitual, even automatic. This is how we learn new behaviors, in an upward spiral.

STAGES IN THE LIFE CYCLE OF A NEW BEHAVIOR

Establishing a new behavior involves three stages: initiating the behavior, strengthening it, and making it self-sustaining.

Initiate New Behavior

Ask the following three guide questions and ponder the answers to help employees begin a new behavior.

What Must Happen?

To initiate a new behavior, employees must either have a behavioral model to emulate (they must see someone demonstrating what "good" looks like) or already have the behavior in their repertoire, ready to apply. Thereafter, they need opportunities and cues to try out the new behavior.

What Makes the Behavior Stronger?

Immediate, frequent, positive consequences make the behavior more likely to happen in the future. Rewards may be intrinsic for the individual ("That was really satisfying for me") or come from others (praise from a colleague, such as, "How did you do that? That was really good work!").

What Weakens the Behavior?

An immediate negative consequence such as failure ("I tried but it didn't work") or punishment (a colleague saying, "That was dumb" or "You goofed that up") will reduce the frequency of an emerging behavior.

Strengthen the Behavior

Apply the same guide questions to ensure that the new behavior is firmly established.

What Must Happen?

Employees must get continued cues and opportunities to practice and polish a complex cluster of behaviors.

What Makes the Behavior Stronger?

Feedback is key. It can come from self-monitoring ("I am getting better and need to make these changes to get improved results") or from the coaching of others ("You did that well. How about adding this approach next time and see if you get even better results?"). Interestingly, positive consequences or rewards don't need to happen with every occurrence of the behavior at this stage. In fact, intermittent positive consequences create the most sustainable behaviors with the greatest resistance to fading.

What Weakens the Behavior?

Setting improvement goals too high, beyond the reach of the learning employee ("I was doing okay for awhile, but now the standards are too high for me" or "How will I ever reach that level? It's impossible!"), reduces the frequency of the behavior. Failing to achieve overly high standards for success reduces positive consequences—which are the critical nutrients for growing strong behaviors. Also, a complete lack of external reinforcement by others, despite improved employee behaviors that meet standards, sends a discouraging message to the individual ("I guess it doesn't make any difference to anyone").

Make Behavior Self-Sustaining

Finally, ask the three guide questions again for self-sustaining behavior.

What Must Happen?

Emerging, tentative, less-than-perfect behaviors must grow up to become part of the everyday functioning of the individual. Or, in other words, these behaviors must become a constructive habit (internalized and automatic). To foster this outcome, the organization must build a set of expectations and processes in which these behaviors are required.

What Makes the Behavior Stronger?

Periodic recognition from others helps the individual internalize the behavior. The individual becomes her own evaluator and coach ("I feel good when I show that I have mastered these new behaviors"). The organization's culture determines what gets rewarded on a day-to-day basis. The culture has to make these behaviors simultaneously expected and rewarded with both formal (evaluations of performance) and informal systems (what people say and actually do). Best Buy came to call this "baking the change in." The behavior must become part of what is overtly encouraged and rewarded by official practice and tacitly reinforced by the organization's culture. Individuals must see that their behaviors line up with their own personal needs (WIIFM?) as well as the vision and goals of the company.

What Weakens the Behavior?

Competing or old behaviors can reduce the time available to learn and apply new behaviors. Moreover, allowing undesirable behaviors to continue sends a conflicting message ("I see Bill is still doing it the old way. I guess they're not really serious about the new stuff"). And finally, in the total absence of any recognition or acknowledgment at all, even sturdy behaviors decline, especially if they take more effort or skills than the former practices did.

DON'T OLD BEHAVIORS JUST FADE AWAY AND DIE?

By now you might be asking, If behaviors can be born and grow up, what about the death of behaviors? What happens to the unwanted or old behaviors in a change process? Don't they just die? No, humans do not unlearn or forget important behaviors. Rather, new behaviors replace them. Old behaviors become dormant and invisible. They still exist, even while new behaviors start to predominate and become visible. The fact that old behaviors lurk just below the surface explains to us why backsliding can happen so quickly. If people sense that the cues and reinforcement for the old behaviors have returned, those old behaviors instantly come out of retirement and go back to work.

Asked about these behaviors, a veteran regional manager said, "The 'dark forces' in our culture are embodied in the attitudes of people who have been successful—and who didn't change. They keep doing the same things that brought them this far in their career. Many of them are reaching their ceiling."

CHANGING HANDS: THREE LEVERS FOR CHANGE

Psychologists have described the process of learning new behaviors in great depth. Rather than use the language of behavioral science or learning theory, here we will simply talk about three interrelated ways to achieve behavioral change. These three levers for change are key to influencing behavior.

1. **Maps, models, and goals point the way.** "What exactly am I supposed to be doing now?" This is the question that comes into the mind of the person who has just grasped the need to change and has a growing motivation to put new behaviors into action. Complex behavior, such as that required by Best Buy's SOP, needs to be understood and learned in patterns rather than as individual behaviors. For example, a tennis player learns to execute an overhead serve as a rhythm and flow rather than as several dozen unconnected movements of the head, eyes, torso, hands, arms, legs, and feet.

    Often descriptions of new employee behaviors are called *profiles* or *competencies* to convey this integrated image. A more accurate term is *behavioral maps*. Maps simplify complexity by including only the most important elements and prioritizing them. Best Buy translated business and operating processes into such behavioral maps. For example, a map would show how a merchandiser (who puts inventory on the store shelves) plans and organizes the ways she gets cartloads of product from the back room onto the shelves—and how she does so in the most efficient manner while coordinating with other employees in the store. Just like tennis players watching the teaching pro, people learn fastest by watching others model new behaviors. Best Buy found or created role models for people to watch. So they provided both maps to follow and models to copy. And along the way, it helps to have well-defined goals or milestones to mark progress in the new learning (more about these goals later).

2. **Make new behaviors automatic with practice and feedback.** Remember when you first learned a new behavior? Can you recall how awkward and incompetent you felt initially? What does it take to make a complex behavior automatic? What leads to its becoming smooth, polished, and effective? First, you need a lot of practice in a supportive and accepting environment in which mistakes and miscues are allowed and even expected. You also need to get feedback all along the way. Again, think of learning to serve a tennis ball. As you practice hundreds of serves, you start to learn exactly what it takes to hit the ball. And your objectives—your criteria for success—evolve. At first, your objective is to hit the ball in the direction of the net, then you want to get over the net, and then you aim for the service box. Much later you work on pace and putting spin on your serve. These mini-milestones in learning are called "successive approximations" of the final behavioral goal. Opportunities for practice, with room for mistakes, feedback, and setting successive approximations of the final target behavior, are the critical elements of making new behaviors automatic.

3. **Bake new behaviors into the culture.** New behaviors that implement change are not sustainable unless the organization consistently supplies the right consequences. From a learning perspective, we know that positive consequences teach us to sustain behaviors, and negative consequences, or even no consequences, lead us to decrease the new behaviors. In the early stages of learning, people need extra attention and recognition for practicing new behaviors. This special reinforcement is like

the temporary scaffolding erected during construction of a new building. Eventually the scaffolding is taken down and the building stands on its own. Similarly, new behaviors must become self-sustaining. Creating an environment that supports self-sustaining behaviors is what we call baking the changes into the culture—or "bake it in," for short. How can an abstract concept like *culture* be useful when planning how tangible, everyday behaviors can become self-sustaining? We address this shortly.

Table 24, Creating Change in the Hands Arena, on the following page, provides an overview of these three levers for change. We will go into more depth on each of these, using examples from Best Buy.

Lever 1. Maps, Models, and Goals Point the Way

Maps and Models

Given the importance of role modeling by managers who are leading change, it makes good sense to put effort into mapping the expected manager behaviors. Modeling means that everything you do and say sends a message. When you say one thing and do another, people will believe what you do, not what you say. Others will trust those leaders who do what they say and say what they'll do—when their words and actions match.

At Best Buy, the culture showed itself in rowdy and undisciplined meetings. Participants expended a lot of energy, but much of it was lost in the chaos and confusion. The consultants and then CIT members consciously tried to introduce some basic behaviors conducive to effective, productive meetings. We had no desire to stifle or dissipate the energy but only to help focus it. Running meetings became a model for a collaborative, efficient, but still enjoyable culture. Following are some of the specific behaviors.

- State the purpose and goal of the meeting. Get confirmation.
- Agree on starting time and stopping time. Stick with these times, unless there is strong agreement that the meeting should be extended.

Table 24

Creating Change in the Hands Arena: Three Levers		
Levers to Change	**Challenge Addressed**	**Techniques**
1. Maps, models, and goals point the way	▪ What do I do differently on Monday? ▪ How do we define the new behaviors required to be successful? ▪ Who are the role models (from exec to frontline employee) for new behaviors? ▪ How do we measure progress? What are the new expectations? ▪ How do I get the personal payoffs (WIIFM?) that I have heard about?	▪ Behavioral descriptions ▪ Behavioral profiles of new leader and manager behaviors ▪ S.M.A.R.T. goals* – **S**pecific – **M**easurable – **A**ction oriented – **R**ealistic – **T**ime and resource constrained
2. Make new behaviors automatic with practice and feedback	▪ How do I learn the new behaviors? ▪ How do I master the new practices? ▪ What is acceptable as I try out the new roles? ▪ What happens if I make mistakes along the way? ▪ How do I know if I am making progress?	▪ Structured training experiences ▪ On-the-job coaching and mentoring ▪ Working toward successive approximations of the final target behaviors (dynamic scorecarding) ▪ Creating climate accepting of mistakes that come with learning ▪ Behavioral scorecarding with skillful feedback on progress and mistakes (discussed in Chs. 9–10)

Table 24 (cont'd)

Creating Change in the Hands Arena: Three Levers		
Levers to Change	**Challenge Addressed**	**Techniques**
3. Bake new behaviors into the culture	▪ How do we get new patterns to replace old practices and habits? ▪ What if managers lack teaching and coaching skills? ▪ How do new behaviors become self-sustaining? ▪ How do we align the culture to reinforce the desired new behaviors?	▪ Map desired new culture ▪ Align right results with right behaviors—recognize and reward those showing new patterns to achieve business results ▪ Thin out rewards; start with high frequency of reinforcement for new behaviors then taper toward intermittent reinforcement ▪ Begin/update professional development plans for key managers

*Reprinted with permission from Crisp Publications Inc., 1200 Hamilton Court, Menlo Park, CA 94025

- Have an outline, in which topics relate to the stated purpose of the meeting.

- Name a facilitator, whose role it is to keep the meeting moving forward and on track.

- Use a flip chart or other visual tool to track key issues, areas of agreement and disagreement, and so on. Use a separate flip chart to track "parking lot issues" not directly relevant to the meeting but worth tracking for the future.

- Summarize points of agreement and disagreements and actions to be taken.

- Conclude the meeting with these questions:

1. How did we do? (How did we treat one another? Did we stay on the topic? Were we able to discuss things at the level of dialogue, or appreciative inquiry?)

2. What did we learn? (New ideas? Discarding of old ideas? What would we do differently or the same the next time?)

Modeling and maps were a start. But this behavior change effort involved more than 30,000 employees, and the number was growing rapidly. The CIT needed a geometrically expanding sphere of influence to reach the thousands of employees. There was no way to focus on each individual. In fact, the CIT began using a motto about leveraging their efforts through managers, "Each one teach one." This became the approach to engaging district and regional management in sharing leadership of the teaching and coaching efforts. The CIT became the ambassadors of change by modeling new behaviors for management, but they nearly sank under the massive effort. It took between six and nine months for the majority of the RMs and DMs to hear that the change implementation was their responsibility—and couldn't simply be delegated to the CIT members who worked in their districts and regions.

We created A *Field Guide to Implementing the SOP* as a written map to help people translate the SOP concepts into clusters of behavior. Different people see and learn things in different ways. There are times when we need to break things down into smaller pieces in order to understand the whole. As described in Chapter 2, The Map Is Not the Territory, one of the major change principles included in the *Field Guide* was that you have to learn your instrument before you can play in the band. With this metaphor, we tried to convey a sense of how each person must learn and practice the behaviors necessary in her individual position so that she can effectively participate in the activities required by the larger group. At other times, we need to see how it all fits together before the individual pieces make sense to us. We need to see our behaviors as part of a collective system that works smoothly and efficiently to achieve a common goal. This requires a disciplined approach to meld individual contributions into a cohesive team effort. See the following excerpt from the Field Guide.

FIELD GUIDE EXCERPT

> To get to the next level of effectiveness, companies have to grow up and move from a chaotic, entrepreneurial company full of Harlem Globetrotter–type employees (who break the rules and do it differently every time, but dazzle the crowd) to a more mature organization that runs like clockwork—efficiently, effectively, and with minimal rework (more like the Chicago Bulls, who generally follow a playbook).

Following is another excerpt from the *Field Guide* in which we tried to convey a sense of how each individual learns the set of new behaviors necessary in her position and then puts those behaviors together with the new behaviors used by other members of the organization.

> **Goals**
> Goals provide focus and direction for our efforts and, when correctly established, have huge value in learning and executing new behaviors. Goals are like the archer's target. The concentric rings around the center are successive approximations to a bull's-eye—the target and the goal for the archer. At first we are happy to just get the arrow on the target. With practice, we expect more of ourselves and aim to hit a bull's-eye.

A note to our readers: many use the term *goals* to mean the desired outcomes of large-scale and overarching initiatives and *objectives* to mean the smaller, intermediate goals and milestones through which one translates general goals into specifics. Such distinctions are useful in practice. Our comments on the use of goals apply equally to the use of objectives.

Setting goals is necessary for effective behavioral change, as specific goals focus individuals' efforts and energies on the necessary activities. Goals define the criteria for success. We know that goals most powerfully align a group's efforts when the people who must actually implement them have agreed to them. Participating in goal setting is a powerful motivator for the people who actually have to do the work. To engage people in effective, participative goal setting, you must give them the big picture, and you must clarify the underlying mental models and assumptions about the change. We will first discuss goal setting and then the role of underlying mental models and assumptions.

Goals without specific action steps are confusing and frustrating. Goals with clear action steps accelerate progress toward reaching the goals. Effective action plans define and prioritize steps that lead to clearly defined goals. To monitor progress and give feedback, you need to define measures of success for both approaching and then achieving the final goal. The early identification of potential obstacles and constraints is critical to keep the change process from derailing and allows for contingency planning. Preventive intervention can help inoculate people against disabling frustrations that might arise during the learning process. Clearly defined accountabilities and assignments establish the actual commitments people need to make in order to reach the goal.

Finally, assigning completion dates for each step helps everyone make the necessary decisions and trade-offs between the types of outcomes desired, the resources available (people and money, for instance), and the time frames involved. All projects and their deliverables are managed on just three variables: time, features, and resources. *Time* is how long something takes. *Features* refers to the features that are included and their quality level. *Resources* is the money, people, and so on available to achieve your goal. Participative goal setting works best when the people setting the goal(s) are explicit about these three variables—time, features, and resources—and about how to make trade-offs between them. Be realistic in your consideration of these variables. Goals that are not feasible inevitably lead to frustration and renegotiation. Clear targets help to ensure success.

S.M.A.R.T. Goals.*

During their work sessions, people at Best Buy found it helpful to use the acronym S.M.A.R.T. to remind them of the characteristics of effective goal setting. S.M.A.R.T. goals are

*Reprinted with permission from Crisp Publications Inc., 1200 Hamilton Court, Menlo Park, CA 94025

- Specific
- Measurable
- Action oriented
- Realistic
- Time and resource constrained

Lever 2. Make New Behaviors Automatic with Practice and Feedback

This lever comes into play when goals are set and people are motivated. How do we get those complex behaviors polished, effective, and at the level of action necessary to achieve the intended business results? Recall those first awkward attempts at the tennis serve? Practice and feedback help you get your serve strong enough to score points. But where do you practice in the business setting? We all recognize the need for feedback, but most of us don't orchestrate anything close to the optimum number or quality of practice sessions in the organizational world. Most employees get some brief instructions and a bit of feedback and are sent off to "serve it up" in the real game with customers or other employees.

Practice Sessions in the Real World

Within Best Buy, role-playing became part of teaching, coaching, or giving any kind of feedback. For example, after describing how to systemically analyze the flow of activities within the store, a CIT member would walk with a store manager as she tried out this new way of seeing for the first time. Then, the CIT member would work with the manager to develop a plan for how she would practice this new skill in the future and how she would track her progress. When new concepts or procedures were introduced at regional and district meetings, the participants first saw the behaviors related to the concept or procedure as role-played by two leadership figures (perhaps the RM and the CIT member). Then the participants were divided into small groups and given scenarios in which they practiced the new skill, with one member of the group as the designated "watcher" who gave them feedback. At the end of each store's scorecarding session, the CIT member would give feedback to the store manager, and then the two of them would step through the feedback with the store employees who were available at that time. Role-playing and practice groups became "grooved" during these meetings.

Successive Approximations Are Stepping-Stones to Goals

Successive approximations, or incremental steps, aid in achieving the final behavior at the desired level of frequency and effectiveness. When you artfully set success standards at progressively higher levels, the learning employee experiences relatively little failure and frustration. Raise the standards as success becomes consistent at each approximation. Successive approximation is summed up by the phrase "Progress, not perfection."

Effective Feedback Accelerates Learning

The three most important things to know about effective feedback in baking in a new behavior are timing, timing, and timing! Giving feedback creates more learning than giving advice. When comments are offered to an employee *before* an event or behavior takes place, we can call it *advice*. For example, "If you ask the customer in a helpful tone of voice about why he is returning the product, you get the best results." Advice will have a mixed reception at best from the learner and only a modest benefit to his rate of learning. Offered immediately *after* an event or behavior, it becomes *feedback*. For example, "The tone of voice you used encouraged that customer to tell you why he wanted to return the product. And then you were able to help them learn how to use the remote control and decide to keep it rather than return it. Did you see how he opened up for you?"

When feedback is offered too long after the behavior, it loses much of its effectiveness. This decrease in effectiveness is evident even when the delay is as short as an hour. Optimum learning occurs when an individual first has a direct, personal experience with the behavior and an emotional reaction (e.g., "I succeeded/failed to meet my standard"), and then they receive feedback to help them digest what that experience is teaching them.

The most effective feedback has a balance of appreciative comments. For example, here is a positive comment: "You approached that customer after she had been looking at the big-screen TV for the right amount of time." And here is a critical comment: "You failed to make eye contact with the customer when you were presenting the big-screen TV." What feels like balanced feedback to the person on the receiving end? The human accounting process here is unique. Five positive comments offered with one critical or corrective feedback point would be perceived as balanced. If you drop below a 5:1 ratio, you risk being perceived as a critic rather than a coach. The receiver, and not you as the sender, determines if there is an adequate balance between appreciative and critical comments and thus if the feedback is constructive. Your positive intentions to give balanced feedback don't count for much if the learning employee doesn't perceive them as balanced.

One more point on timing. When you are outside of a formal training situation, remember to find a time when the recipient is receptive. Feedback offered at times that are convenient to you, but not suitable for the receiver, simply makes the learning process take longer for both parties. What can increase receptiveness? The greatest tool you have for increasing others' openness to and use of feedback from you is modeling the use of feedback in your own behavior. Solicit feedback from others, listen to it attentively, and incorporate it into your own behavior. This is the most powerful tool you have for influencing others.

Descriptive Feedback Supports Learning and Motivation

The best feedback is descriptive and refers to actual behaviors. Descriptive feedback is linked to goals and their business benefits. Here is an example of descriptive, relevant feedback to a technical service representative who had just dealt with a customer returning a computer printer: "When you smiled and took the initiative with the customer, asked open-ended questions about the nature of their difficulty, and then showed them a solution, they decided to keep the printer. You saved a return, which saves the company lots of money. What you just did makes you valuable to both the company and the customer. Great work!" Descriptively rich feedback helps the employee understand the key elements of his experience. It's like helping someone learn directions to a new destination by pointing out landmarks along the route. And since it's usually obvious when you are describing positive behavior, descriptive feedback carries positive reinforcement.

Isn't Criticism Just the Opposite of Praise?

Doesn't criticism work just as well as praise in shaping behavior? No. Criticism in behavioral terms is punishment—providing negative consequences as perceived by the receiver. And criticism has adverse side effects. Punishment can be as simple as making a sarcastic remark or raising your eyebrows. Too much emphasis on mistakes creates an unbalanced communication that is perceived as negative. Though punishment can get a behavior to stop quickly, it simply suppresses that behavior and does not teach the desired new behavior. Remember, old behaviors simply become dormant and invisible, ready to return. Also, punishment teaches an employee to avoid the source of that punishment. In training and development situations, being perceived as a critic reduces rapport at the least and at its worst sets up avoidance between the teacher/coach/manager and the learner/employee. Having employees avoid the source of learning is not what we want! Punishment is best reserved for intentional mistakes and even then should be used only sparingly.

You are always shaping behavior. The key is to learn to do it consciously. Positive reinforcement and balanced feedback work best. And, for most of us, it's more fun to give and get coaching and encouragement than criticism.

Lever 3. Bake New Behaviors into the Culture

Culture never leaves the office. When trainers and managers are not in sight, it's critical that employees continue implementing the new behaviors. In the organizational world, it's a reality that positive consequences become very intermittent. Paychecks and praise do not immediately follow every employee behavior. Employees must internalize the consequences for behavioral change. It's the organizational culture that sustains the rewards (and punishments) for employees' behavior. So, to firmly establish change, you must have an organizational culture that reinforces the new behaviors and vetoes the old.

By *culture*, we mean the deeper, often unspoken values and assumptions that lead to providing recognition, advancement, and attention to employees who model the new behaviors. In other words, culture is the constellation of values and beliefs about what it takes to be successful in the organization. For example, an organization has certain practices regarding time. At one level, there are agreements about setting and attending meetings and appointments: "We value starting our meetings on time." Or, "It's okay to come five or ten minutes late to meetings." At another level are values about the time it takes to introduce a new practice or innovation to the market: "We do whatever it takes to be the first to market with a new store format." Or, "We move as fast as we can and then see where we stand relative to our competitors." Most likely, the organization also has assumptions regarding performance evaluation. Best Buy had put such a high premium on requiring that performances meet or exceed its quantitative standards that an unspoken value or assumption began to surface: "It's better to distort our measuring process than to be seen as not meeting the standards." The most important and powerful dimensions of culture are extremely hard to see as an insider and are even more rarely articulated and written down.

Best Buy was aware of the need to make changes in its culture to make it compatible with the SOP and with the change process overall. The old culture (win, no matter what) was fed by a highly competitive forced-ranking system of all stores on multiple measures. It was strongly reinforced by a compensation structure (bonuses) based on achieving good numbers. The unanticipated side effect of this old culture was that some people would cut corners and misrepresent their achievements in order to look good and get a bigger bonus. The goal became reaching a particular score on a measure, rather than actually achieving the business results the score was intended to represent. In Chapter 7, we discuss specific practices to help managers and leaders change what they pay attention to and thus affect the focus of their organization.

SLIP OF HANDS

Change in the hands arena is the most visible of the changes in the three arenas. You can easily see progress as well as goofs and slips. We hope you can smile at our list of five favorite potential mistakes and misjudgments, listed in Table 25, and not repeat them.

During some "let your hair down" social hours at night, the group created a list of tension-releasing phrases that poked fun at the powers

Table 25

Five Ways to Fail at Changing the Hands

1. Expect people to automatically know what to do once they understand why the changes are needed.

2. Set standards so high that people experience failure in their learning efforts. Don't create early success on successive approximations of end goals.

3. Emphasize finding mistakes. Creating an accepting climate leads to weak employees.

4. Be surprised when old behaviors reappear and the underlying culture is slow to change.

5. Forget that new behaviors need extra and early recognition to make them self-sustaining. Too much recognition can spoil employees.

that be, the consultants, and themselves. The group often referred to "the phrase that pays." A T-shirt was produced with the sayings of the team, and it was illustrated by one of the CIT members who is a skilled cartoonist. As you can imagine, most of these phrases made sense only to the insiders. The number-one phrase was "You're not the boss of me!" Jason explained that members of the CIT used this phrase cynically when "none of this change stuff or influencing without authority was working." Team members did not wear the shirt at work, but no matter. The point was not wearing it but creating it.

CHANGING HANDS ACROSS THREE STAGES

Which comes first, motivation or behavior? Can change occur in the hands arena before change takes place in the heart arena? Is it possible for people to change their behavior (hands) without first changing their internal motivations (heart)? Sure. We all know that it is easier to be motivated to do something before we do it, but we also know that we can change our behavior out of pressures from the situation around us. For many, trying the new behaviors brings positive results that change our internal motivations. And our emotions will follow. You might hear, "I thought the new sales zones were stupid, but my boss made me follow them. Hey, I found they worked okay for my customers and me!" Behavioral scientists have shown that behavior change can change both emotions and cognitions—the ways we think and feel. Getting employees to step through new behaviors can reduce their tensions and concerns with new practices. An integrated change management strategy simultaneously pursues change in all three arenas—head, heart, and hands. Changes in one arena can prepare us for change in another arena.

The importance of the hands arena increases over the three stages. Beginning with stage 1, coming to grips with the problem, most of the attention in the hands arena is on the behaviors and practices that must change—the old hands. The new hands—the new behaviors and practices of the future—are simply sketches associated with the vision and business goal-setting process. During stage 2, working it through, new behaviors are coming into focus at the level of individual employees in different parts of the organization. This is necessary so that people can see WIIFM?—how the new behaviors will create results that have payoffs for them. Behavioral change, the bottom line of the change process, becomes the dominant focus in stage 3, making it stick: maintaining momentum. The three stages and the role of the three levers of change at each stage are shown in Table 26, Changing the Hands in Three Stages.

As we have noted, there is increasing emphasis on hands with each step of the three stages of change. Beware of too much emphasis on the hands early in the change process. Putting too much attention on individual behavior change without first addressing the challenges of the head and heart arenas creates an unprepared audience. Employees will appear to be resistant to change, uncooperative, and self-focused. This can lead to too much attention on "fixing" the employees rather than on having executives and managers communicate an understandable vision and the necessary motivations for change. The importance of fostering understanding and buy-in for the new behaviors was evident at Best Buy when store staff members were especially slow to adopt zoning, the practice of assigning salespeople to cover specific areas and training them in the product knowledge of that area. The sales employees and even their GMs did not understand the why and WIIFM? However, their support for sales zoning increased when they experienced how much it lifted the customers' shopping experience and how that, in turn, made them the beneficiary of improved sales and profitability via bonuses and promotions.

Table 26

Changing the Hands in Three Stages

Stage	Coming to Grips with the Problem	Working It Through	Making It Stick: Maintaining Momentum
1. Maps, models, and goals point the way	■ Identify specific behaviors that you must change ■ Create business case that shows how these behaviors (and their underlying mind-set) must change	■ Define success with behavioral profiles for managers and employees ■ Define new behaviors that will have direct payoffs (WIIFM?) for employees ■ Make it clear that training and achievable steps will be in place so that employees can master new behaviors ■ Further refine behavioral descriptions	■ Set action plans with S.M.A.R.T. goals ■ Involve employees in creating change implementation plans ■ Give opportunities for practice and learning ■ Find and recognize early role models of desired behaviors ■ Continue to refine behavioral descriptions

Table 26 (cont'd)

Changing the Hands in Three Stages

Stage	Coming to Grips with the Problem	Working It Through	Making It Stick: Maintaining Momentum
2. Make new behaviors automatic with practice and feedback	■ Define old practices and behaviors that will be incompatible with new behaviors and practices	■ Provide structured and informal training and coaching ■ Give frequent and rich levels of feedback and recognition ■ Accept mistakes and failures as early signs of progress—taking the first steps ■ Provide opportunities to practice and reinforce new behaviors	■ Move to higher performance expectations ■ Thin out amounts of feedback and recognition to make behaviors resistant to fading ■ Have managers and experienced employees teach new people ("each one teach one") ■ Give balanced feedback in reviewing results of scorecarding

Table 26 (cont'd)

Changing the Heart in Three Stages

Stage	Coming to Grips with the Problem	Working It Through	Making It Stick: Maintaining Momentum
3. Bake new behaviors into the culture	■ Map archetypal behaviors of the old and the desired behaviors of the new culture ■ Identify parts of the old culture that sustain undesired behaviors	■ Redefine people, processes, events, awards, etc., to reshape culture ■ Redefine performance management practices (objectives, performance reviews, feedback, etc.) to sustain new behaviors ■ Discuss culture maps; use reality check sessions (see Ch. 7) to discuss disconnects between behaviors of old vs. new culture	■ Implement refocused performance evaluation and compensation practices ■ Prune out managers/employees and dismantle teams that cannot/will not master new behavioral expectations ■ Emphasize scorecarding results as part of evaluation and reward process

IT'S MONDAY. ARE YOU DOING THINGS DIFFERENTLY? SCORECARDS FOR THE HANDS

Observing people as they attempt new behaviors provides insights for those designing the change program. Behavioral observation and measurement both support this analysis as well as provide the metrics for progress. If behavioral change is the profit line for change efforts, then behavioral measurement is the accounting of the business of change.

How do you measure the way people are behaving? Observing and scorecarding their behaviors can provide measurement, feedback, and motivation for change. To help you develop scorecards for the hands arena, Table 27, Scorecarding Changes Hands, lists questions to address in the process of scorecarding behavior. When scorecarding shows favorable changes, it becomes a powerful reward for progress.

We have now introduced you to the three arenas of change. Though this framework was extremely useful, it first needed to be modeled by the CIT before the rest of the organization would embrace it. The CIT was now well into efforts to change behavior. The

Table 27

Scorecarding Changes Hands

1. **Measure the right things.**
   Are we measuring the behaviors necessary to achieve improved business results?

2. **Measure consistency and strength.**
   How reliable and consistent are the employee behaviors? Are they above the threshold for improving operations and ultimately the customers' experience of the company?

3. **Assess underlying culture changes.**
   Are behaviors being measured that are indicators of the underlying values and assumptions that will help the culture evolve in the right directions?

4. **Gauge sustainability.**
   Are we assessing the extent to which behaviors are sustaining themselves over time, when training and intensive supervision have been completed?

team was feeling increasing pressure and starting to show strain. The team had created a FAQ sheet on the SOP for coaching and training purposes. The FAQ sheet essentially contained the "answers to the test" but without all the specifics. As every student knows, if you get your hands on an advance copy of the test, you can score well by memorization rather than mastery. The CIT decided not to share the sheet outside the team and only to use it in teaching and coaching. One of the team members, Charles, either misunderstood or decided not to remember the agreement. He gave the information to his region, and (not surprisingly) the people in that region began to appear very knowledgeable. Charles insisted that the rest of the team follow his actions.

Charles's region was doing an effective job of communicating and supporting the SOP. But the dissemination of the insiders' FAQ sheet caused other CIT members to question Charles's results. At a CIT meeting, the consultant raised the issue. Charles challenged the consultant, "This should be okay. We should do this everywhere. If we don't hand it out in the other regions, it's going to make my region look bad." "But," said the consultant, "we as a team agreed not to do this." The CIT members were shifting restlessly in their chairs but not saying anything. Charles grew angry and insisted that the consultant and the team capitulate. Looking around the group, it was clear that the other CIT members disagreed with him. The consultant said, "Just look at your team members. They all stayed with our agreement. What message would it send them if we were to make it okay to hand out the FAQ sheet just because you've already done so? We can't do it and we won't do it."

Then Alex spoke up, "The only credibility we have in the company comes from our integrity as individuals and as a team. It's what we stand on as CIT members. It's the only thing we have to keep us from getting divided and pulled apart. We have to stick to our agreements. Otherwise, we are no different from the culture we are trying to change." So the team, except for Charles, stuck with its original practice and became more united in the process. Charles continued to diverge from the team in his practices, causing concern that the organization would perceive in the CIT a disconnect between the heart and the hands. Eventually Charles did leave the team.

7

Foundational Skills for Changing Head, Heart, and Hands

HEAD, HEART, HANDS

The outer challenges—the SOP and its implementation—were the focus of conversations among the CIT and the executives. The inner challenge they confronted was the feeling that they were losing what had made them and Best Buy successful, that is, acting independently, focusing on what was in front of them, and relying on speed to get short-term results. The CIT members had now been out of their former positions long enough that their replacements were well established. If they faltered or were discredited by the resisting culture, they might no longer have leadership positions in the company and they would experience failure. The team needed powerful tools and skills with which to take on their challenges.

The three arenas each have their unique challenges, and we have looked at some ways to meet them. As we worked through the change process at Best Buy, we realized we needed not only a conceptual framework, but also a toolbox of skills and techniques to address these challenges. We began to articulate these skills. They are so important to success that we call them "foundational skills."

THE HEAD: CHALLENGES AND LEVERS FOR CHANGING MINDS

The challenge of the head arena is to confront and break through the conventional mind-set and at the same time generate a new mental model for the future. With the new model must come the rational business reasons to commit to change. As we mentioned earlier, we found that three methods worked especially well in changing the way people were thinking.

1. **New eyes.** Help people see with a fresh, new perspective. Assess, gather data, and prompt questions that explore gaps between the "as is" and "should be" models of the world. Along the way, this requires understanding and challenging deeply held assumptions.

2. **Visioning.** Create a picture of the future organization. We like to get people thinking about this by asking, What does "good" look like?

3. **Dialogue.** Engage in conversations that create an environment of understanding and collaboration in which individuals can look with new eyes and see for themselves the new vision.

THE HEAD: FOUNDATIONAL SKILLS

As the CIT and consultants struggled to change mind-sets, we realized that the head arena put most demand on communication skills that were aimed at achieving two objectives: connection and influence. To achieve *new eyes, visioning, and dialogue,* one must communicate to connect with and then influence the audience. The following three fundamentals of effective communication can help you achieve the objectives of connecting and influencing.

1. **Clarify and confirm**. Also termed *active listening*, the technique of clarifying and confirming helps ensure that you understand and shows your audience that you are listening and understanding.

2. **Express appreciation.** Noting good ideas and points in the conversation keeps up the energy and momentum of the discussion.

3. **Give balanced feedback.** Note positives and points of agreement. Also note areas where change or improvement is needed.

Remember, the underlying purpose of these skills is to connect you with your audience and seek to influence, rather than control, their mind-set. Table 28, Three Fundamentals of Communication, on the following page, synthesizes the use and benefits of these skills. Further discussion of each, with specific how-to's, follows.

Clarify and Confirm

Use active listening to demonstrate that you hear and understand what is being said. You can also use body language that demonstrates attention, use prompts such as "go on" and "uh-huh," take notes, nod encouragingly, and apply many other techniques. Clarifying and confirming are ways of obtaining the information you need to gather information in the "new eyes" mode. These techniques also help to make the connection necessary for engaging in dialogue. As you clarify and confirm, assume there is value in what others say. Most people are rational and will not make suggestions that do not have some merit, even if their reasons are not immediately clear. Listening with a positive attitude is the basis for clear and open communication. If you have trouble seeing the value in another person's remarks, you might not fully understand what is being said or why. Table 29 summarizes when you can most effectively use these skills.

Misunderstandings are common in interactions between people. Remember, confirming ("So, my understanding of your idea is . . ." or, "In other words, . . .") does not necessarily mean you agree with what has been said, only that you *understand* what was said. When you use the skill of confirming, you keep channels of communication open and avoid discouraging the other person. Confirming is especially

Table 28

Three Fundamentals of Communication		
Communication Fundamental	**How It Works**	**Key Benefits**
Clarify and confirm (active listening)	**Clarify** by seeking additional information, and **confirm** by stating your understanding of ▪ What has been said/happened ▪ Why something occurred	▪ Conveys interest and builds rapport ▪ Increases understanding and reduces misunderstanding ▪ Opens channels of communication
Express appreciation	**Recognize** and appreciate specific behaviors or ideas that support the change by noting ▪ What it was (specific examples) ▪ What it took (personal attributes) ▪ What it means (resulting benefits) **Express appreciation** when ▪ You see something that promotes change ▪ Someone exceeds expectations ▪ Someone expresses thinking/action rarely seen	▪ Builds morale and readiness to entertain new ideas and behaviors ▪ Reinforces new approaches and mind-sets ▪ Maintains momentum and energy of discussion

Table 28 (cont'd)

Three Fundamentals of Communication

Communication Fundamental	How It Works	Key Benefits
Give balanced feedback	First confirm and clarify your understanding, then **give feedback** to — **Specify merits** of what you want retained — **Specify concerns** you want eliminated Explore ideas for retaining merits and eliminating concerns	■ Provides constructive feedback while managing denial or defensiveness ■ Improves ideas and plans while preserving creativity and avoiding negativism

Table 29

Clarify and Confirm at These Pressure Points

1. When a conversation is moving too quickly for you to understand everything
2. When you feel negative emotions or disagreements building
3. When the other person frustrates you because he or she appears to be
   a. Illogical or unreasonable
   b. Vague or contradictory

valuable before responding to proposals with which you disagree. Confirming demonstrates that you seek to understand the other person's position. In turn, this tends to encourage the other person to keep an open mind when you respond with your own ideas.

Table 30

Express Appreciation at These Pressure Points

1. When a conversation is about to stall and lose momentum
2. When a person is showing an overly strong attachment to an old mind-set (find something positive in them to recognize, e.g., their loyalty or consistency)
3. When the other person indirectly shows a need for encouragement because he or she is

   a. Being hypercritical or cynical

   b. Reluctant, whining, or otherwise showing a lack of self-confidence about change

Express Appreciation

Point out ideas and contributions from others that you find positive. Remember that recognition is important to all people, regardless of the work they do or their level of responsibility. Recognition builds self-esteem, gives people a sense of satisfaction, and increases the likelihood that they will repeat the behavior and thinking. Recognition for a positive idea, raising a difficult topic, or solving a problem helps a conversation retain momentum. The positive morale this builds leads to even higher performance in thinking and action.

Express appreciation to let people know how you want them to perform. When you express appreciation to someone, you increase the chance that the person will continue to exceed standards. Positive recognition can be spoken or written, planned ahead of time or given immediately. By being specific, you avoid possible misunderstandings about which behavior or idea is being recognized. Identifying and mentioning particular qualities that contributed to a successful performance will let the person know what qualities you like to see demonstrated. Mentioning the resulting benefits to the department and/or the organization enables the person listening to you to see the results of his or her efforts. This provides the person with a feeling of accomplishment and reinforces the link between the desired behavior and business goals. Table 30 provides a summary of when to express appreciation.

Table 31

Give Balanced Feedback at These Pressure Points

1. When you need to identify a disagreement or area of concern

2. When you are encountering resistance or denial regarding change

3. When you sense a person is at a critical turning point in his or her thinking and needs some additional momentum to embrace the changes

Giving Balanced Feedback

Providing feedback is an important component in the daily interactions among members of any work group. Without feedback people will not know how you feel about their behavior or what you would like them to do differently. Communicating feedback effectively is not always easy, because people often react defensively, making it almost impossible for them to hear and evaluate feedback objectively.

The most positive results occur when the way you suggest the other person change defuses his defensiveness by closing the potential gap between your constructive intent and your effect. You can reduce defensiveness through balanced, two-sided feedback. People can't improve their performance if they don't know what they're doing right. Balanced feedback means that you recognize what's positive and has merit along with what needs improving. What has merit and is worth preserving should be mentioned first. Then talk about what needs to change, how it needs to change, and what it will look like in its final state. The more specificity you put into the feedback, the more valued it becomes. Table 31 gives a reminder of critical times to provide feedback.

When you itemize merits and concerns, be clear and specific. Remember, your intent is to provide information the person can use to upgrade or change her thinking and behavior. The person listening must be able to understand both what you like and what concerns you. Then explore ideas with the other person about ways to retain the merits and eliminate the concerns. Actively involving the other person brings the judgment and imagination of two people to bear on the issues and makes it more likely that the other person will be committed to carrying out the final course of action. Note that the impulse to reject or disagree is your clue to first *clarify* and *confirm* and then move toward *balanced feedback*.

The Power of the Foundational Skills

Using the three foundational skills helps ensure powerful communication, which can create change. Powerful communication conveys empathy and acceptance, which are necessary precursors to change. A sense of acceptance often precedes the most dramatic changes in an individual's thinking. Empathy creates a sense of acceptance and freedom to change. When challenged and pressured, the mind spends its energies defending instead of "unfreezing" and preparing to change. Beyond the communication fundamentals, some behaviors that the CIT used to convey empathy include the following.

- Suspend your need to be right in order to more deeply understand the other person's perspective
- Be patient, be respectful, and don't interrupt
- Try to be aware of your internal filters (mental models, assumptions, biases) that can block your hearing
- Maintain good eye contact
- Be responsive
- Hear the entire communication before interpreting or judging it

These skills can be used in two different ways: *communicating to control* or *communicating to connect*. Communicating to control uses all these skills, but its subtle message is one of direction and control, which decreases the readiness of your audience to change. Humans tend to resist anything that appears to reduce their choices or their freedom to make decisions. Communicating to control, at its worst, is sophisticated manipulation.

Communicating to connect, however, involves a more pure form of empathy and engagement. Understanding is its primary objective. This is the appreciative enquiry we mentioned earlier. A team or an individual who feels real connection becomes dramatically more ready to listen to new ideas, entertain them, and then implement change in all three arenas: head, heart, and hands.

CHALLENGES AND LEVERS FOR THE HEART

The key challenge of the heart arena is to increase the readiness of individuals and teams for change. This involves overcoming resistance to letting go of the old and trying on a new mind-set, a new vision, and the specific behaviors of implementation. To accomplish this challenge, one must deal with the central question in everyone's mind, What's in it for me? or WIIFM?

You can't directly control the way people feel or how the forces of a culture affect them. But there are three major levers to address the challenges of the heart and to help create commitment to change.

1. **Rebalance gains versus losses.** Provide opportunities and experiences that help individuals rebalance their gains-versus-losses equation regarding the "new order."

2. **Surface and release fears.** Help release the fears that underlie the anger, uncertainty, and skepticism that are usually the visible emotions during change.

3. **Realign rewards.** Rewards, both monetary and psychological, define motivations. To change the motivational landscape, shape the culture and management practices to reward the new behaviors. At the same time, remove rewards and recognition that reinforce the old mind-set and behaviors.

THE HEART: FOUNDATIONAL SKILLS

As we have stated throughout our discussion of the heart arena, change readiness can be assessed and modified if one is willing to deal directly with the emotions of those experiencing the changes. The foundational skills in the heart arena provide opportunities for these emotions to be brought to the surface and worked through. For individuals to understand their readiness for change, they need to recognize their balance of gains versus losses. Change does not automatically occur when people see what is in it for them, but they do change when they see that the pain of changing is less than the pain of *not* changing or, in other words, when the new WIIFM? outweighs the old.

We found an opportunity to apply all of these foundational skills in a forum that became known as "reality checks." Reality checks are carefully designed and skillfully executed meetings to address these issues of the heart. Such sessions are typically held with groups but can be adapted to work with individuals. Of course, such activities also build on the communication skills that we discussed as foundations for change in the head arena. Reality check sessions explore emotions and resistances (through emotional venting) and perceptions (through gains-versus-losses charting) and seek the leverage points for change (through negotiation). Though they often focus on issues of the heart, if such sessions are handled well, they also link to changes that must occur in the areas of the head and the hands.

Table 32, on the following pages, provides an overview of reality checks and the foundational skills that make them successful.

Gains Versus Losses: Charting the Balance

As we've mentioned before, the sales zoning process included in the SOP met with a lot of resistance when first introduced. The CIT encouraged managers to use the gains-versus-losses charting to help employees work through their resistance and understand the WIIFM?—specifically, how the benefit to customers and increasing competence in their roles would be more satisfying and effective than the current practice of "floating" through the store.

Table 33 is representative of a gains-versus-losses analysis between a sales associate and her manager. Typically, this comparison of gains and losses would be done in an informal conversation and not presented in a formal handout. In this example, we compare the *overall* gains and losses, and thus a gain in one column need not be compared to the loss adjacent to it in the table. Normally, a gains-versus-losses discussion requires an overall, weighted comparison of the two columns, not just a simple count of the number of gains versus the number of losses.

When an individual weights each item in the list, the chart can be used to determine the relative change readiness of that person. As you

Table 32

Reality Checks: Foundational Skills for Changing the Heart

Key Element	How It Works	Key Benefits
Gains-versus-losses analysis	**Write it down** ■ Individually or as a group ■ Gains in one column, losses in the other ■ Push to get complete lists ■ Check the balance; what will it take for gains to begin to outweigh losses?	■ Brings the light of reality to reviewing gains and losses ■ Reduces emotionality as losses and gains are written down and objectively discussed ■ Clearly shows degree of change readiness by determining the balance of gains vs. losses (WIIFM?)
Emotional venting	**Make a visit to "Pity City"** ■ What are the losses and problems? ■ What are the frustrations and negative emotions? **Work through emotions** ■ What underlies the feelings? ■ What emotions are reasonable given the circumstances?	■ Provides forum for expression of feelings; legitimizes the resolution of emotions in the arena of the heart ■ Emotions, once allowed expression, first expand but then can be released as they are talked through

would assume, when gains are perceived to outweigh losses, change readiness is greater. If you add up the gains versus losses among a number of individuals, you get a sense of the change readiness for a team or an organizational unit (see Figure 11 in Chapter 5, Increasing Readiness for Change).

Table 32 (cont'd)

Reality Checks: Foundational Skills for Changing the Heart		
Key Element	**How It Works**	**Key Benefits**
Negotiate for change	**Define what will increase change readiness** ■ What obstacles and concerns need resolution? ■ In what ways can gains be increased or strengthened? **Build an action plan** ■ What are next steps? ■ How best to monitor progress and ensure commitment to follow-through?	■ Links changes in heart to changes in other arenas ■ Builds trust and commitment to change

Emotional Venting: Reality Checks Change the Heart

Reality check meetings are divided into two parts. In the first part, people are encouraged to "vent" with no holds barred and no repercussions. (As Jeanie Daniel Duck noted in a 1993 *Harvard Business Review* article titled "Managing Change: The Art of Balancing," "You can visit Pity City but you aren't allowed to move there." As we have noted so often, this process is critical for bringing to the surface negative emotions and resistances and allowing the emotional charge to be released.

Moving forward, groups (or individuals) work through a gains-versus-losses analysis. This moves the conversation from one focused on losses to one that is balanced—that includes both pluses and minuses. Initially, getting people to talk about how to make the change work, rather than venting their frustrations with it, is slow going. The group may pressure its members to continue with the camaraderie of griping. To speak counter to the group's normal ways of behaving takes

Table 33

Gains Versus Losses for Sales Associates (sample)

How It Works	Key Benefits
▪ Increased clarity of job performance expectations ▪ Increased recognition for sales results coming from their zones ▪ Sense of mastery on new product knowledge and positive customer feedback; increase in self-esteem that comes with skill building ▪ Increased availability of merchandise to meet customer requests eliminates need to apologize for out-of-stock items ▪ Systems approach across all departments provides an opportunity to understand store operations at a broader level; greater sense of ownership and being in the know about what leads to store's success	▪ Reduced time to cluster with other associates to socialize, chat, etc. ▪ Less room to hide behind fuzzy accountability for sales results and goals ▪ Uncertainties (fear) about abilities to master new expectations/skills and availability of opportunities to learn this new information ▪ New expectations to team up with merchandising staff—new, unfamiliar individuals; need to build collaboration skill is threat to sense of competence

courage. You may need to "prime the pump" and have your own examples ready to initiate this discussion of what is going well—what is working, how someone is making it work, and what the gains are for the organization and for the individuals involved. In the final part of the meeting, continuing obstacles—both emotional and behavioral—are discussed. The group negotiates commitments to action steps that they clearly see will have payoffs for them as well as for the organization. We've provided a sample agenda on the following page from a reality check session.

FIELD GUIDE EXCERPT

Agenda for a Reality Check Session

1. Start by talking about the SOP.

- Explain that this meeting is to help with the implementation of these practices.

2. Let participants take a trip to Pity City.

- Explain that for 15 to 30 minutes it's time to vent. Then do so— no editing allowed.

3. Have participants do a gains-versus-losses analysis.

- Can be done as group or individuals working their own flip charts
- Facilitate discussion to draw out full lists
- Promote discussion of emotional impact of gains and losses
- Ask participants to evaluate their change readiness based on balance of gains versus losses
- Assist participants in working toward a commitment to add positives or address selected losses

4. Individually, each person makes two lists: what is working well regarding the SOP and what isn't working well. If the SOP has not yet been implemented in their district, ask them to anticipate what will work well and what will not.

- When they have finished, ask each person to share one item from his or her list of what is working well. Each person shares until there are no new items. Write each on a flip chart.
- Do the same thing for what is not working well.

5. If major issues come up, highlight those that are hindering the implementation of the SOP. Have people vote for the top 2 or 3 they feel are the biggest obstacles to successful implementation in their store. These should be things that people in the group can affect.

- Items that cannot be affected by people in the group should be charted and dealt with at another time.

- To do this voting, divide the number of issues by three; this is the number of votes each person should get.

6. Lead a discussion of the top 2 or 3 issues.

- Ask the group to suggest an action plan for each issue that would help ease the implementation of the SOP.

7. Assign responsibilities for carrying out the action plans, with agreed-upon follow-up dates.

8. Finish with a quick review of head, heart, and hands concepts and change readiness.

Negotiating for Change: Influencing Without Authority

In negotiations on change issues with individuals or groups, attitude is (almost) everything. Try to see the negotiation as a potential opportunity for you to change and to expand your worldview. Treating the negotiation as a joint problem-solving process, rather than a battle to be won or lost, frees you to think of collaborative solutions that are mutually beneficial. Be clear on what you need: what your limits, degrees of flexibility, and goals are. What seems critical to the success of the change effort? Learn as much as you possibly can about the other party. What are his needs and goals? What sorts of pressure might he be experiencing?

Explain your position and reasoning, as well as the consequences you foresee. Try to be as objective as possible. Ask for the other party's point of view. Listen fully to him, using active listening, and try to generate empathy for his situation. Try to suspend your own position momentarily. Be flexible in your conversation, as this will help to keep the discussion moving.

In proposing, counterproposing, and reaching agreement, the discussion cycles back and forth as needed. Be open to generating and discussing new possible solutions or agreements. Shared and compatible interests, as well as opposing ones, can lie behind conflicting positions. Actively look for these shared interests, even if you end the negotiation by agreeing to disagree. To ensure action, agree on follow-up steps and dates.

Building shared agreements and a personal sense of control over change is the foundation for our commitment to the change process. Sincerely involving others enhances their understanding and buy-in. Too often we ask people to implement something when we haven't involved them in defining the problem or creating the solution. Involving people close to the beginning will increase their interest and commitment to making the change work.

Foundational skills have greatest value when delivered at the right time. As we mentioned before, in the psychology of change, the three important things to consider are timing, timing, and timing. As with all of the change tools described in this book, there are prime times for reality check sessions. Table 34 lists the key times to use these foundational skills.

There is also a best time to work with the person who is unwilling or unable to adapt to the change, and that is when the organizational momentum has turned toward the change, and that person is being left behind. Often this individual will decide for himself that it is time to leave the organization. On the other hand, turning around a highly resistant person, especially if he has a good deal of visibility in the organization, is much more effective than asking him to go. Resisters usually have very strong value sets, and their resistance is usually at the emotional level. Usually this is the level at which conversion must take place. It is worth the effort to try, and try again. But if a sincere effort has been made and the individual is still resistant, then it is time to ask him to leave.

CHALLENGES AND LEVERS FOR CHANGING BEHAVIOR

The challenge of the hands arena is to help people understand, "What, exactly, am I supposed to do? How do I learn and master these new behaviors?" This involves helping people work through a learning cycle that sets goals and provides practice and feedback, while allow-

Table 34

Use Reality Checks at These Pressure Points

1. When a group seems almost ready to make a quantum leap in change readiness but needs a nudge or extra energy to make this jump

2. To increase the readiness of a key change agent, opinion leader, or even a resister (certain individuals will warrant individualized attention)

3. When emotions in a team are running so high that progress cannot be made on other dimensions of the change process; the group is stuck at some point in the change process and the emotions, and thus change readiness, are either backsliding or are caught in an endless eddy with little or no progress

ing room for mistakes. The following three levers are most important in this arena.

1. **Maps, models, and goals point the way.** "Maps" are behavioral descriptions of new employee activities—profiles or pictures. Maps prioritize and simplify. Goals and milestones give direction and measure progress.

2. **Groove new behaviors with practice and feedback.** The critical elements for "grooving" new behaviors are opportunities for practice with room for mistakes, feedback, and setting successive approximations of the final target behavior.

3. **Bake new behaviors into the culture.** The new behaviors must become self-sustaining. Creating an environment that supports self-sustaining behaviors is baking the changes into the culture.

THE HANDS: FOUNDATIONAL SKILLS

It's when change stalls that change managers really earn their pay. Remember that home do-it-yourself project that went well up to a point, then something didn't go as planned? And you were left feeling stuck without the problem-solving skills and the deeper understanding needed to directly solve or work around the obstacle? Does it ever happen that a change process seems to have all the key elements in place, but your employees are showing up on Monday and not executing the new behaviors? Yes, and it happened on several occasions at Best Buy. Out of these experiences, we have summarized the foundational skills of the hands arena essential for analyzing behavior.

Behavioral analysis is not something reserved for those with impressive resumes in organizational and human behavior. It is an approach to thinking through why people are either failing to do the "right" things or are doing the "wrong" things (or a combination of the two). Following analysis comes the behavioral redesign work to get the desired new actions happening and to eliminate the old, "wrong" behaviors.

What Is Behavioral Analysis?

Here is the headline on behavioral analysis: our behavior is under the influence of the consequences or responses those behaviors bring to us. To understand behavior, understand the consequences that sustain or eliminate the behaviors. Let's take a simple example. On a shopping trip, you see a child throwing a temper tantrum even though the parents are trying to suppress the wails. Why does that child throw a temper tantrum? Because the child's parents are giving him what he (or what every child) craves—attention. Sometimes the parents give a treat on top of that and the tantrum becomes a likely feature of every trip to the store. Behavioral analysis is about understanding what encourages or discourages behavior. You can imagine the power of this approach to understanding why employees might not be engaging in the desired behaviors of change.

Now You See It, Now You Don't

The first step in analyzing behavior is to simply watch carefully. Are the desired behaviors happening or are they not? What other behaviors are going on at the same time? Are there undesirable, counterproductive behaviors taking place? This sounds so simple. All I have to do is devote observation time? But this is often simply not done. Conclusions are drawn from quick impressions ("I spent a few hours in the stores, and what I saw was . . .") rather than careful observation

("I spent an hour in each of the departments and carefully tracked the behaviors that were taking place and by whom"). Sometimes decisions are based on hearsay or other superficial or nonfactual information. We have talked before about scorecarding, which is the quantification of behaviors. Here, to use a Minnesota metaphor, we are simply talking about the equivalent of sitting in the duck blind, watching how the ducks are flying in and out of the pond.

CEO Brad Anderson is softspoken but highly poised and confident. Brad became the teacher, even senior professor, in the first year of the SOP implementation. He accepted an invitation to sit in on part of a meeting of the CIT. He felt an inner confidence and let the CIT know that, for the first time, it seemed possible for Best Buy to become the kind of organization he had envisioned—a learning organization. He saw the seeds and possibilities in a way that no one else seemed to do. He was able to encourage and motivate the team with his enthusiasm. Even when the new behaviors were not in place, Brad felt he could see them coming. That might have been his greatest contribution—to see what was possible even when encouraging signs were not on the surface. In Table 35, Behavioral Analysis, we have summarized the elements of analyzing behavior and its underlying dynamics.

Behavioral Analysis:
A Page out of the Change Team's Notebook

Behavioral analysis need not be staged like a massive government-funded research project. It's better seen as the practice of careful observation combined with thoughtful inferences about what is leading to the observed behavior. The Big Question, the *Field Guide* excerpt on pages 170–71, gives you some questions to ask of yourself and others when making observations on the front lines of change implementation.

Use Behavioral Analysis at These Pressure Points

Foundational skills can have their greatest value at the tough transition points in the change process. Some key times to use these foundational skills are summarized in Table 36, Use Behavioral Analysis at These Pressure Points, on page 172.

Table 35

Behavioral Analysis: Understanding Hits and Misses

	Desired Behaviors Required by Change	Undesired, Old Behaviors
Behaviors *Are* Happening	**A "hit": desired behaviors are happening** **Analysis** ■ What positive consequences are following these behaviors? ■ Are these behaviors sustainable? ■ Do people understand why they are doing these things? **Actions** ■ Slowly reduce (but do not eliminate) the amount of positive reinforcement ■ Will the new culture begin to reinforce these behaviors? ■ Can these people teach others?	**A "miss": undesired behaviors are happening** **Analysis** ■ What consequences follow these behaviors? ■ Are these behaviors being reinforced by the old culture and beliefs? ■ Are people aware of what they are doing and why? Is fear involved? **Actions** ■ Uncover the causes of the behavior ■ Make explicit the assumptions that lead to these behaviors; change those assumptions ■ If absolutely necessary, and then only selectively, provide negative consequences for these behaviors (punishment)

Table 35 (cont'd)

Behavioral Analysis: Understanding Hits and Misses

	Desired Behaviors Required by Change	Undesired, "Old" Behaviors
Behaviors Are *Not* Happening	**A "miss": necessary behaviors are not happening** **Analysis** ■ If the behaviors occur, do any consequences (positive or negative) follow? ■ Are new behaviors being punished? ■ Are cues or reminders necessary? ■ Are necessary skills in place? **Actions** ■ Provide more and stronger positive consequences ■ Reward successive approximations of desired behaviors ■ Realign underlying assumptions and culture to support desired behaviors	**A "hit": undesired behaviors are not happening** **Analysis** ■ Are undesired behaviors just temporarily suppressed? ■ Are people getting their necessary recognition and reward from new, desired behaviors? ■ Have old assumptions and culture been deeply changed? **Actions** ■ Continue to carefully monitor behavior ■ Call attention to and celebrate successful change/elimination of old behaviors

The Big Question

What needs to happen so that all the new desired behaviors and practices are being applied, and so that the old and undesired behaviors and practices are *not* happening?

Smaller questions to help answer the bigger question:

1. Do these individuals have the skills and knowledge to succeed with the desired behaviors?

- Do they understand the need for change, or do they repeat old behaviors? Do they give rote answers that lack insight? (Head)

- Do they show interest or lack of enthusiasm? (Heart)

- What exactly are the people doing? What are their desired and undesired behaviors? (Hands)

- Ask what they do during the day. And ask for demonstrations and role-plays. If direct observation is not possible, then ask them to demonstrate or role-play their daily activities.

2. Ask people directly to speak about what they are doing.

- What are they able to do? With what level of mastery?

- What do they need training on? What do they need coaching on?

- What is getting in their way?

- Have them show you how they do it.

3. Ask people about why they are taking a particular approach.

- What leads to their approach?

- What are the rewards and benefits of those behaviors? For the customers? For the employee?

- Who do they model themselves after when it comes to these particular skills or practices?

- What are their biggest concerns about learning and applying these behaviors?

- What is it that they uniquely can see, given their [fill in particular] role, that others may not? What do they think management does not fully understand about what it takes to get the job done here? And for them, personally, to be evaluated as successful?

- If they could be the manager of the department/ store/region for a day, what would they do differently to make these changes be even more successful?

4. Make inferences, but with great care.

- What is leading to what they are actually doing (desired and undesired behaviors)?

- What might lie behind what they are not doing (that you want them to begin)?

- What are the cultural issues and dynamics supporting and undermining the desired behaviors?

- What adjustments will increase the flow of positive consequences to support the new behaviors?

- What adjustments are needed so that undesired behaviors will not inadvertently lead to some positive results for people?

Behavioral Analysis as a Foundational Skill: A Recap

Getting employees to change behavior is the ultimate goal of any change effort. Deep and lasting behavior change requires the insights that come only with the careful observations that some people refer to as "watching with the third eye" or "listening with the third ear." This means combining careful observation with sensing what might not be immediately apparent but is central to influencing what is happening. Why are behaviors happening? Are they for the reasons the change architects intend? And when behaviors are not changing, what adjustments are needed in the culture and work environment to sustain the flow of these behaviors?

Head, heart, and hands each have their challenges and their foundational skills that change leaders must master to address the

Table 36

Use Behavioral Analysis at These Pressure Points

1. When it's time to move to behavioral change but none of the new, desired behaviors are occurring yet

2. After a period of intensive training or practice and it's time to reduce the high levels of feedback and positive praise that typically come during a training process; it's now time for the organization and culture to sustain the new behaviors

3. When there is backsliding, and undesired behaviors resurface

4. When an important individual is continuing to persist in old, undesired behavior (this person might be an intended early adopter of change) or later on in the change process, when "heroes" of the old culture might need additional attention to make the shift to the new culture—their readiness to change will provide a rich source of insight into the progress of the culture change

challenges. The measurement process is itself a fundamental skill for leading change. It is so important that the measuring tool, what we call dynamic scorecards, and measuring process—scorecarding—require a separate discussion.

Changing Yourself

THE BUCK STOPS HERE

As a leader, manager, employee, or consultant—working at any level of an organization—you will need to change, too, if the organizational change effort is to be successful. If you think that you can delegate change or hire someone to do it for you, you're wrong! No one is exempt—not the top officer or officers, executives, managers, workers on the front lines, or consultants. The change process requires first that you know yourself and then that you change yourself. At Best Buy, everyone involved in the change effort changed—the executives, the CIT, the managers, and the consultants. The learning and changing accomplished and demonstrated by the executives and senior management were absolutely pivotal.

It might seem easier to undertake to change yourself first before leading or participating in an organizational change, but the reality is that we usually don't change deeply until we absolutely have to. And it may not even be possible to change yourself until you are working through the process with others. The process of changing yourself is messy and nonlinear and requires feedback and correction. Does this sound familiar? It should, as the personal change process parallels the organizational change process.

IT'S NO ONE'S FAULT, BUT IT'S EVERYONE'S RESPONSIBILITY

Since we are all part of the systems we live in, we're part of what needs to be changed. To recognize and accept that you are part of the status quo, part of the system of behaviors and interactions making up the whole, is to accept that you are a human, social being. Wittingly or unwittingly, you are participating in whatever it is that keeps the system going, even if you are the sponsor and champion of changing the system.

As part of the system, your behaviors will be caught in a struggle between the need to change in constructive ways and the natural inclination to preserve the status quo. We are all creatures of habit and a product of our experiences. Our habitual behaviors are not something that we consciously do to inhibit change; they're simply part of our current or previous way of being. Think about some familiar topics of dissension that keep surfacing with your spouse or other family members. Have you ever found yourself in the midst of a familiar disagreement with the other person and realized that you are both saying things you've said before and that you know what pattern the discussion will follow? It's like living a rerun, in which you know both your and the other person's lines.

It's not easy to recognize these patterns of behavior when they start, and it's even more difficult to try to replace them with new behaviors. The more senior you are in an organization, the more likely it is that you are unconsciously following the practices and mind-set of that culture. And since sustained change requires culture change, you must change. As challenging as this will be, it *is* possible to change your behavior, especially if you can get honest feedback from people you trust and if you practice the new behaviors. Having a behavioral expert coach you through the process is valuable, but it's not always possible. Fortunately, there are other sources of feedback to assist you, which we will discuss later in this chapter.

If you are involved in a change process, it is critically important to understand yourself and your approach to change. Why? If you are to influence others to make changes, especially in their behaviors, you must first understand yourself and why you do things the way you do.

You need to manage yourself throughout the change process and, if you're in a leadership position, be an effective role model for others. Within Best Buy, the executives, managers, members of the CIT, and consultants had to confront and work through their own reactions to the change while making every effort to pass the change along to the rest of the company.

Successfully changing yourself is the most powerful instrument for influencing others to change. Either consciously or unconsciously, you will be a role model to others for how to respond to the change. It is crucial to maintain your integrity as a leader. Your employees will know if you don't support the change initiative. You must be honest with yourself regarding how you feel about the change. Make explicit any uneasiness you have. Write your concerns down and develop a plan to address them. As you work on changing yourself, you will demonstrate your support and commitment to the change effort, which is essential to get others on board.

This "simple" truth can come as a powerful realization when it hits home. About four months into the Best Buy SOP change implementation, a regional manager was invited to sit in on a CIT meeting in Denver, during which he had a revelation: "I finally get it—in order for my people to change, I have to change!" Hearing that, some of the other team members later told the CIT member who worked in that region, "I wish I had your RM."

THREE ARENAS: HOW TO CHANGE?

The head, heart, and hands are the three arenas of change for you, as well as for others. In the head arena, how do you think and ask questions about the change process? In the heart arena, how do you feel about the change and/or the change agent role, and how does it motivate and/or discourage you? And in the hands arena, what are the skills you need to develop in yourself and the behaviors you need to change to be effective? Head, heart, and hands provide a framework for organizing questions to ask yourself as a way of handling your own change process. By learning and applying the tools and techniques of these arenas to yourself first, you will be more effective in using them with others.

Use Your Head

How well do you understand and believe in the business reasons for the change? How well do you understand the nature of the change itself? In Best Buy, the CIT explored the head arena as they educated themselves and researched the change. They investigated the following questions.

- What does the change involve?
- What are the mind-sets that I have now? What new mind-sets will be required with the change?
- What benefits could the change possibly bring?
- What will each person have to give up?
- What will be expected of individuals and work groups?

If the CIT couldn't articulate the answers to these questions for themselves, then they wouldn't be able to help others find answers to their questions. They realized, too, that they needed to understand the change intellectually at both conceptual and concrete levels.

Try to clarify what you do and don't know, and then work to understand what you don't. If you understand the new model, you will be better able to make educated decisions and answer the following questions for yourself.

- Can I support this?
- What will it require of me?
- Can I learn what it takes?

Look into Your Heart

What are the challenges and difficulties that you face as an agent for changing yourself? What makes this role of being an agent for change especially difficult? For some people, the need to change one's self is obvious; for others it is not. Whether or not you readily come to terms with the need to examine and initiate changes in yourself will depend on your individual psychological makeup. There are, however, some useful skills and techniques to help you address the common, often unseen, challenges to changing yourself.

Adjust Your Self-Concept

Your self-concept may not allow you to admit to yourself or others that you are less than perfect. The organizational culture you work in may demand that its leaders be heroic figures that never show hesitation, self-doubt, struggling, or learning. Even if you don't face these particular internal or organizational barriers to self-examination and change, you probably feel some pressure to look good in the eyes of your organization. It can be tough to be a role model who needs to change in the midst of change. Doing so takes a good sense of self, maturity, and courage.

Identify Role Models

Try to find at least one role model either within or outside of your organization. The best role models are capable and self-confident — yet humble and honest enough to solicit feedback, discuss their need to change, and ask for the support of others. These role models seem to grow in stature and self-respect from the process of changing themselves. Try "acting as if" you were that person or at least how you think that person is. "Borrow" her attitude and behavior and try them on for size. This can be a refreshing approach to changing oneself, and the benefits to you can be immense, including

- A sense of freedom, as if a weight is being taken off you
- Experiencing the possibilities of trying things you've never tried before
- Releasing energy to be used in new, constructive ways
- Connecting with people in meaningful new ways
- Connecting with people you've never been able to connect with in the past

Learn to Deal with Resistance

With any change effort, resistance is inevitable. This is a normal reaction for all of us, and you may be kidding yourself if you think that you have no resistance. Self-honesty is crucial. Every change carries within it the potential for loss and usually the potential for gain. As we've explored in Chapter 5, Using the Heart for Emotion and Motivation, you will likely identify more losses than gains in the beginning of a change, since that is what you experience first; your loss of the familiar feels more real than what you might gain. It is difficult to look into the possible future and imagine the potential payoffs of the change, but the results are almost always gratifying, and this exercise can bring renewed energy and momentum to the change effort.

Step by step, the CIT explored their areas of resistance and worked through their doubts. If the CIT couldn't resolve an issue as a group, the team members talked it over with someone who was at a higher level in the organizational or who simply had a different perspective than they did. This process of surfacing and working through their own doubts and resistance gave the team the confidence and experience they needed to help other people deal with their resistance. The CIT members used their own, real-life struggles as material for authentic discussions with their internal clients. By sharing their own experiences with others outside the team, the CIT made it okay for others to be honest, to express their concerns without fear of being branded as negative, and to see if they could genuinely move beyond their resistance.

Maintain Perspective

There are some things you can change and some things you can't. Writing down your concerns and making your gains and losses explicit makes them easier to build on or to deal with. If you know you are losing something, make a plan to deal with it. Change what you can; cope with the rest.

You've heard it before, but here it is again: change is stressful and it becomes doubly so if we abandon our health-sustaining habits. Why do we let this happen? Stress creates a short-term perspective due to fear, uncertainty, and doubt. You are thinking about just getting through it in the near term. We get caught up in the race, not realizing that we're in a marathon instead of a sprint, and that we need to conserve our energy for the long haul. Most healthy, stress-reducing behaviors require a long-term perspective because the payoffs of these behaviors are realized over time rather than instantaneously. When stressed, we focus on the urgent and immediate and use short-term stress releases like eating, watching TV, or drinking, and we often neglect behaviors that payoff in the long run. If you can, maintain stability in other parts of your life while embarking on a major change. You will need to guard your energy supply and recharge it regularly. It's best to refrain from sacrificing long-term effectiveness for short-term gain. Use stress-reduction techniques and try to maintain the basics of good health: moderate exercise, enough sleep, and a balanced diet.

An essential attitude needed by all change agents is the ability to see that resistance from others is aimed at the changes and not at the change agents personally. Early in the change process, members of the team had to learn to not take resistance too personally and to not respond defensively when blamed for things that made people uncomfortable. Rather than look for someone to blame, the team learned to shift the focus to "Where is the system breaking down?" Usually, if people are upset, they are upset with the change process, *not* with the individual who is trying to help them make the change. That person just happens to be there at the time and might seem to represent the change.

One of the members of the CIT encountered a difficult, even hostile audience when he first addressed the leaders and managers in his region. He went to his consultant/partner for advice and coaching: "How am I not supposed to react and get defensive when they're blaming me for their poor results and problems?" She counseled him, "Imagine that the person they're attacking is a couple of steps over to your right. And imagine that they're directing all of their anger, frustration, and emotion toward that person, not at you. Because that's really what is happening. That other entity is 'the change' and it's the real target of their fears and uncertainties. Try to see beyond their anger to their fear and concern. Respond to that concern and fear, not the anger, and try to treat the situation as one of mutual problem solving." It took some practice, but this CIT member became extremely skilled at transforming confrontational and challenging encounters into mutual problem-solving sessions.

Apply Your Hands

What new know-how and skills are required by the change? How will you do things differently? Even after the CIT had developed a clearer understanding of what the change process involved, there was a point at which they still did not know exactly what they were supposed to do differently. They needed to delve into the arena of the hands.

Remember, at the time no one knew what it would look and feel like to work effectively in the new environment of the SOP. The assumption, however, was that they all did. When they eventually realized that, in truth, no one really knew what "good" would look like in all its manifestations, this was a major breakthrough. It opened the door for the CIT, managers, and employees to begin working both individually and collectively to define and envision their own picture of what "good" looks like. This new picture had implications for how each person did his job, regardless of where he worked—on the front lines or in the executive suite.

As we've mentioned before, the CIT began asking questions such as, What leadership style is required? and, What new skills might you or I need as a leader? Fundamentally, the team had had to ask itself, What does it take to lead change at Best Buy? Although many resources were used, the answer to this question had to come from the experiences, learning, and mistakes of the team.

Once a working version of "good" was defined, the next step was to learn how to get there (from *what* to *how*). It's easy enough to say, "Oh, I know about _____ " (fill in the blank, e.g., with "French," "legal contracts," "fire fighting," or "the three arenas of human change"). Here "to know" means "I know something about it." It's the kind of "knowing" that you might get from reading a book, seeing a movie, or taking a class on the subject. Another meaning of "to know"is to have know-how. Peter Senge describes "know-how" as "the capacity to take effective action." There is a world of difference between "knowing about" French, legal contracts, fire fighting, or the three arenas of human change and having the "know-how" to speak French effectively, write a viable legal contract, fight major fires, or manage change through the three human arenas. In short, knowing how to do something is another way of defining behavior, the arena of the hands.

The skills the CIT needed to know how to use to be effective leaders in the new, emerging Best Buy included being able to coach and develop people and being able to think about and analyze situations in terms of interacting systems. In Best Buy, we began to hear the terms *coaching* and *developing people* more and more frequently. It was a beginning for the leaders to say, "We need to coach people and develop people in our company." But it was easier to say it than to do it, and especially to do it well. The other emerging leadership competency, which also required new ways of thinking and behaving, centered on working with systems and interacting processes. Understanding the basics of systems thinking is not difficult, but applying the theory beyond the basics can be quite challenging.

LEADING IN THE NEW BEST BUY

The CIT developed a working profile for an effective leader in the new Best Buy, and they used it to direct their own behavior. The personal growth model of the CIT members became their guide to helping others change. The team members served as real-life models of what it takes to learn a new way of being and working.

Several members of the CIT changed substantially. One of them, Tom, had been a streetwise general manager from an urban market who had successfully managed and turned around a tough, "high octane" store. He was smart and savvy. About five months into the SOP change implementation, he approached the lead consultant and asked to talk with her. Emotionally, he told her, "Initially, I thought I needed to be tough and even tricky in this job to be successful. Earlier in my life I wanted to be a teacher, but I didn't think I could support my family on a teacher's salary. Being part of this process has taught me that I can be successful in my work and also be the person that I always wanted to be."

This CIT member was later offered a couple of promotions to district manager after he'd been on the team about a year. Before his experience on the CIT, Tom would have set his sights on such an opportunity. When he actually was offered the promotion, however, he decided to pass. He wanted to give himself more time as a member of the team—building relationships with his fellow team members and the regional staff and making sure that his new perspectives and skills had grown strong roots.

Another CIT member summarized the parallels occurring between individual and organizational change: "It's now okay to not be perfect and to not have all the answers—and for your region to have less than perfect results (which we always did anyway). Being on the right path, knowing what you don't know and owning up to it, and knowing how to learn and to find the answers is a good thing. Now it's even honorable. This is a deep culture change."

When the situation called for it, the members of the CIT even confronted some of the retail senior executives about problems stemming from the executives' old ways of behaving. A huge shift occurred in Best Buy's perception of successful leadership when these senior executives listened to the team and started to let others see how they, as the leaders, received feedback, learned, developed, and changed themselves.

Here are some questions to ask yourself and others to start defining the new leadership attributes and skills necessary to be effective in your changing organization.

1. **How do you have to change to be effective?**

   At Best Buy, as the change started taking hold, the following categories of leadership attributes and skills became more important.

   - Leading change
   - Skilled coaching and developing of people
   - Understanding systems dynamics to guide decision making
   - Building systems and processes

2. **What leadership style is required?**

   You will probably need to tease apart this broad question to find out what it really means. At Best Buy, we used the following types of questions to get into the nitty-gritty of what the broader question implied.

   - What skills will you need?
   - What behaviors will you need to exhibit?
   - How do we work together? What remains unchanged? What remains the same?

START WHERE YOU ARE

Pointing fingers at others and playing the blame game was not unknown in the Best Buy culture. The CIT was in a dangerous position. The team could become the scapegoat of the organization if the change effort was not successful. And, if people had the mind-set that the CIT was solely responsible for the change effort, it would not succeed.

Things began to get really tense when the CIT realized that the district and regional managers were actually undoing the team's efforts. Management was still acting under the influence of the old culture. The DMs and RMs were rewarding old-culture behaviors with their own outdated behavior. The retail executives were also reinforcing the status quo—by virtue of what they paid attention to—even though they were the sponsors of the change initiative.

One of the team members reflects, "We started at the wrong place, but that was the place we had to start. We started at the store level. It was the place we were comfortable. We figured on a push upward from the stores. We really needed to start at a higher level, but that wasn't possible. We weren't ready. We weren't capable of doing this at that point. It was easy to coach peers but not to coach my previous boss and his boss."

In retrospect, the CIT members agree that the crucial turning point in the SOP change implementation was "realizing that we couldn't do this only in a bottom-up, grassroots way, and accepting that we had to get feedback to the executives, as well as to the RMs and DMs, that their behavior needed to change, and how and why it needed to change." The CIT was learning that in addition to their need to change themselves, the CIT needed to get the message to senior management that they needed to change, too.

Jason, a member of the CIT, recalled this challenging realization made by the team: "After the second round of scorecarding, some of us had become aware that we needed to address the leadership behavior of the retail executives. The team worked out a plan and agreed on it. Melanie met with one of them, and I met with the other. This was *the* big turning point. If they ignored us or didn't believe us, we could see that the change effort was doomed."

Melanie said, "I was touring stores with my executive in his market and giving him feedback. And I was learning how to give him feedback in a way that he could hear it. Early on, I'd told him to focus on the process and that the results would come. We both took extreme positions about this." The executive remembers, "I read the book [of new store procedures], but I didn't understand what behavior it translated into or that I needed to model the new behaviors."

Melanie tried a different approach with the retail executive. "I told him, don't change your expectations about output, just put it into a different frame. Ask, 'What processes are breaking down?' We were able to move from being caught up in 'punch lists' [simplistic, results-only–oriented scorecards] and focus more on what the managers and leaders were doing."

The other retail executive agreed to a closed-door discussion with Jason. Jason recalled, "Leading up to our attempt to effect a change in the top leader's behavior, the consultants had begun teaching us how to influence without authority. I used what I had learned with my retail executive."

Here's a re-creation of Jason's "closed door" session.

Jason hesitated and then began, "The way you look at things and the way you tell people what they're doing wrong during your store visits is undoing our work." He quickly added, "I'm not saying that you're doing this on purpose."

"Run that by me again," the executive replied.

Jason said, "Well, last week when I was with you, the first thing you asked each person on the floor was, 'What were your accessory sales today?'"

The executive looked skeptical. "Yes, that's true, and your point would be . . . ?"

Jason replied, "When you ask people things like 'What were your accessory sales today?' you're directing their attention to isolated activities and individual results instead of how they used the SOP as a system that allows them to manage processes to get all kinds of results—and instead of thinking in terms of a 'complete solution' for the customer."

The executive frowned, "I still don't get it."

Jason explained, "Selling accessories is just *part* of the salesperson's responsibilities. It fits in sometime after greeting the customer and before he walks out the door. How about asking the salesperson to describe her last interaction with a customer? Ask her to take you through it step by step. Then, you'll hear the overall flow of how she does (or doesn't) connect with the customer. You can get a lot more information and you can also land the point with the salesperson that the

SOP helps her manage her overall activities and helps her to achieve each particular result."

"Mmmm," the retail executive said. "Okay, I think I see your point. So what else am I doing wrong?"

Jason answered with his own question, "Are you sure you're up for this?"

"If I can dish it out, I better be able to take it and to learn from it," the executive stated.

"All right," Jason continued. "You walk in and pound on people for bad shrink [lost and stolen product] and poor financial results. You put people on the spot and accuse them, 'Why can't you do this?' You say, 'Get it fixed!' and it sounds like a threat."

The retail executive commented, "I'm just holding them accountable."

"Well," Jason told him, "That's the way we define the word *accountable* around here a lot. It comes across like you're pounding on them. We've had to operate here at Best Buy with a lot of inadequate and broken systems. How about, instead of pointing the finger at the person, you work with her to find out where the system is breaking down first? You can always blame them later, there's plenty of that going around.

"Think about it," Jason continued. "You could be asking the store manager questions like, 'What could this be linked to? What other problems does it cause?' And your RMs and DMs are doing the same thing. Nobody is thinking about how to use the SOP to tackle the underlying causes and problems in that store or region."

The executive listened. He was quiet for a long time, looking out the window beyond his desk and past Jason into the parking lot and the gray, overcast winter sky. "Okay," he said finally. "Let's start by making some more store visits together. I think I'm teachable."

In public forums, each of the retail executives became willing to role-model his learning in front of his entire leadership team. This forum let them showcase the executives listening to the feedback, changing their behavior, and giving credit to the CIT.

For example, at a divisional management meeting in Santa Barbara, one of the executives role-played himself absolutely laying into a store manager. He really got into his role, and there were knowing chuckles in the audience—this was *too* familiar. Then one of the members of the CIT called a halt to the scene. He asked the executive what effect he thought he was having on the store manager and suggested that the executive proceed in a different way. They replayed the scene, but this time the retail executive worked with the store manager to investigate where the problem was originating and what to do about it. They concluded by talking about what each had learned from the process and how they felt about it. The experience of seeing the executive laugh at himself and acknowledge how he needed to change his own behavior to be more effective was electrifying. This group of leaders saw that even their most senior leader was open to feedback and learning. As one CIT member recalls, "We all began to understand what change was really about. Before, we expected that we would tell people what to do and they'd do it."

One of the other retail executives remembers this time also. "When I ask myself, 'What was the major turning point?' it comes to me that it was when Melanie came to me, and Jason went to the other retail executive, with feedback about how our leadership behaviors were derailing the change effort and how we needed to change, too."

A member of the CIT added, "Once it became the thing to do and the executives started 'walking the talk,' it made our jobs as the CIT so much easier. Then, the RMs finally got it, and we started getting cascading sponsorship from every level." The success or failure of the SOP change implementation effort turned on this point—leaders started acknowledging that they needed to change, too, for the change effort to succeed.

FEEDBACK: ASK FOR IT AND YOU *MIGHT* GET IT

Why is feedback necessary? As someone involved in or responsible for changing your organization, you need thoughtful, objective feedback from the people you work with to accurately gauge the impact and implications of your leadership behaviors. Often, though, these people may be reluctant to share with you how they really see you. It may be that their high regard for you causes them to hold back, or they may be afraid of repercussions if they're honest, or they may simply not know how to do it. They might think you'll label them as negative, when they're actually trying to be positive and constructive.

The leadership paradox is that the more you could benefit from feedback, the less likely you are to get it. That is, the more senior your position, the greater the impact of your leadership behaviors and the greater your need for input but the less likely that people will offer it. The most effective leaders turn this paradox upside down to find the truth. They ask for, take, and use sincere, critical feedback on their style, behavior, and impact. A consistent, underlying characteristic of highly successful leaders is their ability to manage themselves—that is, they are willing to look at, and change when necessary, their own mind-set, emotional reactions, and behaviors.

We all have blind spots, and in very successful people these blind spots often are the flip side of the strengths that have gotten them where they are and have contributed to their success. For example, in Best Buy, leaders were used to taking care of a problem and quickly moving on to work on the next big thing. This attitude and behavior enable them to successfully build an entrepreneurial company. Sometimes, though, they could miss the fact that a problem might require their more sustained attention and effort.

An executive from another function was recruiting a retail executive to work on a new, major corporate undertaking that would require substantial time and commitment. To take on this new duty, the retail executive was planning to stop coming to the CIT executive briefings. However, this could send the message that he was withdrawing his support for the SOP change implementation. The culture was pulling the retail executive to move on to something new and exciting rather than sustain something already in progress.

Another retail executive confronted the executive being recruited: "Damn it, you're falling into our usual trap. We move from thing to thing without finishing the first thing *first*. If you back out of the CIT meetings, you'll be sending them and the rest of the organization the message that you're not supporting them anymore."

The recruitee shot back, "That's bull. Of course I'm still support-ing them!"

His confronter stood firm. "No, you have to keep attending the CIT meetings. You can't just start something, recruit the CIT, bring in consultants, and then walk out and expect it to be hunky-dory. You can't delegate leadership of this change effort. Think about the people on the team. They're taking tremendous risks with their careers. They're working to and past the point of exhaustion. They need to know that you believe that they're important and that what they're doing is important. Your leadership is required; your presence and at-tention are required. The culture is pulling you onto the next interest-ing thing. It's the quick-fix culture that says, 'I don't have to change myself.' No need to be complete or thorough. This is a dangerous time for you and for all of us!"

The retail executive thought it over. "You're right," he said. "I need to stay the course."

The change agent faces a great deal of complexity and may be in a special role in which there are new skill requirements. Yet the feed-back necessary to master these skills may be less likely to be forthcom-ing. Developing avenues for feedback and forums for learning and practicing new behaviors is a necessity for the emerging change agent. Being coached by someone who is skilled in changing behavior and influencing others without having direct authority over them is one way to help the change agent develop the necessary skills quickly. An-other powerful way to learn is to be part of a team in which dialogue and team learning are emphasized.

LEADERSHIP FEEDBACK IS BUSINESS DATA

As a leader, you need a "control panel" that gives you up-to-date infor-mation on key aspects of the business. Feedback to you on the impact of your leadership behaviors is one "dial" you need to monitor. It is key business information. Accurate, candid, leadership feedback gives you

- A status report on which aspects of the change objectives and methods the people you lead or work with understand—and which ones they don't

- Insights into what others expect of you—both as an individual and as a member of a group

- How your role is seen and how playing this role influences the ways others see you

- Clarity on what things you're doing as a leader that you should keep doing

- A mirror to see your leadership blind spots—those behaviors that obstruct you from achieving your goals and the business's goals

Leadership is about people: how you interact with them and how they interact with one another. Leadership change is behavioral change, and we know that changing behavior requires feedback about what to change, how to do it, and how well you're doing.

FINDING FEEDBACK

Viewpoints on your behavior from other levels and positions in the organization can give you different perspectives on your role and your effectiveness. Feedback is most valuable if it's focused on current behaviors and can be applied right now or in the near future.

To provide you with an accurate and unbiased reflection of your leadership style and impact, feedback needs to come from those people who have frequent, meaningful interactions with you. In the Best Buy SOP change implementation, some members of the CIT were able to earn the trust of the leaders in their areas and to build their own confidence enough to provide healthy, helpful feedback to the regional, district, and general managers they worked with.

One RM said, "I think what the CIT did that had the most impact is that they held up a mirror. The problem was *me*. I had to realize that these behavior pieces weren't about the people in the stores; they were about me and my regional team. This helped me and it still helps me tremendously as a leader—someone holding up the mirror. The connection between the head, heart, and hands became real to me."

He continued, "We started getting it. About a year into the SOP change implementation process, we [the RMs as a group] really got it.

One of the things that led to that awakening was that people who were using the SOP were getting business results!"

SETTING UP AND USING FEEDBACK LOOPS

How do you change yourself? This isn't a trick question, but it is a tough one to answer. We've already described some of the steps to take in Chapter 6, Using the Hands to Make Change Real, but we will reframe them here for your use.

1. The first step is to ask questions such as, "What leadership style is or will be required?" and "How do I have to change to be effective in the new environment?" Then ask the questions embedded in those broad questions.

2. Using your answers to the above questions, how do you evaluate yourself as a leader of change and as an effective leader in the changing organization? What are your strengths and areas for improvement as a change leader and a leader in the new order?

3. How would others evaluate you on all these questions?
   - How do you know?
   - Who can you ask that will give you an honest, unbiased answer that you will trust?
   - What is your organizational relationship with this person?
   - Have you asked her for feedback about yourself before?
   - If so, how did you react to the feedback she gave you?

4. How are you going to get at the unvarnished truth? If you can only speculate as to how others would evaluate you on the changing leadership questions, then you need to set up some ways of getting timely, honest feedback to help you grow and change.
   - Who do you trust in the organization? It needs to be someone in the organization who wishes you well yet won't whitewash his feedback to you.

- Is he in a good position to notice your leadership behaviors on a regular basis?

- If he's ever given you feedback in the past, especially critical feedback, how did you react to it?

5. Be proactive. Ask for feedback more than once. Assuming that you have one or more people who could be reliable, informed, and honest sources of feedback to you regarding your style and impact as a leader, you will need to ask them to observe you and give you feedback. Even then, in a lot of cases you will need to go to that person to solicit feedback. If you wait for him to come to you, you could be waiting (and delaying your own growth and improvement) for a long time.

6. Assuming that you find some areas in which to develop yourself as a leader, try to choose only one or, at the most, two areas for improvement.

We all need some structure to help us change our behavior. Table 37, Stuck? Steps to Change Yourself, contains a summary of these points, plus a few reminders from earlier chapters.

It sounds so straightforward. But is this really how people change? In reality, it is seldom this linear and planned. However, referring to these steps might be useful if you find yourself stalling out and need to refocus your energies. Essentially, changing yourself—your own behaviors—is about learning. Using a stepped approach to learning, especially in learning new skills, is the most practical way to proceed.

Table 37

Stuck? Steps to Change Yourself

1. Identify your goal. "What will I look like if I'm successful?"

2. Break down your goal into concrete, achievable steps. Put a time frame to each.

3. Describe how you will measure your success for each step, including your final goal.

4. Define the rewards for being successful at each step.

5. How will you continue to work this on your own?

USING A STEPPED APPROACH TO CHANGING BEHAVIOR

If you don't run or jog on a regular basis, and you set for yourself the goal of being able to run five miles in fifty-five minutes, how would you go about it? If you know something of sports training, you would know to start with jogging about two miles a day at about a twelve-minute-per-mile pace. Then to gain distance and speed, you would need to add to your workout over time—but never more than a 10 percent increase over yesterday or last week. If you went out and ran five miles now, you'd probably quit the next day and you'd hate running. What's the lesson here? If you *slowly* build up the frequency and intensity of a behavior, the behavior is more likely to stick.

A stepped approach to changing behavior is based on the reality that even transformational change, especially if it involves changing human behavior and if it is to be successful and sustainable, often occurs in steps. Transformational change in organizations reflects the combined behavioral change of many individuals in the organization. Up close, the change is stepwise, but in the big picture, it's curvilinear.

It's beneficial to increase your confidence and readiness to change at the very outset. This is a legitimate step, because if you skip this you are much more likely to relapse or fail. But how do you do that? Beginning with the end in mind is helpful. Create a tangible image of success. Try to answer the question, "What will I look like if I'm successful?" Try to think of examples of people who exhibit aspects of leadership you need to learn, and decide what parts of them you want to be like. One person may not have all the qualities you're looking for, or a person may have some qualities you want to emulate and other qualities you don't. Pick and choose what you want to learn from different people.

Define your end state, your eventual goal. Then break down your end goal into concrete, achievable steps to move toward it. Ask yourself, "What small step can I take to get me there?" and, "What further step after that?" You'll need to have small successes to stay motivated to change your behavior. If you are able to start changing some aspect of your own behavior, your commitment to change and your confidence in your ability to change will increase. We guarantee it. But, just in case you want to maintain your status quo, you can use the "five ways to fail at changing yourself" found in Table 38.

Table 38

Five Ways to Fail at Changing Yourself

1. Act like change applies only to others. After all, you are an agent of change.

2. Expect that you will be personally immune to the culture that acts to circumvent change. You are above it all.

3. Demand deep change of others. But you need only make superficial change. Others cannot see the difference.

4. Never ask for feedback. It will diminish your leadership authority.

5. If you do decide to change something, skip the incremental stuff. Do it all at once.

FEET OF CLAY: THE CONSULTANTS' STORY

Consultants have it even tougher. They sometimes share the belief with their clients that, as consultants, they are exempt from the change process. Or, if they *do* have to make some changes, they (being experts) can do so nearly effortlessly and without the need for feedback.

But in the Best Buy SOP change implementation, the consultants found that they, too, changed in the process—a lot. In trying to "meet the clients where they were," the consultants could easily jump into a reactive, emergency-overdrive, "ready, fire, aim" mode. But, when this happened, the best response was to model using feedback and resilience to recover from inevitable mistakes—to change themselves. It didn't always happen this way. Mistakes are the system's way of telling us what needs to be changed.

The consultants fell into the trap of fragmenting everyone's efforts by trying to respond to too many emerging needs and wants, a familiar characteristic of the old culture. During a CIT meeting, one of the team members confronted the lead consultant, "You're supposed to help us learn to work differently—better and smarter—but you're turning into us. You're acting too much like us." Ouch! This was good, strong feedback about the balancing act the consultants needed to play between fitting into the culture enough to have rapport and staying mindful that part of their role was to introduce new ways of thinking and acting.

Trying to meet all the needs and keep things on track took a major toll on team members. One of the members, Jason, had thirty-seven stores to cover in nine states. Here's what he had to say about his situation: "We tried to move too fast and nearly burned out some people. One of the retail executives liked the baseline scorecard so much that he wanted to scorecard, scorecard, scorecard, and we tried to comply. We got caught up in the culture. For example, the consultants were urging some of the team members to do two stores a day, which was crazy."

Another way the consultants got caught up in the momentum of the change effort was in trying to be expedient, at the expense of good human relations. Nine or ten months into the change implementation process, the two most senior consultants decided they needed to give feedback to each CIT member and to let each know if the consultants were recommending that the member stay on the CIT, be promoted, or be returned to his previous role. The consultants took time out of a team meeting to see each individual, give him feedback, and send him back to work with the team. The group was tremendously uncomfortable as, one by one, they were called in for feedback. And when the whole team reconvened, the atmosphere was so gloomy, nobody could focus on the work at hand. So much for developing teamwork. The consultants had fallen into the trap of sacrificing diplomacy and good judgment for efficiency and speed. They had not factored in the individuals' needs for privacy and time to digest the feedback.

As any leader does, you run a risk when you give people the benefit of the doubt. Some people will—for whatever reasons—manage or manipulate your image of them. The lead consultant fell into this pit. From one of the members of the CIT: "She was having the wool pulled over her eyes by one of the team members. This person was manipulating her. She wasn't seeing what he was really like. He had done some really destructive things in the market, beyond the meeting sessions. When rolling the numbers up, he had not filled in some required media merchandise observations—he just left them blank! The rest of us had worked our tails off getting good, reliable observations."

Responding to the cultural forces in organizations is inevitable. Even though consultants or seasoned change agents know the classic mistakes, they still keep making them. Why? Because no one is immune to systemic, social pressures and especially social norms. If an external consultant is responding to social forces within a client organization he is working in, just think how intensely these social forces are affecting people who are internal to the organization. Also, the more you care about the client organization, its people, and the goals, the more emotional energy you develop. These emotions have the potential to energize your work as well as misdirect your efforts or cloud your vision. To provide the best service to the client, consultants can monitor their awareness of the organizational norms and their responses to the norms. Having trusted colleagues to turn to for feedback in order to regain some constructive distance and objectivity can be essential to a consultant's effectiveness.

Here's some straight talk from a retail executive: "The real danger is that the consultants go native. The moment the consultants are seen as an employee, 50 percent of their effectiveness goes away. People start wondering, 'How are they seen? Do they have too much influence with the boss? Who are they really working for?' There's a little bit of secrecy. They're not just reporting to someone in the business; they're really reporting (usually) to someone like the CEO."

Mistakes illustrate the forces interacting in a system. It is wise to treat them as instructions to be learned from and not something to be eliminated. One saying common among consultants who work with organizational behavior is "Everything is data."

PART

3

LASTING
CHANGE

MAKING IT STICK

Tools for Measuring Change

MEASURE CHANGE?

Why measure change? Is it even possible? Allen Sloan, Wall Street editor for *Newsweek*, said, "As they teach you in Business 101, what gets measured gets managed." The Best Buy retail executives agreed with the tenets of Business 101 and were adamant about needing a way of tracking the progress of the SOP change implementation. Maybe it could be done; there are techniques for measuring changes in people's thinking, feeling, and behavior and their advances in learning. Perhaps these techniques could be put to use in new and different ways?

Implementing change requires that people learn new ways of being, and people learn more efficiently when they get accurate feedback on how they're doing. Assessing the state and progress of learning provides the necessary feedback, but it must be used carefully. Measuring change in itself is strong medicine for change. It is a potent process that can do much good, but if it's not done appropriately or skillfully, it can harm or kill the patient. Even when it works the way it's intended to, you must anticipate the possible side effects. Any time you measure (pay attention to) something, you are sending messages to the people involved about the importance of what's being measured.

Best Buy measured business results such as sales, profits, productivity, and efficiency to assess how well managers, stores, and the company were performing. These business measures were called *scorecards*. At that time, a scorecard was a checklist that measured an outcome. An informal company slogan was "Winners keep score." At one time, there were more than thirty scorecards in use just in the stores, and store managers were expected to perform well on each and every one. Some of the scorecards' criteria contradicted other scorecards' criteria, but unfortunately no one was keeping track of that. In the fiercely competitive environment at Best Buy, individuals' and groups' stars rose and fell weekly, according to how well they were performing on various scorecards. People's bonuses were tied to their scorecard results, and "beating the scorecard" (whatever it was measuring) became an end in itself. The scorecards had been so manipulated that the results, although used, were viewed with skepticism.

The scorecards used in Best Buy prior to the SOP change implementation, as in most businesses, tracked the business results but not the behaviors that got the company its desired results. Remember the equation developed by one of the Best Buy executives? $B + P = R^3$, or, *behavior* plus *process* equals *results* exponentially raised by 3. The scorecards/business measures typically used in Best Buy prior to the SOP change implementation measured the R^3 of results. The certification checklist used to assess compliance with the SOP immediately after it was introduced measured, in addition, the P of processes. But to develop new ways of working in the stores would require attending to and measuring the B of behavior. The notion of measuring behaviors (what people do, beyond process compliance) as well as measuring results (outcomes) was a revolutionary concept.

Because the culture put pressure on its employees and managers to look good, many of the operational measures suffered from huge score inflation. This inflation of supposedly objective quantitative indicators of performance precluded the reality testing of the company, and the company's denial of reality kept it from taking any actions that might deal with that reality. Inflation was worst on measures and in stores where performance was most in need of improvement—where the "true" results would not look good.

The challenge to build new scorecards to assess the degree and success of the change effort generated several questions.

- How do you build a scorecard that is not distorted by social pressures to get certain results?
- How do you capitalize on the power of effective measurement—measurement that it is objective, reliable, and impartial?
- What behaviors are most important?

Fortunately, there are ways to measure the intangible. Powerful, proven techniques exist—techniques that no one had yet applied to the human arenas of organizational change. The Change Scorecard would turn out to be very different from any scorecard previously used in Best Buy.

When the SOP was first introduced at Best Buy, all stores were required to pass the certification checklist/audit with a score of 90 percent or better. The audit consisted of yes/no and closed-ended questions such as, "What percentage of your time do you spend on non-selling-related activities?" (This question typically was asked of a sales associate.) The "correct" answer was 70 percent. This meant that the sales associates were supposed to be engaged in behaviors to stock merchandise and keep their area tidy when they weren't assisting customers. Earlier, we mentioned the Kansas City regional operations manager who used the certification checklist in a store. He asked an employee a standard question from the checklist about the SOP, but when he rephrased the question to require a different (opposite) answer, out came the memorized answer to the expected question—exactly the opposite of the correct answer to the revised question. "Prepped" employees were giving memorized answers to the evaluators.

The employees could give "right answers" but did not understand at a deeper level why the items in question were important, and they were not engaging in new behaviors. This was not so much a display of lack of personal integrity, but rather an indication of how strongly the magnetic field of the culture was affecting people's thinking and behavior. First, it was not clear to managers why the new processes (SOP) were in place or what the importance was to the company of using similar processes in all the stores. Second, managers were still rewarded for doing whatever it took to get results. Failure to pass a certification checklist was so culturally unacceptable that people felt compelled to look good regardless of the reality. The retail managers looked at the checklist as one more number to hit and one more scorecard to beat.

The retail executives needed a tool to measure what had never been measured before. Not only that, the new tool or scorecard had to be good enough to overcome the company's severe skepticism of scorecard results. The consultants realized that a fundamentally different kind of scorecard was needed. This new scorecard would have to be specially built to withstand the huge pressures of the Best Buy culture to distort the measurement and kill reality testing.

MEASURING THE B IN $B + P = R^3$

Specifying what behaviors to measure provides the focus necessary to achieve the intended benefits of change. Defining the behaviors makes explicit the link between employee and organizational behavior change—and the intended benefits to corporate stakeholders (customers, financial community, etc.). To achieve different results from what you've been getting, the behavior of people and teams has to change. You cannot get new results from the same behavior.

Rather than measure outcomes (R^3), Change Scorecards are designed to measure the $B + P$ of a change effort. In doing so, they can be put to work as learning (teaching, coaching, and feedback) and diagnostic tools. This new and different type of scorecard is difficult to "beat," and there is little reason to try to do so. The only way to "beat" the SOP Change Scorecard was to do well on it, and that meant learning and using the new SOP—understanding why to use it and what it was, both in the big-picture sense and in the details, and to behave in ways that supported it.

The exercise of measurement and the definition of what must change are inextricably linked. If you cannot figure out what to measure, you do not yet know what you need to change. What can be clearly explained is more likely to be well understood. "What do we need to do differently?" and "How will we know we are being successful in implementing this change?" are flip sides of the same coin of measurement and change.

What behaviors do we select to measure if we want to gauge the progress of a change effort? The analogy with a human patient would be, What measures do we use to assess the patient's immediate state of health and her response to treatment? You would probably take readings of her blood pressure, heart rate, respiration, and so on. Why? Because if you measure these, you are measuring key indicators of the patient's status and getting information about other things that are important but not as accessible. You are measuring her vital signs.

What are the vital signs to measure in a change process? How do we translate the key challenges of the head, heart, and hands into something we can hear or see? We find answers to the following important questions.

- **Head:** Do people understand the reasons for change? Do they understand what their roles and responsibilities are?

- **Heart:** Are they motivated? What is motivating to them? Do they have the level of desire they need to engage in the new behaviors?

- **Hands:** Do they know how to do "it" (the new set of behaviors)? Are they doing it?

Once you understand how essential it is to find out the answers to these questions, the importance of measuring change is apparent. See Table 39, Why Change Must Be Measured, for a summary.

DESIGN SCORECARDS TO MEASURE CHANGE

The first and foremost issue to consider in building a Change Scorecard is whether or not you are achieving the desired business results. At the beginning of the change process, the ultimate business goals and objectives should be defined (this is part of stage 1, coming to grips with the problem) and the business results identified that will be most reflective of the change and improvement. The correlation between the selected business outcomes and the results of the scorecard should

Table 39

Why Change Must Be Measured

1. Makes necessary changes real

2. Teaches people what to change: what behaviors to start, stop, or adjust

3. Clarifies expectations for change

4. Provides standards against which to create accountability for making/not making desired changes

5. Provides feedback on progress

6. Pinpoints areas of successful/unsuccessful change implementation, and why those areas exist

7. Gives change process leaders key indicators to either stay on or adjust the current course

be assessed at regular intervals. At Best Buy, the business reason for introducing the SOP was to increase the profitability of the stores and the company. Profitability was the goal, and the results of the Change Scorecard needed to be aligned with the measures used to assess profit. Improved shopping experiences for customers was also a key goal.

Reaching the desired business outcomes can necessitate integrating additional attitudes, perspectives, and behaviors in your change effort, including

- Promoting a universal sense of urgency
- Developing problem-solving, thinking, and interpersonal skills needed to cope with implementation chaos
- Consciously creating a culture based on values compatible with the new business model
- Overcoming rifts between employees of different departments and increasing collaboration among teams
- Increasing the organization's capacity to manage future change efforts

Translating business plans into goals for the changes needed in people's thinking, feeling, and behaving is the essence of a Change Scorecard. Some knowledge of the basic building blocks of behavioral measurement is also essential. Creating meaningful measurements — that are reliable, meaningful, and feasible, so that employees can measure themselves and others — is the heart of successful change measurement. Keep in mind that every time you measure and evaluate something, you are sending messages to people. To measure is to intervene and to have an impact on the system.

In the following paragraphs, we describe five elements that are essential aspects of designing Change Scorecards. These are

- The framework (or model) to use
- Basics of effective measurement
- The building blocks of Change Scorecards
- Evolving the Change Scorecard
- Embedding knowledge and know-how

The Framework

The framework on which to base a Change Scorecard should be familiar by now. The Change Scorecard needs to assess how people are thinking, feeling, and behaving (head, heart, and hands) in relation to the change. Since change is continuous and not an event, the evolution of the Change Scorecard parallels the evolution of the change process. Earlier in the change effort, how people are thinking about the change is emphasized, but not to the exclusion of how they are feeling about the change and how they are behaving. In the midst of the change process, all three arenas are given equal weight: How are people thinking and feeling about the change, and are they learning and performing the necessary new behaviors? Later in the change process, determining if people are behaving in new, appropriate ways, and if they're doing so skillfully, predominates. In effect, the Change Scorecard corresponds to the shift from "knowing about" the change to developing "know-how" (the capacity for effective action). See Table 40, Technology for Measuring Change.

Table 40

Technology for Measuring Change			
Stage	**Mind-Set/ Thinking**	**Emotional**	**Behavioral**
1. Coming to grips with the problem	Assess people's understanding and knowledge about the change	Determine readiness for change	Find out who and how many are using new behaviors and how well they are working
2. Working it through	Find out if people understand the change well enough to problem-solve with it and teach it	Assess how people feel about the change	Determine what people's notion of "good" is and if they are behaving in ways that will support "good" performance
3. Making it stick: maintaining momentum	Determine if people new to the organization are learning the new	Determine people's level of acceptance of the change	Assess how many people are exhibiting new behaviors, how frequently, and how well

Basics of Effective Measurement

Behavioral change, just like any other change, such as an increase in revenues, must be reliably (accurately) measured. Reliability or accuracy is usually defined as the ability of two or more well-informed and experienced person(s) to agree on what they are observing or measuring. A measure that lacks reliability can never become valid or meaningful, because people can't trust it or rely on it. It's fairly easy to reliably measure tangibles, such as the number of customers coming through the door or the number of employee hours worked. Achieving reliability in measuring complex human and organizational behavior is difficult. It requires a high level of specificity in behavioral terms. Whoever is taking the measurement needs a clear picture of what "good" behavior looks like, and if more than one person is doing the measuring, all need to agree on "what 'good' looks like." The internal consistency of the person doing the measuring and the consistency between people measuring the same things are critical. These topics will be more fully addressed in the next chapter.

Validity, or meaningfulness, of what is being measured is also essential. An important principle applies here: the ease and reliability of measurement are inversely proportional to the meaningfulness (importance) of what is being measured. Often the behaviors that are easier to measure, such as whether or not an employee is staffing a service counter or the number of salesperson-customer interactions, fail to address critical, underlying issues, such as the service attitude that leads to customer retention or a positive shopping experience.

As we try to achieve rewards for meeting behavioral change targets, we concentrate on doing exactly what gets measured (and rewarded). People do what they are rewarded for doing. Thus behavioral measurement, if not focused on core objectives, will lead to misinterpreting the results. What can inadvertently happen is that the goal becomes exhibiting the measured behavior rather than meeting the underlying objectives of change. For most people, this is an unconscious side effect of being observed and evaluated. For a few, it's conscious corner cutting.

Building Blocks of the Change Scorecard

Behavioral anchors and behaviorally anchored rating scales are the main building blocks of the Change Scorecard. Behavioral anchors describe a behavior in a way that captures its essential aspects. The person asking the question or making the observation will be listening and looking for words or actions that fit the criteria specified somewhere on the behaviorally anchored scale. (Keep in mind that answering questions *is* a type of behavior.) Behavioral anchors are used to avoid ambiguity and describe specific on-the-job behavior. They are a system for sampling a person's know-how, or capacity for taking effective action in a particular skill or knowledge set. Scorecard example 2 is a lighthearted example of behaviorally defined measurement.

Scorecard Example 2

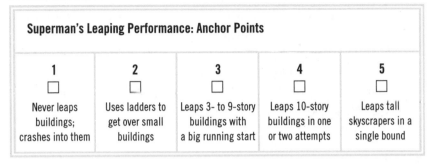

Some powerful aspects of behavioral anchors are that they engage the raters in the rating process and that the anchors on rating scales must be meaningful and clear to the raters who are using them. Developing behavioral anchors requires that the people developing the rating scale collaborate with supervisors—those who know the demands of the job involved, who can put into words the job demands in terms of performance criteria, and who understand what kinds of job behavior a variety of people might exhibit. Beyond that, developing and using behavioral anchors requires reaching consensus on what performance behaviors to look for and how to interpret them. In other words, raters have to agree on how "good" to "poor" behaviors are defined. The behavioral anchors will then represent the range of expected behaviors necessary for success in the changing organization. In other words, in the behavioral anchors, you are defining what good looks like, as well as not so good, mediocre, and unacceptable performance behaviors.

What about those behaviors that are new to the organization? Defining new, expected behaviors is fundamental to successful change implementation. Determining what those behaviors are (or will be) requires harvesting best practices from within and outside of the organization. Table 41 gives an example of a rating scale that is not behaviorally anchored.

Scorecard example 3 shows a behaviorally anchored rating scale. Note that a specific component of effective communications, the use of questions, is used instead of the vague term *communication skills*.

Developing behavioral anchors is a lot of work, but it pays off. You are clarifying what it takes to be successful in the new organization in

Table 41

An Unanchored Rating of Communication Skills

	Strongly Agree	Agree	Strongly Disagree	Disagree	Don't Know
1. This person communicates effectively with his/her teammates.	○	○	○	○	○

Scorecard Example 3

A Behaviorally Anchored Rating of Effective Questioning Skills

Observe the person interacting with his/her peers in at least three different situations and rate him/her using the descriptions below.

1	2	3	4	5
☐	☐	☐	☐	☐
May ask no questions, only makes statements, or asks only yes/no or other closed questions	Mainly asks yes/no questions or closed questions (that require very limited answers)	Frequently asks open-ended questions that open up a dialogue	Frequently asks open-ended questions that solicit people's thoughts and feelings; listens carefully; checks out what he/she hears for accuracy	Makes highly effective use of questions to exchange information and facilitate group dialogue; moves a group forward past difficult points

terms of thinking and acting. (For each of the Change Scorecard questions used as examples in this chapter, you will find the corresponding behaviorally anchored rating scale in Appendix B, Embedding Knowledge and Know-How in a Change Scorecard.)

Evolving the Change Scorecard

Change changes over time, and the tools we use to measure it also need to evolve with it. We know that as change and learning move forward, the emphasis shifts from understanding new models and concepts to working through feelings to defining and learning new behaviors, and so must the emphasis within the Change Scorecard change.

In stage 1, coming to grips with the problem, people are trying to understand why the change is necessary and what it means for them, so the greatest emphasis is on the head, with some emphasis on the heart and a little on the hands. In stage 2, working through the change, the scorecards start to bring in more "doing" (the hands), and the heart issues are specifically addressed by using short Change Progress Surveys (shown in detail later in this chapter). In stage 3, making it stick: maintaining momentum, the emphasis is on developing new skills and practicing new behaviors, but the head and heart are not ignored.

Successful change implementation requires constant integration of the three arenas of the head, heart, and hands throughout the change process, as well as shifting the emphasis from the head to the heart to the hands. The rate at which the emphasis shifts will be different from person to person and group to group. And, a person or group may move back into the head from the hands, or the heart might interfere with the hands learning a new behavior or skill. For example, if someone fears looking stupid in front of others (and who doesn't?), then trying to do something new for the first time can be an emotionally charged situation that requires understanding of and skill in dealing with the heart. At the same time, some of us learn best by simply doing something—by trying it out. We are therefore going to develop understanding and comfort with something new by first doing the specific behaviors and then trying to understand why they are important.

At Best Buy, the CIT found that when they were well into the SOP change implementation and had evolved the scorecard to emphasize observing behavior, there were newly hired associates who needed to be worked with in the head arena and evaluated appropriately. The CIT realized that they would need to move back into modes of understanding and feeling when the behaviors were not forthcoming, especially when the behaviors were modeled and coached by people's direct supervisors but still weren't taking hold.

Here are some questions from a Change Scorecard used in the first several months of a change implementation. These questions focus on the head arena: understanding why the change is necessary, knowing the essence of the change well enough to problem-solve with it or teach it to someone else, and understanding what it takes to lead the change effort.

- "In your opinion, what is the purpose of the Standard Operating Platform in each discipline? For the store as a whole?"
- "What benefits have resulted in the store from implementing the Standard Operating Platform?"

As people start to come to terms with the change in the head and heart arenas, they still need to learn what they need to do differently and how to do it. Fortunately, we know a lot about what it takes to unlearn old habits and learn new habits and develop new skills. Even though many techniques can be used in this arena, changing behavior is never easy. Remember, for people to learn something new, they need to have a model, picture, or example of the new behavior; they need opportunities to practice the new behavior and get feedback on their progress; and they need coaching and encouragement.

In the next chapter, we address how to meet these requirements for learning and skill development and what that implies for the organization's processes and culture. Here, our main point is that in developing items for the scorecard and in using it wisely, the raters and managers need to rely on observing behavior, including verbal behavior. To observe people and what they're doing, you have to take the time to do so and be in a position to notice (observe) what they're doing. Realizing and promoting this idea was just one of the many lessons the organization learned and embedded in its evolving, new culture. In Best Buy, the phrase "position to notice" became part of the company vocabulary, as in, "Are you (as a manager or supervisor at any level) in a position to notice?"

Examples 4, 5, and 6 show items from a scorecard used later in the change implementation process (nine or ten months into it). In these items, the stage of change is somewhere between stage 2, working it through, and stage 3, making it stick: maintaining momentum, and the arena emphasized is behavioral, the hands.

Scorecard Example 4

In each department, observe a product specialist and rate the quality of his/her current activity. If Quick Serve, look for	
Contact ■ Customers in the zone being acknowledged immediately (10 ft, 10 sec) or if overwhelmed, he/she seeks help from another zone, department, or manager *Yes = 1 point, No = 0 points* ■ Practicing greet and release with *all* customers (3–5 minute presentation) *Yes = 1 point, No = 0 points*	_____ /2 **TOTAL**

Presentation
 	
■ Use of the noncommission statement
Yes = 1 point, No = 0 points
 	
■ Is the customer offered:
  – Accessories?
  – Warranties?
  – Appropriate install/tech services?
  (all that apply)
Yes = 1 point, No = 0 points
	_____ /2
	TOTAL

Notice that the scorecard items and ratings are based on observable behaviors. These new items look and feel very different from the understanding-based questions emphasized earlier in the change process. However, all the items are anchored in behaviors; some of the behavior is simply verbal behavior.

Embedding Knowledge and Know-How
The content of a Change Scorecard will also draw on multiple sources of knowledge and know-how, including the following.

- Organization and culture-specific knowledge
- Industry-specific knowledge

Scorecard Example 5

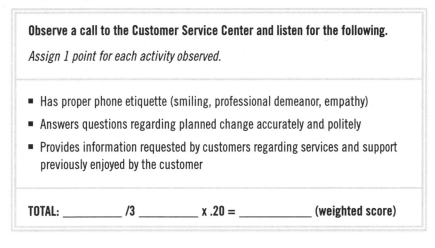

Observe a call to the Customer Service Center and listen for the following.

Assign 1 point for each activity observed.

- Has proper phone etiquette (smiling, professional demeanor, empathy)
- Answers questions regarding planned change accurately and politely
- Provides information requested by customers regarding services and support previously enjoyed by the customer

TOTAL: _____ /3 _____ x .20 = _____ (weighted score)

Scorecard Example 6

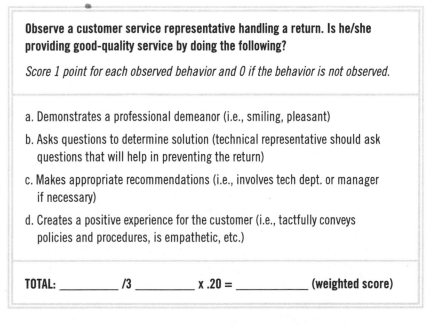

Observe a customer service representative handling a return. Is he/she providing good-quality service by doing the following?

Score 1 point for each observed behavior and 0 if the behavior is not observed.

a. Demonstrates a professional demeanor (i.e., smiling, pleasant)

b. Asks questions to determine solution (technical representative should ask questions that will help in preventing the return)

c. Makes appropriate recommendations (i.e., involves tech dept. or manager if necessary)

d. Creates a positive experience for the customer (i.e., tactfully conveys policies and procedures, is empathetic, etc.)

TOTAL: _____ /3 _____ x .20 = _____ (weighted score)

- Organizational structure: levels and functions
- General change management know-how and know-how relevant to specific types of change

In the following paragraphs, we briefly describe what we mean by these various sources of knowledge and know-how that can be embedded in a Change Scorecard. If you are interested in designing and using a Change Scorecard, see Appendix B, Embedding Knowledge and Know-How in a Change Scorecard, in which we go into these areas more deeply and provide examples.

We mention these additional types of knowledge that are part of a Change Scorecard in order to alert you to one of the dangers of using scorecards. The questions you ask and observations you make may look simple, but by focusing on particular areas and asking questions in particular ways, you are sending multiple messages to people that you may or may not be aware of. And you may be strengthening basic mental models and behaviors that actually need to change.

Change Scorecards are powerful medicine and need to be developed and applied by people who know about designing and asking questions. They know, for example, that the way in which you ask or phrase a question can influence the answer you get. And, the way in which you structure a question and its behavioral anchors can challenge or reinforce certain assumptions and values or, alternatively, challenge people to consider options they've never thought of.

Organization and Culture-Specific Knowledge

You can get the most payback from the effort required to develop and use a Change Scorecard, and lay the groundwork for future successes, by embedding in the culture the deeper learning principles, values, and attitudes necessary to successfully implement a change process. To build in the capacity to shape people's thinking, feeling, and behavior, as these things relate to the organization's values and capacity to learn and adapt to change, requires a deep understanding of the organization—including its foundation, culture, leaders, and strategy—as well as skill in choosing and constructing questions.

Industry-Specific Knowledge

In the Best Buy example, the industry is consumer electronics retail store operations. In determining what industry-specific know-how to embed in a scorecard, you need to have an understanding of the industry's best practices, the current practices, and what the new processes and behaviors should be. Determining the industry-specific best practices and how they should work within the organization requires collaboration between the industry experts and the experts in changing and measuring human behavior.

Using external consultants who are specialists in the industry, running tests of specific practices in different parts of the organization, and finding the best practices within the organization are all useful in determining what goes into this aspect of the scorecard. Using your best performers as your source of know-how and making this known throughout the organization helps to increase organizational buy-in to the practices rated highly in the scorecard. Keep in mind that these best practices, standard operating procedures, or "the new way we're doing things here now" need to be explained and taught to the people in the organization before they are evaluated on the practices.

Organizational Structure: Levels and Functions

Here's a guideline to use in deciding if different parts of the Change Scorecard need to be designed to assess particular levels or functions within the organization: a Change Scorecard should incorporate the key ingredients of understanding and working through the change for *any person who is expected to change his behavior.* And, the parts of the Change Scorecard that are applied to each person should be relevant to his or her work. If different levels within the company have different roles to play and if what they do in those roles is changing, then the Change Scorecard will need to address those changes. If, with the change, differing functions require specific behavior changes, then there need to be components of the Change Scorecard that address those behaviors specific to particular functions.

Change Management Know-How

Earlier we made the case for leaders who are involved in a change effort at any level becoming knowledgeable about how change effects people in the organization. The term *know-how* means more than simply "knowing about" change. It implies that the person has the capacity to take effective action. The key challenge for leaders, then, is, How well do they understand what it takes to lead and manage change, and how skilled are they at doing it? We also emphasized that becoming a skilled, successful leader of change means that you know how you approach and work through change and how it has the potential to change you. It is likely that some aspects of managing change will be the same regardless of the type of organizational change being implemented, while other aspects of managing change are likely to be specific to the type of change being implemented.

PUTTING THE CHANGE SCORECARD TO (MORE) WORK

Measuring the progress of the change effort is the most obvious use of the Change Scorecard. When we stop to think about it, we know that changing requires learning. When we learn something new—really learn it—it changes us. And conversely, when we change we often learn something new—about others, our world, or ourselves. The Change Scorecard can be used for feedback, learning, and diagnosis in the following ways.

- **Feedback.** Are people getting feedback about how they're doing? To teach and coach people, and for them to learn effectively, you need to give them feedback.

- **Learning.** Are people learning? Is the new learning being shared and celebrated? People need feedback, as well as opportunities to practice and forums in which to practice, with feedback, in order to learn. The progress of the change effort is contingent upon learning.

- **Diagnosis.** Can we diagnose what the problem is? Can we spot and analyze problems that are blocking the progress of learning and change?

When people set out to measure the effects of change on business results such as productivity, sales, profit, and employee turnover, they are measuring the outcomes of a process. Measuring results does not provide much information on how the change is proceeding or what issues might be impeding or furthering the change process. And, measuring results generally does not help people learn and improve their game. Knowing the score at the end of a game gives you limited information about how the individuals played, where they need to improve, or what's getting in the way of their achieving a better score.

In business, measuring results early in a process is the norm, but it's not particularly useful in implementing change. In fact, too much emphasis on the results early in a change process can be dangerous, since it does not measure the behaviors that must be learned to achieve those results. We've already pointed out that people will behave in whatever ways they believe will be rewarded. This can mean taking shortcuts, learning only about the superficial aspects of a change (memorizing information, for example), or temporarily mimicking a behavior. To really learn something usually means that you will struggle with it to some degree. And, in learning something new, your performance often gets a little worse in the short term. As you struggle with the new learning, you need feedback on where and how you are moving forward (even though it may feel like slipping backward). The Change Scorecard gives people feedback on their progress, so they're not off the hook, and it encourages their improvement, bit by bit. But, it doesn't encourage warped behavior.

ADDITIONAL TOOLS

The Change Scorecard is one tool to use in measuring and managing change. For measuring the heart arena we use an additional tool. The science of measuring people's honest emotional reaction to something is still in its infancy. It isn't desirable to use a polygraph to assess people's level of reaction to different questions, nor would it be legal. In any case, all that a polygraph tells you is that a person is having an emotional reaction to something, not what type of emotion they're experiencing.

To find out how people feel about the change and how they're handling it, you can interview them, observe them, and ask about their feelings in a short, anonymous survey. Throughout the change process we use a survey we call the SOP Change Progress Survey (see Table 42). We administered it in July and October of 1997. Using the survey early in the process gives a baseline measure of people's reactions to the change. It also sends a message to them that the issues raised by the survey are important. Using the survey later in the change process, both in stage 2, working it through, and stage 3, making it stick: maintaining momentum, gives you information about how people's feelings about the change have or have not shifted. Using this type of "heart"

Table 42

Best Buy Co., Inc.—SOP Change Progress Survey

	Strongly Disagree	Dis-agree	Neutral	Agree	Strongly Agree
1. I see the urgency to implement the SOP in my department.	○	○	○	○	○
2. Cooperation and teamwork among departments (OPS, Merchandising, Sales, Inventory) in the store is better than it was a month ago.	○	○	○	○	○
3. I understand the benefits of the SOP.	○	○	○	○	○
4. There is a spirit of cooperation and teamwork within my department.	○	○	○	○	○
5. I have already seen some improvement in my department as a result of the SOP.	○	○	○	○	○
6. My store manager is really in touch with employees.	○	○	○	○	○
7. There is a spirit of cooperation and teamwork between departments within Best Buy.	○	○	○	○	○
8. The person I report to is helping eliminate obstacles to implementing the SOP.	○	○	○	○	○
9. I understand our store's plans to implement the SOP.	○	○	○	○	○
10. Our customers have a great experience in our store.	○	○	○	○	○
11. I know what I must do to help implement the SOP.	○	○	○	○	○

12. In which area do you work?

○ Inventory (incl. Loss Prevention)   ○ Merchandising/Media

○ Leadership: GM and AM   ○ Sales

○ Loss Prevention   ○ Operations/Administration (incl. Install)

survey can help you to identify trouble spots and to design appropriate interventions throughout the process. Just as in the Change Scorecard, underlying messages are embedded in several of the questions on the survey, such as "2. Cooperation and teamwork among departments in the store is better than it was a month ago." Other questions ask if the person realizes the urgency of the need to change. And, not surprisingly, there are questions about how the person's boss is managing and communicating the process.

One of the things that the CIT learned time after time was that the quality of leadership was the determining factor in how effectively the change was being implemented in a particular store, district, or region. Although it may seem like we're stating the obvious, the team learned the truth of "It all depends on the leadership" again and again from multiple angles. Consequently, another tool that the team started using (after being in the field for about four months) was a leadership questionnaire: a short, "pulse" survey that gathered information and was used to give feedback to the managers within the stores. The CIT member would give the questionnaire to a predetermined number of store employees during a scorecarding session. She would then collect the questionnaires and tally the results. She used these results to give feedback to the managers in the store about how their leadership was affecting the change process. The results of the leadership questionnaire were not used as part of the process of "keeping score" but only to give information to the CIT about how to best work with the managers. Examples of the types of leadership behaviors the CIT looked for and the questions that stem from them are shown in Table 43, SOP Leadership Survey, on the following pages.

MEANWHILE . . .

The team was ready to take a baseline measure of the SOP implementation effort. They had established the new and very different SOP Change Scorecard that they believed would support new ways of thinking and behaving. As usual, everyone was under pressure to get good results. Every store, district, region, and division would be posting its results. Remember, score inflation had been the norm in previous Best Buy measurement practices. The executives wanted to see positive scores. But they also wanted to see the truth.

Table 43

Best Buy Co., Inc.—SOP Leadership Survey

	Strongly Disagree	Dis-agree	Neutral	Agree	Strongly Agree
1. In thinking about my Supervisor, he/she:					
a. Explains our goals and objectives clearly	○	○	○	○	○
b. Holds people accountable for maintaining standards and meeting objectives	○	○	○	○	○
c. Recognizes the quality of my work	○	○	○	○	○
d. Offers new ideas, which help me improve at my job	○	○	○	○	○
e. Does a good job of keeping us informed about department and store issues	○	○	○	○	○
f. Does what he/she says he/she will do	○	○	○	○	○
2. In thinking about my Assistant Manager, he/she:					
a. Explains our goals and objectives clearly	○	○	○	○	○
b. Holds people accountable for maintaining standards and meeting objectives	○	○	○	○	○
c. Recognizes the quality of my work	○	○	○	○	○
d. Offers new ideas, which help me improve at my job	○	○	○	○	○
e. Does a good job of keeping us informed about department and store issues	○	○	○	○	○
f. Does what he/she says he/she will do	○	○	○	○	○

Table 43 (cont'd)

Best Buy Co., Inc.—SOP Leadership Survey

	Strongly Agree	Agree	Strongly Disagree	Disagree	Don't Know
3. There is a spirit of cooperation and teamwork between the departments within the store.	○	○	○	○	○
4. If I should be doing things differently, I get feedback about it at the time.	○	○	○	○	○
5. I understand what I need to do in my job to help my department execute the Standard Operating Platform.	○	○	○	○	○
6. My store's management team maintains a sense of urgency to execute the SOP, even between SOP Change Scorecards.	○	○	○	○	○

The CIT members' bonuses were tied to the success of the implementation. The scorecard results became the obvious criteria for determining the size of their bonuses. The consultants also had an agreement that the size of their fee would be tied to the success of the implementation. And, naturally, scorecard results were the way to measure success.

The national scorecarding plan was set, goals were established, and work schedules were in place. But in a series of wrenching meetings on the executive floor at headquarters, the entire credibility and validity of the proposed scorecard results was called into question. And so, too, were the value and efforts of the CIT. The old culture said that people could not be trusted to give accurate measurements. Everyone was in it for himself or herself. Just having a different type of scorecard or improved results was not enough to prove the integrity of the results. The CIT and their scorecards could not be trusted. From that perspective, there was no one left inside the company who would be free from the influence of the culture.

By now the CIT was operating as a cohesive unit. But this, too, could be dangerous. Maybe there was no longer enough interregional competitiveness in the team to make the cross-regional scorecarding objective. Maybe the team members would start to cover for each other. No one inside of Best Buy was really immune from the pull of the old culture, including the consultants.

From his first involvement, one of the retail executives doubted that the CIT or the consultants could or would evaluate the stores objectively, especially since part of the CIT members' bonuses and the consultants' fees were contingent on the scorecard results. He'd seen too many manipulated scores in the past. Surely it wouldn't do to have the fox guarding the henhouse? He proposed hiring an outside firm to "audit" the CIT and the consultants. The use of external auditors was a direct challenge to the credibility and integrity of the CIT. It would weaken confidence in the ability of the CIT and the organization to create deeper change. If the CIT had to be audited, the change process was forced compliance, not genuine endorsement. In some ways, the proposal to use this outside audit felt like a slap to the CIT and the consultants. It meant that the old culture was prevailing and that they had failed in their efforts to create a new approach in which measurement was both valuable and valid.

The CIT was in a squeeze. If the national scorecard results came back high, team members might get bonuses. The outcome was of keen interest to the consultants as well. But if the results came back high, questions of credibility and validity would surely arise. The CIT could bring back results that were too successful and that would discredit them.

The team worked harder to understand and agree on "what 'good' looks like." Since the scorecard involved making judgments on what looked like subjective measures, the team was vulnerable if its members saw and scored things differently from one another. The CIT knew that inevitably individual team members' scores would be challenged. The consultants and the CIT applied even more stringent standards for achieving and periodically retesting interrater agreement, as free of bias as possible. (These methods are described in Chapter 10, Measuring Change.) The executives agreed to hold off on the independent auditing until after the first wave of scorecarding. If the results looked "reasonable" to the executives, the work of the CIT would be considered successful and independent audits would not be necessary.

In this chapter, we've described how to design and develop a Change Scorecard. Although we've said it before, the following axiom bears repeating: every time you measure and evaluate something, you are sending multiple messages. To measure is to intervene, and it has the potential to impact the system. Here is another axiom: how you communicate about and apply a Change Scorecard is just as important as what goes on it. How to use Change Scorecards skillfully and successfully is the topic of the next chapter. As a reminder of what we've discussed so far, the excerpt below summarizes some tips for measuring change.

FIELD GUIDE EXCERPT

Tips on Tools for Measuring Change

1. Measurement and feedback are powerful change tools.
2. Those who design new processes must deeply understand the underlying change objectives.
3. Designing change measurements is iterative; it gets better (i.e., you never get it right the first time).
4. You can never get the method too simple. But simplification creates the risk of easy but trivial metrics.
5. Each arena must have clear behavioral descriptors—behavioral anchors. If these core behaviors are present, associated behaviors must also be present.
6. Measurement methods do not have to be perfect to be useful. Even flawed methods can have the power to create change. Give up trying to make them perfect.

Measuring Change

TAKING THE MEASURE OF CHANGE: APPLYING THE CHANGE SCORECARD

The Change Scorecard was well built and in trained hands, but it was up against a formidable culture that had defeated other change measurements. Would it pay off this time? Building and evolving a valid, powerful Change Scorecard was vital to the success of change. But how a scorecard is applied is just as important as *what* goes on it. Scorecards are potent tools and when used correctly can promote remarkable, transformational change. Used incorrectly, they can be useless or even destructive. In this chapter, we describe our approach to using the scorecard and explain how it helped define key new behaviors and demonstrate emerging learning. We also speak to the benefits of scorecarding to improve the performance of teams. And we see how Best Buy measures up to the test.

Scorecarding is, by nature, evaluative and judgmental, and thus it tends to put people on the defensive. When people are defensive, they shut down their learning processes. To realize the benefits of a Change Scorecard, as well as build trust and promote learning, we learned to be very careful about the way the scorecard was used and the way in which feedback was delivered.

CHANGE SCORECARD VERSUS THE CULTURE

What do we mean by the "correct" or "skillful" use of a Change Scorecard? Change and learning go hand in hand; seldom do you have one without the other. The Change Scorecard can be used to inform people about the why, what, and how of the change as it evolves over time. As we mentioned in the last chapter, a tremendous amount of knowledge and know-how came to be embedded in the scorecard. Transferring this know-how to managers and employees required using the Change Scorecard as a tool for learning, as well as a tool for measuring the progress of the change effort. We believed the Best Buy culture would be changed as much by how the scorecard was used as by the actual numbers coming from it.

To use the Change Scorecard successfully, the people applying it needed to be seen by managers and line staff as allies in helping them learn and make the transition successfully, and the scorecard needed to be seen as a tool for feedback and learning. The CIT found it best to adopt an attitude of mutual problem solving and collaboration. CIT members were constantly reminded that the active listening skills described in Chapter 7, Foundational Skills, were essential in the communication and scorecarding processes, and they continually asked themselves, What messages are we sending?

As we've mentioned in earlier chapters, before the CIT was formed, a certification audit was initially used to assess the stores' compliance with the SOP. At that time, the district managers claimed that all stores had passed the audit with a score of 90 percent or better. In reality, however, not much had changed in terms of how the stores were operating. The need to comply had been hammered into the retail organization with an authoritative "because I said so" attitude. However, when you try to drive change into an organization, you run over a lot of people. Best Buy had complied on the surface without doing what it would take to actually change.

CULTIVATING IS BETTER THAN DRIVING CHANGE

As we joined the efforts to implement the SOP, we aimed for a mindset of cultivating rather than driving change. We asked ourselves and the CIT, How do you grow people's awareness of the need to change, their willingness, and the skills they need to be successful? We pretested our messages on key critics in the field, asking them how they interpreted the message, and we looked for misinterpretations that would require us to use a different approach.

We knew that Best Buy people were good at figuring out how to beat scorecards, so we needed to find a way to make the scorecard valid and to reflect real changes. One of the CIT members suggested that we make unannounced visits to the stores to apply the scorecard. His reasoning was that if store managers were told in advance when CIT members would be visiting, they would put only their best and brightest people on duty at that time. Then we would not be likely to get an accurate read on the use of the SOP in the store.

However, if the CIT was simultaneously trying to establish a working relationship with the store management based on trust and respect, what message would surprise scorecarding visits send? What chance did the CIT have of promoting an atmosphere of collaboration and mutual problem solving if they were seen as the SOP cops? Little to none. Operating in this way would pit the CIT against the store management in an adversarial relationship. So the team decided to publish an advance schedule of their store visits and build in the necessary safeguards against artificially inflated scores.

In preparation for the first round of scorecarding, the retail executives and the CIT spent significant time refining their approach. They spent long hours hashing out exact agreements on what language they would use as a team to introduce the Change Scorecard. Team members practiced their speeches and explanations with one another using role-playing. They also practiced active listening and behavioral interviewing. They challenged one another if a conversation sounded suspicious, punitive, or condescending. Together, they forged a mindset, ways of behaving, and an identity that declared, "We're here to help you improve your game. We'll work through this with you and we'll get it done. And we're not going away until we're all using the SOP every day in every store."

The CIT members grew into their role, defining it as they went along. Here are some of the guidelines they used to aid their work.

- Make sure your words and actions match. *Say* and *do* should be the same.

- The SOP and the Change Scorecard are serious business.
- The SOP and the Change Scorecard are about improving, and they can be used to help you learn.
- Every question is a good question and will be met with sincere efforts to promote understanding.
- Every person deserves to be treated with courtesy, respect, and dignity.
- We won't let you off the hook, but we won't let you sink, either.

Making significant changes in a functioning organization is like trying to change a tire on a moving car. Best Buy needed to take care of daily business and at the same time change the way it was doing that business. Added to that was the reality that although Best Buy had a clear idea of its goal, the company had never experienced it before — what the organization would look, feel, and function like once it had changed. How do we measure progress toward a constantly moving target? We had to make the measuring tool dynamic and evolve it to be in sync with our target. And we used the process of measuring and giving feedback as a culture change tool itself.

THREE ARENAS: HOW TO MEASURE?

You need to be very clear on what the central elements of the change are in each of the three arenas: head, heart, and hands. And be careful about selecting what to measure, because what gets measured gets done, and this will ultimately determine what the change process amounts to. Just as important as the information being gathered by the CIT was the approach the team took in seeking and interpreting the data. As expert interviewers know, the way in which you ask a question can have an impact on your audience and influence the answer that you get.

The Head

To assess a store employee's understanding of a change, you need to ask him about it. And to get at his degree of understanding and know-how, you need to ask the types of questions for which he can't easily memorize the answers. The open-ended questions used in the under-standing-based Change Scorecard are examples of questions used in behavioral scorecarding. In most of these questions, you are asking the manager or employee to describe an action he's taken or his thinking about a particular issue. As a scorecarder, you need to pay attention to a variety of signals. First, listen to the content of his answers—what he says and fails to say. In addition, listen to word choice, tone of voice, and other nonverbal cues. Scorecarders must be excellent at using effective communication skills (described in Chapter 7, Foundational Skills), such as clarifying and confirming (active listening), expressing appreciation, and giving balanced feedback.

A skilled observer will notice the way the person is expressing himself. Some people are more verbal and expressive than others, and it took the CIT some practice to be able to ask probing questions without asking leading questions. Encouraging the person to elaborate or to give real examples from his experience is a good way of looking under the surface of his initial response. When you are satisfied that you have gotten to the essentials of what the person knows, you have to make a judgment call on how to rate his answer.

What we're describing here are sophisticated skills not generally needed by people in retail sales management. And, quite honestly, Best Buy's leadership did not have the time or the inclination to send the members of the CIT through intensive training courses. What we did, instead, was partner each CIT member with his or her own consultant. Early in the project, the CIT member and consultant spent long days in the stores jointly interviewing people, using the SOP Change Scorecard. The consultant would model, coach, and give feedback to her Best Buy partner as the two of them worked together over a number of days. And the Best Buy CIT member would coach the consultant on how to read the culture and how to present issues to Best Buy people. This type of mutual learning by watching, practicing, getting feedback, and trying again created the transfer of know-how from person to person and across the company.

We describe this type of knowledge as *know-how* rather than *knowing about*, because know-how conveys the sense that the person has the capacity to take effective action. Earlier we gave the example of learning a foreign language. There is a difference between knowing something about that language and speaking it fluently. With this in mind, we designed the Change Scorecard process so that the expertise in behavioral scorecarding techniques could be transferred to the CIT and then throughout Best Buy. Without this continuing transfer of know-how, we would not be able to achieve sustainable change.

So far, we've talked about developing skills in scorecarding in the head arena and interpreting the results. In the Best Buy SOP change implementation there were nine CIT members using the same questions across nine regions. How could we get those nine individuals to agree on what a "good" answer is? We had to insure that the person applying the Change Scorecard in Washington, D.C., and the person applying it in San Diego were judging a particular score on a question in the same way. Later in this chapter we dig into this question.

The Heart

People often do not have the vocabulary or insights to reliably describe or evaluate their own motivations or feelings about change. Compounding this problem is the fact that being emotionally aware and expressive are not generally encouraged in the workplace. And how do you assess your emotional state in comparison with someone else's? Evaluating emotions and motivations is a challenging endeavor that requires a skilled combination of asking people questions and observing them. We took the approach of asking people how they felt about something in a structured way. We also knew that people would express themselves more accurately if they could respond anonymously. Using the Change Progress Survey (described in Chapter 9, Tools for Measuring Change) and comparing the results obtained at different times in the change process also provided us with a reading of the emotional temperature of the organization at all levels.

The Hands

The most accurate way to assess behavior is to watch and listen for specifically defined behaviors to occur (including verbal behavior). For a variety of reasons, we humans generally are not accurate at recalling what we've done or when and how often we've done it. Therefore, independently observing people while they work and measuring the outcomes of their work provides the surest measure in the arena of the hands. To scorecard behaviors accurately requires that the behaviors you are looking for be described in enough detail to be recognizable and that the scorecarders agree on what constitutes a specific behavior.

Some of the value of the Change Scorecard is that, in building it, you have to think through and test what new behaviors will be appropriate and constructive as the organization changes. Just as the CIT did in the SOP change implementation process, you will have to define and agree on the behaviors to measure and then paint the picture of what they'll look like in action. Then the scorecarders need to practice observing and rating behaviors and comparing their results with their colleagues. Given that people will figure out new and better ways of accomplishing tasks, the target behaviors will naturally change and evolve over time. The Change Scorecard evolves to keep up with the new learning and behaviors.

BEING IN A POSITION TO NOTICE

At Best Buy, managers were so busy putting out fires that they often could not or did not take the time to observe their people in action. When the CIT started observing people in a purposeful way, offering constructive feedback, and providing coaching, they realized that the behavior of the managers needed to change, too. The CIT learned it was necessary to be in a "position to notice" what was going on in order to understand, evaluate, and improve the behavior of employees. They shared this insight with the retail managers, and the simple, powerful question that became obvious was, Are you in a "position to notice"? The question emerged as the CIT engaged in the scorecarding process, and it was transmitted swiftly by word of mouth throughout the entire retail organization.

It's easy to jump too quickly to the arena of the hands (observing behaviors). When we started measuring the change process too close to the outcomes, we realized we didn't have access to information we needed about why and how certain things were happening. The lesson is that if you focus on results too early, you won't have the diagnostic information you need to assess and address emerging problems in the change process or to capitalize on emerging opportunities.

WHY SHOULD I LISTEN TO YOU?

The CIT encountered significant challenges when trying to influence others. As we mentioned, "You're not the boss of me!" merited the number-one position in their top twelve phrases. What would it take for the CIT to develop and maintain enough credibility in the organization so that their feedback was trusted and their support solicited?

People in organizations can wield authority in several different ways. An individual may have power because of her position or her expertise, or she may have a track record of success. When the CIT began using a Change Scorecard, they were concerned with how they would establish their authority to develop the scorecard, administer it, make judgment calls about their colleagues, and be taken seriously. CIT members were giving feedback to people who outranked them in terms of positional authority in the (very hierarchical) organization. Why should these leaders listen to the CIT? The CIT knew that if the retail leaders didn't take the team's input and feedback seriously, neither would the larger constituency of the organization.

The CIT, without a track record as a team or as individual change agents, had to develop their skills at influencing others over whom they had no direct authority. We found that the key indicator of whether or not someone would be effective on the team was her performance and credibility as a store manager. The rule of thumb we discovered as useful in this regard is: you want and need the people that the company can't afford to give you. No other people will be respected or listened to by the rest of the organization to the same degree.

At the beginning of the SOP change process, the "currency of influence" in the CIT's account was based largely on each member's past performance and standing. Given the highly competitive and numbers-oriented nature of the Best Buy culture, the CIT members could expend this limited capital very quickly. How would they create more "credibility capital" within the organization?

Through two critical means, the CIT established strong and lasting credibility within the company. First and foremost, the team was in close, regular contact with their sponsors, the retail SVPs. They and the rest of the organization needed to know, on a continuing basis, that the team was acting under a mandate from top management and that what was being measured in the SOP Change Scorecard was aligned with the strategic business goals of the company.

Monthly CIT and retail executive meetings were scheduled up to six months in advance, in various locations across the country. The team spent two or more days together before meeting with the executives to explore and discuss what they were seeing emerge in the company. The team worked hard to craft their message to the retail executives so that it was clear, understandable, supported by facts, and followed by the team's recommendations. The visible support that the three executives gave the team members gave credence to the team's reliability and authority.

Second, and much more difficult to achieve, was the team coming together as one entity with a united front. Achieving unanimity among the team members—at least to the degree that they could agree on what they would say and do in the field—required significant time, effort, patience, goodwill, and skill.

TEAM INTEGRITY BUILDS FROM INTERRATER AGREEMENT

The members of the CIT were not used to thinking of the company as a whole; they typically focused on the performance of their region, district, or store. The narrowness of this view was even more extreme among different functions, which people referred to as "silos." One of the first steps we took to focus the team on the big picture (called "The Big Win") was to base part of their compensation on what the team and company achieved as a whole. This step was necessary, but by no means sufficient, to overcome the mind-set of being individual "stars." In fact, a major change that many of the CIT members underwent was realizing that they would succeed not by being individual heroes, but by helping *other people* to improve and succeed.

Back in their regions, the members of the CIT were subject to forces ("Don't you want *your* region to look good?"), old ties and friendships, and peer pressure of all sorts. Most of the team quickly realized that their credibility and ability to influence others would be based on functioning as one unit, with one voice. This is easier said than done, but it was a goal that the team by and large agreed on. Some of the agreement, unfortunately, was more in the head than in the heart and hands arenas.

The central idea for the CIT was that they needed to all agree on what "good" was. This was not a simple task. Instead, it was a process of comparing notes, discussing problems and possible solutions, agreeing on the basis for making judgment calls, and determining how to deliver feedback to their internal clients. The CIT members started emphasizing the need to make objective decisions in the field and to rely on the team's input when any member was uncertain about how to evaluate something. Specifically, the members of the team all had to try to administer the Change Scorecard in the same way, using similar scorecarding techniques and rating the responses the same way across the country. This is essential when asking open-ended questions, such as those shown in scorecard example 7.

Scorecard Example 7

- In your opinion, what is the purpose of the Standard Operating Platform in each discipline? For the store as a whole?
- What benefits have resulted in the store from implementing the SOP?

Agreement among raters is also essential when evaluating behaviors, as illustrated by the following item in scorecard example 8.

Scorecard Example 8

- Observe a morning meeting and rate the following elements on a scale of 0–5 . (0 = nonexistent, 5 = outstanding)

a. Interactive	0	1	2	3	4	5
b. Positive / upbeat	0	1	2	3	4	5
c. Informative / topical / a learning experience	0	1	2	3	4	5
d. Attendance	0	1	2	3	4	5

How do you look inside every team member's head to see (a) what the rating is, (b) how she is actually making the rating, and (c) how to calibrate each team member's rating with all the others? Another way to say this is, How do you achieve an acceptable level of interrater agreement? What level of interrater agreement is "good enough" to build and preserve the credibility of the group of people doing the rating?

In the business world, the issue of the level of interrater agreement is a practical (rather than a scientific) one. The scientific process for establishing an acceptable level of agreement (usually defined as a 0.9 correlation coefficient of agreement on a scale ranging from –1.0 to +1.0) is quite detailed, thorough, and painstaking. We need not go into it here. Instead, we will describe the practical way we applied it in the Best Buy change implementation process.

1. We started by having the CIT review and discuss each item on the initial version of the Change Scorecard. Each team member described what he would look for in determining how to rate each item. If we heard more accurate or relevant descriptions of behavior that the team agreed on, then we revised the scoring criteria for the item and verified the revision with the team.

2. We practiced making ratings, using videotaped excerpts of role-played and actual scorecarding. The group would watch a video, and each person would rate the interviewee's answers on her individual scorecard. After signing and turning the scorecards in, the group compared and discussed their ratings for each item. The group worked toward a shared picture of what "good" looked or sounded like for the items. This process was something we would continually need to revisit to maintain the validity of results.

3. For subsequent rounds of scorecarding, the team first analyzed and agreed on any modifications to be made to the scorecard. Then we practiced rating the items and comparing our ratings, although less formally than we had done in the beginning of the process. If a score was markedly different (for example, by at least one full point on the five-point scale), the CIT member with the dissimilar score was asked to explain the rating and justify it to the team.

The steps the team took to develop a shared vision and rating system for the application of the SOP might sound like the team put one another on the spot. They did. But they did so with a strong spirit of collaboration and mutual support. One of the skills the members of the team developed and passed on to the rest of the organization was the ability to challenge their own and one another's thinking or actions without belittling others (or themselves). The emphasis in the organizational culture shifted from having to be right and have the answers to focusing on mutual understanding, problem solving, and learning. This was exciting.

THE TEAM'S GLUE

The team's pride in its fairness, objectivity, and shared vision of what "good" looked like became part of the essential glue holding the team together. Members of the team became committed to developing and evolving this shared vision, realizing that it was the bedrock of their new credibility in the organization. It was not all smooth sailing, though. Bringing together strong personalities who looked at the world in different ways was challenging, but it also helped the team avoid the trap of "groupthink." As the team moved through the phases of team development—from coming together initially (forming) to establishing the group norms (norming) to challenging the leader and each other (storming) to achieving their goals (performing)—some of the members of the team were unwilling or unable to accept what was becoming the group's code of ethics.

About two months into the process, one of the CIT members brought to the team meeting a videotaped scorecarding interview he had done with one of the district managers in his region. He shared it with the team as an example of what "good" really looks like. The team viewed the videotape and rated the DM's answers individually. When the team's ratings were compared to how the original CIT member had rated the DM's responses, all hell broke loose. It was clear that the majority of the CIT members saw the responses as far below normal. The discussion very quickly became heated, and we all agreed to call a time out. Eventually it became clear that the DM and CIT member in question were very good friends, and that the CIT member's objectivity had been compromised by their friendship. Fortunately, the group was able to make it through this issue as well as many, many others.

PRACTICING WHAT THEY PREACHED

The lesson we all learned and relearned was that the price of success-ful change and adaptability was constant vigilance. People at Best Buy were generally too "nice" to give each other tough, constructive feed-back. The CIT knew that they needed to learn how to do this and that they needed to be the active role models for this behavior in the or-ganization. Most of their practicing and role modeling occurred daily in one-on-one or small group settings. However, the team also decided to find out how effective their internal client base thought the CIT was. Using a short, anonymous survey, the CIT polled people regard-ing both the entire team and individual members. They discovered how others viewed them and how they could improve their impact, while sending a strong signal to the organization that asking for, listen-ing to, and using feedback was a powerful tool for improvement. The consultants also modeled this process by surveying the CIT and a range of executives to get feedback on the consultants' role in the change process. One learning point that came through loud and clear for both the CIT and the consultants was: when in doubt, check it out. Don't assume what people are thinking—ask them what they are thinking.

TEAM LEARNING AND SYSTEMS THINKING

One of the things that is useful and stimulating about working with a team is that the issues and dynamics that surface within the team are a pretty good indicator of the issues and dynamics occurring throughout the entire organization. This certainly proved true with the Best Buy CIT. Shortly before the SOP change implementation effort started, Brad Anderson asked us this question: If there was one attribute or skill that you could introduce within the organization to improve it, what would that be? We answered quickly, "Systems thinking."

As in many sales-driven organizations, the Best Buy way of doing things was to move quickly, rely on intuition, and get the job done. It was a novel, even strange idea to take the time to explore what was causing a problem, especially a reoccurring problem, get to the root cause of it, and find out if other problems stemmed from the same root. At a CIT meeting about three or four months into the SOP change implementation, the team came up with an array of seemingly unrelated and insurmountable problems occurring in the field. Here's a partial list of the problems voiced by the CIT at that time.

- Lack of two-way communication
- Selection and promotion decisions based on only one, narrow criterion
- Competing and even conflicting priorities
- Efficiency down
- Confused career path
- Inconsistent message: no in-store connections being made
- High turnover
- Assistant managers within a store don't see their common goal(s)
- Competitiveness and unwillingness to share
- Poorly defined roles
- Misalignment of pay and recognition/rewards

Sheer energy and brute force wouldn't work to solve these problems. They were too wide ranging, and the staffing was limited. The issues were overwhelming for some of the team members. We listed all the problems on a white board, and the team started lumping problems together that seemed to have something in common. Soon, some categories emerged. Before these categories were set, the team started listing the criteria they were using to categorize the problems. They found that the problems they had identified, as well as others, could be grouped into the three following categories.

- Tactical leadership overemphasized
- (Apparent) change in focus/direction; "flavor of the month" mentality
- Lack of teamwork

The jumble of problems (symptoms) was untangled by applying organizing principles (although we didn't know what they were in advance) to group the problems into categories. This process tapped into the team's tacit organizational knowledge as individuals and as a group and was a clear example of team learning. We then needed to make these tacit organizing principles explicit. Once we could describe how the categories were formed, we were close to describing a possible root cause, or causes, of the problem category (a diagnosis). In this case, the team defined the root cause as "a lack of big-picture thinking/not seeing how the SOP fits together/a lack of systems thinking."

Next the team asked, What should we do about this underlying problem? Many possibilities were discussed; some were dismissed and others survived. Then the team categorized the potential solutions (remedies). As the CIT applied possible solutions (in theory) to the problems, some of the solutions needed to be adjusted to fit particular instances. The team's tacit organizational knowledge was applied again in the principles they used to tailor a solution to fit a particular situation.

We called this "diagnostic thinking." We used the "bridge" diagram shown in Figure 13, Diagnostic Thinking, on the following page, to illustrate the pattern of our thinking (systems thinking), which was a bridge to cross over a torrent of problems.

Another way of trying to get to the root cause of the problem(s) that the team used was the "Five Whys," as described by Peter Senge in *The Fifth Discipline Fieldbook*. Applying the Five Whys is straightforward, but it requires tenacity. When you encounter a problem, ask, Why? When you have a credible answer, again ask, Why? to that answer. When you've taken the whys as far as you can, without getting ridiculous or irritating someone, often you'll uncover a problem that affects a number of people, processes, and outcomes in the organization. In other words, you are uncovering systemic problems, or issues affecting many aspects of effective organizational functioning. Here's an example from our CIT work session.

- "People in the stores are just competitive and not willing to share." Why?

Figure 13

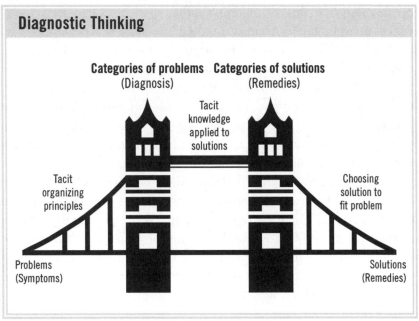

- "They (and their managers) don't see what their common goals are." Why?

- "They lack teamwork." Why?

- "No one has communicated to them, in a meaningful way, that they have shared goals, responsibilities, and especially shared opportunities." Why?

- "Because their management doesn't think in terms of the big picture. They don't see how things fit together and interact." And so on.

Following the Five Whys line of reasoning and uncovering systemic issues was an eye-opener for the team. Without being aware of formal systems thinking, the team started asking systemic questions, such as, If we make this decision, who else might be affected? And, What might be some side effects that could happen because we took this action? And, What kinds of things might happen later on because of this action? This wasn't detailed systemic thinking, but it was practical and expanded the team's concept of the big picture. Their new perspective allowed them to see the organization as a whole made up of many interacting parts that affected one another.

RHYTHMS AND ROUNDS

Retail organizations like Best Buy are broad oceans to cross. Scorecarding multiple dimensions of every store was a huge challenge. Since the early scorecard focused on evaluating the level of understanding of the change (the why and what for), the data were gathered through multiple interviews of people in each store. At this stage of change, each application of the scorecard took from eight to twelve hours per store.

Nine Best Buy people were on the CIT, and each of them was responsible for scorecarding from twenty-four to thirty-five stores. Putting all the pieces together, we found we could apply the scorecard on a national basis a maximum of three times per year. We also designed the process so that there were intervals between each application of the scorecard. During these intervals, the CIT was engaged in activities to support people's learning about the SOP and about managing change, including

- Comparing notes and creating a shared picture of where the company was in terms of the change
- Working directly with the most problematic stores
- Investigating the higher-performing stores to find out how they did it, and then sharing these insights across the company
- Finding opportunities to deliver the message and teach and support others, without making people attend any extra meetings (for example, the CIT started attending district and regional meetings)
- Coaching the district and regional managers
- Accompanying the DMs and RMs, and eventually the retail executives, on store visits
- Holding reality check meetings (described in Chapter 7, Foundational Skills) to help people work through their emotional reactions to the change

- Facilitating workshops, such as "Managing Change on the Front Lines" and "Foundations of Influence" (influencing without authority), to teach and practice the new skills needed to successfully implement the change

- Working on individual leadership development with the consultant partners

- Staying connected as a team—talking with one another on a weekly, sometimes daily, basis

The diagram in Figure 14 depicts the cycle of activities the CIT engaged in.

All rounds and versions of the Change Scorecard were anchored in aspects of the SOP implementation, but the specific emphasis shifted according to the progress of the company. As we described in Chapter 9, Tools for Measuring Change, earlier in the change process the scorecard was heavily weighted with items focusing on whether or not people understood why the change was necessary and what the change consisted of. When at least half of the company seemed to grasp and could articulate the "why and what for" of the change, we replaced most of the understanding-based items with behavior-based items. These items were still anchored in the same change; they were just focused on other aspects of the change and its implications, and the difficulty increased according to the company's progress.

The only way you can make it "fair" to use a changing yardstick to measure the progress of the change is to let people know, in advance, your intentions and the reasoning behind them. What this meant in Best Buy was communicating frequently and repeatedly about the phases and arenas of change and about how the Change Scorecard would continue to be modified as appropriate to the state and progress of the change.

CHANGING!

Even with all the preparations to create an objective, fair scorecarding process, a few executives challenged the validity of the process, suggesting that the old culture was too strong, even for the CIT to overcome. The old culture was not about to let in this new approach

Figure 14

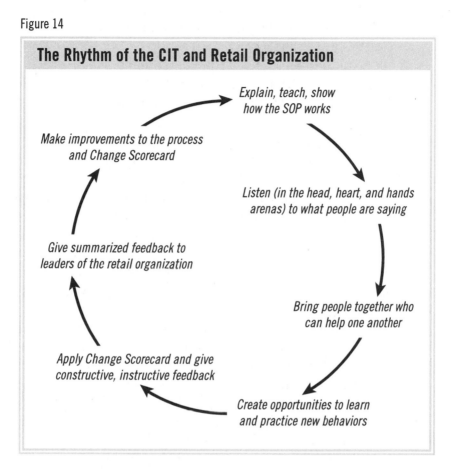

The Rhythm of the CIT and Retail Organization

Explain, teach, show how the SOP works

Make improvements to the process and Change Scorecard

Listen (in the head, heart, and hands arenas) to what people are saying

Give summarized feedback to leaders of the retail organization

Bring people together who can help one another

Apply Change Scorecard and give constructive, instructive feedback

Create opportunities to learn and practice new behaviors

without an all-out challenge. These executives claimed that, just like every other scorecarding initiative, this scorecarding data would be biased and unreliable. And if so, the credibility of the CIT would be lost.

The CIT felt as if their personal integrity were being questioned. Months of effort to create a valid scorecard and build their objectivity as change evaluators had potentially been a waste of time or worse. It was upsetting that the company did not feel it could depend on the CIT or their tools. When an external audit was suggested to confirm the results of the CIT's scorecarding, the team felt like they were suspects on trial, rather than valued members of a team that was supported in its efforts. Although discouraged, the team did not give up. Instead, it took up the challenge of facing an audit, even though they doubted that an external firm, unsophisticated in the issues of change management or behavioral measurement, would be able to use the tools in a reliable and valid way.

With no turning back, the CIT plunged into the national score-carding, working day after day while waiting tensely to see how the results would accumulate. A command center to collate the results was set up in the consultants' San Francisco office. The walls were covered with reports and posters as the data emerged from the first round of scorecarding. Over all, the scores were low! After taking a few hours to regroup, the consultants and team realized this was both bad and good. The good news was that this was the true status of the company. It would take time for such a massive change to take hold. The score-carding was producing valid results. The bad news was that everyone's bonus would take a hit.

In this first round of scorecarding to establish the baseline, we saw some big differences between some regions in the composite scores. Our question was, Is this difference in composite scores due to actual performance differences in the region, or is it due to differences in how the CIT members were rating performance? We had to get to the bottom of this. In the regions that had scores noticeably different from stores in other, similar regions, we did another round of scorecarding on a representative sample of stores. This time we either sent two CIT members together or a CIT member from another region to repeat the scorecarding. The conclusion we reached was that the CIT members who did the original scorecarding had rated a number of stores in their regions higher than they should have been rated. Their picture of what "'good' looks like" was distorted. Their colleagues worked with them to bring their internal calibration in line with the rest of the team.

Jason commented about this process, "A real trial for the team was when our interrater reliability was questioned. The RMs were saying things like, 'I got that [lower] score because my CIT member scores harder.' We then went back to practicing with videotapes and also hav-ing CIT members cross over and do parts of other regions in their scorecarding."

After one or two more rounds of scorecarding, it became clear that the stores' operations were improving and that the results of the Change Scorecard reflected real change and improvement. The changes weren't dramatic, which meant that they were believable.

The stores were changing and the scorecarding was being accepted as accurate. Even the most skeptical retail executive acknowledged that the CIT and the consultants were honestly and accurately evaluating the degree of the stores' implementation of the SOP.

The change wasn't reflected in dramatically increasing results that can occur when measurements are biased. It was real. And it showed how a new culture was unfolding. With subsequent rounds of scorecarding, the scores increased slowly and laboriously compared to the "shooting scores" seen on previous measures. And, the way the stores "felt" when executives and retail leadership visited them seemed to verify and validate the scores. The idea of an independent audit of the scoring was dropped for now. The CIT members celebrated their achievement by working even harder—and there was at least one celebratory baseball game, a fishing trip, and some raucous dinners, too.

SCORECARDS TELL THEIR STORY IN COLOR

Hundreds of stores, thousands of managers, tens of thousands of employees—the CIT and consultants had to find a simple but meaningful way to communicate the scorecard results to all. Iterating several prototypes led to linking the scorecard measures to a color coding that showed the level of success in implementing the SOP. See the 1-to-5 ratings in Figure 15, SOP Change Scorecard Rating Scale. Results can range from failure (red), shown as number 1, to caution (yellow), shown as number 3, and "green to go," number 5 for a high level of success. To get started, some awareness and success was considered an initial achievement.

Scorecard results were presented at several levels. They could be presented at store level for focusing store improvement discussions. The results for larger pieces of the organization could also be presented, for example at the district level, shown in Table 44, or the regional level. And finally, the results could be summarized for the entire company, shown in Table 45. Representatives from the CIT also presented the overall results on a quarterly basis to the entire group of Best Buy officers. The identifying numbers have been changed to

Figure 15

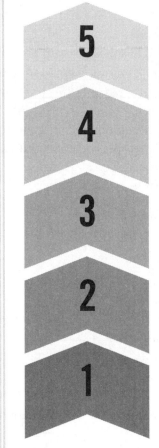

SOP Change Scorecard Rating Scale

5 — Enhances SOP for entire company
Capable of Improving Standard Operating Platform (SOP) within core guidelines. Clearly factors impact of adaptation on "system" within store and within broader company context/system.

4 — Applies thinking to store-specific issues
Clearly has understanding of SOP and skills for implementing it. Proficient in applying SOP knowledge to real store situations. Gives specific examples of issues related to implementation and can solve them using SOP guidelines.

3 — Understands and can apply basics
Understands the SOP and has the skills needed to implement. Actively integrates SOP into daily activities. Implements within narrow guidelines. Does not apply SOP beyond own role or function.

2 — Demonstrates basic understanding
Understands the basics of the SOP but lacks skills. Knows the "what" but not the "how." Can outline SOP but not how they are using it. Observable SOP behaviors limited or absent.

1 — Lacks understanding or basic skills
Limited or no understanding of SOP and how it relates to position/function. Knows SOP exists, but old operating behaviors remain visible.

respect the identity of the stores and people involved—and to promote a continuing emphasis on learning rather than blaming.

An interesting phenomenon occurred as the scorecarding proceeded. The CIT and senior retail management kept raising the bar of performance. What was considered acceptable early on later became substandard. The CIT kept recalibrating themselves to ensure they retained critical interrater reliability. Table 46, Average Company Rating on the SOP Change Scorecard, shows how the scores increase over

Table 44

District-Level Baseline Assessment

District # [A1]

Store #	1000	1001	1002	1003	1004	1005	1006	1007	1008	District Average
Change Leadership	3.50	3.67	4.00	3.33	3.00	3.50	3.30	3.75	3.50	3.51
Mgmt. Know. of SOP	3.42	3.50	4.00	3.58	3.63	3.44	3.13	3.47	3.08	3.47
Merchandising	3.27	2.80	4.60	2.93	3.27	3.93	3.00	3.33	3.00	3.35
Sales	3.19	2.36	3.80	2.93	2.90	3.19	3.07	2.86	3.01	3.03
Operations	2.63	2.75	3.50	2.25	3.75	3.25	3.25	2.88	2.75	3.00
Inventory	3.50	3.33	4.33	3.17	3.50	3.67	3.33	3.67	3.33	3.54
Functionality	1.67	1.33	2.67	2.00	2.00	2.00	2.00	2.00	2.00	1.96
AVERAGE	3.02	2.82	3.84	2.88	3.15	3.28	3.01	3.14	2.95	3.12

Table 45

Company-Level Baseline Assessment

Region	A	B	C	D	E	F	G	H	I	National Average
Change Leadership	3.48	3.20	3.50	3.07	3.59	2.98	2.82	3.43	3.24	3.25
Mgmt. Knowledge of SOP	3.48	3.25	3.33	3.29	3.65	2.87	3.03	3.39	3.15	3.27
Merchandising	3.31	3.37	3.08	3.27	3.09	2.88	3.08	3.29	3.19	3.17
Sales	3.02	3.02	3.08	2.95	2.93	2.71	2.59	3.17	3.04	2.95
Operations	3.14	3.04	3.08	2.86	3.32	2.67	2.70	3.19	3.07	3.01
Inventory	3.63	3.49	3.14	3.38	3.31	2.95	2.78	3.33	3.05	3.23
Functionality	2.22	4.01	2.80	2.79	2.13	2.76	2.71	2.60	2.77	2.75
AVERAGE	3.18	3.34	3.14	3.09	3.15	2.82	2.81	3.20	3.07	3.09

time. Note that the results are not eye-popping. The gradual increase in scores did not undermine the credibility of the process, as we initially feared, but rather enhanced it. The measurements are less dramatic than old-culture data might have been—but far more real. (Keep in mind also that as the company improved its ability to meet the demands of the scorecard, the difficulty of the measure was increased with each round to bring about additional improvements.)

Table 46

Average Company Rating on the SOP Change Scorecard								
Apr 97	Nov 97	Apr 98	Nov 98	Apr 99	Nov 99	Apr 00	Nov 00	Feb 01
3.08	3.51	3.85	3.82	4.18	4.22	4.24	3.71	3.88

TRANSFORMING CHANGE

The stores were being transformed. The shelves were now well stocked with merchandise, partly due to a new inventory management system and partly due to the SOP implementation. The shopping experience for customers was very different than it had been six months earlier. The stores looked clean and well organized. It was easier to get to the service counter and be helped by knowledgeable people. Customers could more easily find someone in the aisles if they had questions. Salespeople had a better grasp of the products in their areas of the store. The lines were not so long at the cashiers—not because there were fewer customers but because the processes were running more efficiently.

There was now an atmosphere of learning in the stores. At each scorecarding visit, there was a debriefing and problem-solving session with the CIT member, the store GM, and, over time, the staff members in the store. The store GM heard the results of the scorecarding at the same time as everyone else. At first, the CIT member would model a problem-solving way of working through the results. After a while, the store GM took on this role, becoming a coach and not getting involved in "blame games."

With the hope of keeping the SOP change process alive, an SOP scoreboard was produced for each store. The scoreboard was hung in a place where most of the staff would see it at least once a shift, usually in the break room. Keeping the SOP scoreboard current became a behavior-based item on the Change Scorecard. The CIT also provided useful tips and tools in a weekly column on "SOP Best Practices" that was published in the store newsletter, *The Weekly Source*. Naturally, when a best practice or tip came from someone in the stores, that person was acknowledged and celebrated in the column.

The stores were managed in a different way now in that they were all dancing to the same tune and in the same rhythm. Stores could go through assessments and feedback without being defensive. Negative scores were accepted as long as management had a plan to understand what was causing them and how to change them.

Additional changes, such as the creation of the Gatekeepers group, supported the SOP change effort. The Gatekeepers provided coordination among store initiatives so that they did not conflict with one another and thus kept the stores from being deluged with multiple initiatives at any one time. This was systems thinking put into practical application.

Management time and energy was freed up, as there were fewer fires (and less fire fighting) on a daily basis. GMs and DMs reallocated their time to coach their direct reports and help develop their talent.

THE PROCESS OF LEARNING ALSO TRANSFORMS

The entire process, especially the use of the Change Scorecard, was positioned and experienced as a tool for learning and improvement. One important forum for learning was the end-of-day meeting each CIT member had with the store management. The CIT member walked through the day's results on the Change Scorecard in depth and explained why particular items were scored the way they were. The CIT member solicited and answered questions and held brief, spontaneous training sessions, if the need arose. Together, the CIT member and store manager consolidated the results into a concise, targeted SOP improvement plan. Over time, the CIT member's end-of-day scorecarding discussions with store management expanded to include all available staff, because more and more people wanted to join in. Why? Because they were learning.

The discipline of writing an SOP improvement plan for each store really paid off. The CIT reviewed each of their SOP store improvement plans regularly to look for general themes as well as to see if particular instances of brilliant or substandard performance were showing up. The entire CIT reviewed the composite results and was able to form some well-grounded hypotheses about what was occurring, why it might be occurring, and what to do about it. Measurement and feedback were nonevaluative. They had become learning tools that faced, rather than denied, reality.

In the next chapter, we'll look at how the SOP scores correlated with the business measures used by the company. But first, here are some of the learning points from the consultant's notebook on measuring change.

FIELD GUIDE EXCERPT

Tips on Measuring Change

1. Anticipate that many people will feel pressure to consciously or unconsciously distort the results—to try to show new behaviors without true, underlying change.
2. Those who measure change are under tremendous pressure (from bosses, peers, those being evaluated) to shift their ratings in a favorable dimension. The more important the change, the greater the pressure. The system must have a way to manage this distortion.
3. Measurement standards "drift" over time. The internal standards that observers and interviewers use shift. They may drift toward being either more or less demanding depending on the forces at work on the observers.
4. No consequences, no change. There must be rewards for progress and costs for lack of progress on change measurements.
5. When the change process gets off track (or fails to get started), the measurement process always takes the heat (it's wrong, unreliable, etc.).
6. Conversely, when change is successfully accomplished, skeptics will question the measurement process (it's wrong, unreliable, etc.).

Sustained Change

WHAT DOES SUSTAINED CHANGE LOOK LIKE?

What qualifies as a sustained change? How would you define it? What does it look like? Imagine you are holding a rubber band. When you exert force on it, you stretch it. What happens when you let go? If the rubber band were to remain stretched out after you let go of it, the stretch would be self-sustaining.

We all know, however, what typically happens when you let go — the stretched-out rubber band snaps back to its original shape and size. A similar phenomenon can happen when you use force to drive change into an organization. When you remove the dedicated resources, the assisting consultants, and the pressures exerted to make the change happen, you often see the organization, its culture, and the associated behaviors snap back into their previous shape. Of course, the metaphor of the rubber band stretches only so far. With organizational change efforts, some aspects of a forced change may remain after the pressure is removed. However, because the future viability, vitality, and even survival of the organization can depend on the strength and sustainability of the change effort, a significant degree of change has to take hold to bring about the necessary results.

There are several possible indicators that a change has, indeed, been sustained over a substantial period of time. These indicators

Table 47

<table>
<tr><td colspan="1">

You Know It's Sustained Change When . . .

1. Over the course of years, the business goals for the change are being met and the positive business benefits continue.

2. The change and its associated ways of thinking, feeling, and behaving are woven into the fabric (the culture) of the organization. The "change" is the accepted way to do things in the company.

   - After the original internal change agents and the external consultants leave, the behaviors associated with the change continue.

   - The language used in everyday work life reflects the language introduced with the change.

   - All levels of management take responsibility for sustaining the change, as part of their everyday role.

3. People *know how* to make the change work. They don't just *know about* it.

</td></tr>
</table>

range from the overarching and always important business goals to the language that frontline employees use on an everyday basis. In Table 47 we provide a working definition of the characteristics of a change that has been sustained.

Does the SOP change implementation effort at Best Buy qualify as a sustained change, given the above criteria? Yes. The SOP results, measured over nine successive waves of scorecarding, rose slowly, in small increments, rather than shooting up. These were believable results, the kind that you see in reality rather than those that come from score inflation. The improvement in the look and feel of the stores was incremental, but when looking at the progress of the change effort after two years, the "before" and "after" difference between the stores was dramatic. And finally, although barely perceptible at first, the operating results improved (sales, profits, shrink, turnover, employee survey results, and customer experience rating). We know that Best Buy likes to measure results, but now they are measuring the *right* results and measuring *how* people got those results.

THE BUSINESS GOALS

Businesses, as social systems embedded in larger social systems, are exceedingly complex, with many, many different variables affecting the ultimate business results. Although it is tough to "unscramble the egg" to determine exactly what aspects of Best Buy's performance on business measures were enhanced by the SOP change effort, we can gain a rough idea. The overall business results since the change implementation began have been consistently outstanding. Between January 1997 and January 2000 the stock price increased by more than 1,000 percent. Executives and industry pundits credit a good deal of this turnaround to the makeover in store operations and the change leadership practices that accomplished and sustained the new approaches.

Table 48, Five-Year Financial Highlights, shows Best Buy's performance on key business measures over a period from March 1996 (FY97) through February 2001 (FY01). The CIT was formed in April 1997, and the Change Scorecard was first administered in May of that year.

CRUNCHING THE NUMBERS OF CHANGE

When we hear a lot of hype about a change process, we skeptically think that the actual changes were probably small. Rather than trigger this skepticism in you, we will present the quantitative analyses without the superlatives. Our main point, in one sentence, is that the SOP change implementation was sustained over four years, as measured by the Change Scorecard and other standard business metrics (e.g., store profitability, employee turnover, and so on).

Now for some details. We conducted quantitative analyses (statistical correlations) over the nine waves of scorecarding, which spanned four years. We focused on three important retail business results: the profitability of each store, the turnover of employees in each store, and the company's stock price. The store metrics are a focus because the SOP was specifically introduced to increase profitability in the stores.

What should we expect? Stores that are operating better presumably are more satisfying to employees and provide a better experience

Table 48

Five-Year Financial Highlights

Fiscal Year [1]	2001 [2]	2000	1999	1998	1997
Statement of Earnings Data (000)					
Revenues	15,327	12,494	10,065	8,338	7,758
Gross profit	3,059	2,393	1,815	1,312	1,046
Selling, general, and administrative expenses	2,455	1,854	1,463	1,145	1,006
Operating income	604	539	351	166	40
Net earnings (loss)	396	347	216	82	(6)
Per Share Date [3]					
Net Earnings (loss)	1.86	1.63	1.03	0.46	(0.04)
Common stock price: High	88.88	80.50	49	15.30	6.56
Low	21.00	40.50	14.75	2.16	1.97
Operating Statistics					
Comparable store sales change [4]	4.9%	11.1%	13.5%	2.0%	(4.7%)
Inventory turns [5]	7.6	7.2	6.6	5.6	4.6
Gross profit percentage	20.0%	19.2%	18.0%	15.7%	13.5%
Selling, general, and administrative expense percentage	16.0%	14.8%	14.5%	13.7%	13.0%
Operating income percentage	3.9%	4.3%	3.5%	2.0%	0.5%
Average revenues per store[6]	39	37	34.0%	30.0%	29
Year-End Data					
Working capital	214	453	662	666	563
Total assets	4,840	2,995	2,532	2,070	1,740
Long-term debt, including current portion	296	31	61	225	238
Convertible preferred securities	–	–	–	230	230
Shareholders' equity	1,822	1,096	1,034	536	429
Number of Stores					
Best Buy	419	357	311	284	272
Musicland	1,309	–	–	–	–
Magnolia Hi-Fi	13	–	–	–	–
Total Retail Square Footage (000s)					
Best Buy	19,010	16,205	14,017	12,694	12,026
Musicland	8,772	–	–	–	–
Magnolia Hi-Fi	133	–	–	–	–

Source: Investor Relations—Financials
(1) Both fiscal 2001 and 1996 included 53 weeks. All other periods presented included 52 weeks. (2) During the fourth quarter of fiscal 2001, the Company acquired the common stock of Musicland Stores Corporation (Musicland) and Magnolia Hi-Fi, Inc. (Magnolia Hi-Fi). The results of those businesses are included from their dates of acquisition. (3) Earnings per share is presented on a diluted basis and reflects the two-for-one stock splits in March 1999, May 1998, and April 1994, and a three-for-two stock split in September 1993. (4) Comparable stores are stores open at least 14 full months and for all periods presented reflect Best Buy stores only. (5) Inventory turns reflect Best Buy stores only and are calculated based upon a monthly average of inventory balances. (6) Average revenues per store reflect Best Buy stores only and is based upon total revenues for the period divided by the weighted average number of stores open during such period.

for the shopper. Better experiences for employees are likely to be associated with reduced turnover. Better experiences for shoppers would translate to higher profits (reflecting both sales and efficiency in operations). The numbers bear this out. Stores with higher SOP ratings, as measured by the SOP Change Scorecard, had better business results—lower levels of employee turnover and higher levels of store profitability.

Finding substantial correlations between the SOP, employee turnover, and store profitability is noteworthy given all the other factors that affect turnover (e.g., competitiveness of wages, manager effectiveness, etc.) and those that affect profitability (competitor stores, advertising, site location, etc.)—any of which could have destroyed the relationships we found between SOP effectiveness and business results.

Another intriguing finding came out of this research. Best Buy conducted store employee surveys to assess employees' views of their local store environments. As expected, employee survey data is linked to turnover. Stores whose employees gave more negative evaluations of their stores had higher turnover. Surprisingly, the results of the SOP Change Scorecard are more strongly related to turnover and profitability than to employee ratings of the store environment. Possibly, the behavioral observations that make up the Change Scorecard process are better predictors of the store environment than are employees' opinion surveys. Though one study is not conclusive, it does show the power of the SOP Change Scorecard. And perhaps when the culture is better aligned with the business strategy, performance-oriented employees in an organization that is more performance oriented will be more likely to stay. Knowing that their behavior is in line with the desired results for the company may encourage employees to want to stay and be a part of the company.

How about stock results? As the scores on the SOP Change Scorecard went up over time, so, too, did the stock price. The correlation is very high, as you can see from the shape of the two lines in Table 49. As every investor knows too well, stock price and operating results have a complex and far from linear relationship. And, as anyone who knows even a bit about statistics will tell you, correlation does not prove causality.

Table 49

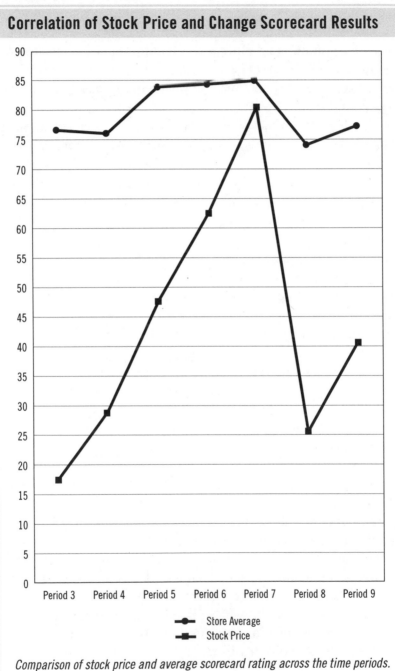

Comparison of stock price and average scorecard rating across the time periods.

However, we do know that stores that most successfully implemented the SOP had higher profitability and that the overall company was getting better at implementing the SOP, as shown by the scorecard results. Thus sustained implementation of the SOP is associated with increasing stock prices. Many stock analysts (and the market, in general) compare year-to-year same-store results before making predictions about the future of a retail stock. To the extent that implementing the SOP, as measured by the SOP Change Scorecard, led to better same-store results, there would be a causal link between the SOP implementation/Change Scorecard and the price of the stock.

In summary, the number crunching and the Change Scorecard results confirmed that the company was changing—and that these changes were occurring at the store employee level. When the SOP and all the changes that went along with it were successfully implemented, the store environment was more positive for employees, they remained with the company longer, and the store enjoyed higher profitability. Though customer experience was not part of our analysis, we would expect to hear that customers' shopping experiences improved as well. Thus, all parties would have a profitable experience.

LANGUAGE REFLECTS THINKING

In addition to performing the quantifiable analysis of sustained behavior, we returned to Best Buy after four years and met with the people who were part of the original SOP change implementation. We asked them questions such as, What is the culture like now, after the change? What's different, today? What do you use now that you learned when the SOP change effort was in full swing? and, How has the learning been passed on? Given the amount of continuing growth and change at Best Buy, we had modest expectations of what people would recall. We were astounded to hear how much the language and methods remained alive. We heard the following types of responses.

- "We have a framework for thinking and a framework for managing large challenges. And we have increased the value we place on hiring people with discipline as managers."

- "What's different? Process and discipline are important. Now the retail leaders understand change. First, they understand the head, heart, and hands arenas, and second, they understand that they have to change, too."

The consultants had withdrawn from the SOP change implementation in a planned way, gradually reducing the amount of consulting support for the CIT and the individuals on the team. About a year into the SOP change effort, the leadership of the team was handed off to two members of the CIT. The transfer of know-how from the consultants to the CIT reached a milestone when a member of the consulting team came to the lead consultant with these questions: "What do I do now? How do I (we) distinguish myself (ourselves) from the members of the CIT? We do most of the same things." When these kinds of questions are asked, you know there has been a successful transfer of know-how into the organization.

WHAT DOES IT TAKE TO SUSTAIN CHANGE?

The short answer to the question What does it take to sustain change? is that the people of the organization must not only change how they get their jobs done, but also must work through—in an integrated way—how they think and feel about the change. Changing how you think, feel, and behave about change is, in itself, part of what's required to successfully make the change. And the organization must "keep the movement moving" through all the stages of change in every part of the system.

The Head

One of the key changes that we often need to make in our thinking about change is realizing that change is almost never an event; it is a *process*. Change usually doesn't have a recognizable end. If you expect it to be neatly wrapped up, like a package with a bow on it, you'll be unpleasantly surprised when it unwraps itself. Change isn't over until it's over, which is usually when the next big change comes along that affects the same systems as the current change.

Some people tend to get stuck in the head arena (usually people who are more academically and analytically inclined) and others short-change it. In business organizations, after the business rationale has been established in the upper levels of management, the importance of communicating the "whys" of the change and exactly what the change consists of (in language and examples relevant to people at each level of the organization) is often overlooked. On the other hand, thoroughly working through the arena of the head, for all levels of the organization, can reap the following benefits.

- A vision shared by a wide variety of people in the organization
- An understanding of the implications of the change for each person in each job/role
- Development of basic thinking skills, such as analytical and systems-thinking skills
- Increased ability of many people to transfer what they've learned to other types of situations and changes

The minimum downside of not really attending to the head arena is that the individual and the organization will not reap the benefits listed above. The maximum downside of failing to work through the head arena is that the change effort will fail. To sustain progress in the head arena, it is essential that new people coming into the organization are also exposed to the whys and whats of "how we do things around here," and that issues associated with the change are continually addressed as they emerge.

How has attention to the head arena fared at Best Buy? As one SVP explains, "Best Buy has always had a bias for action. Now we have learned to focus our bias on understanding, problem solving, and learning. For example, before the SOP, the regional staff meetings were straight 'downloads.' Now, the staff meetings are forums for the business leaders and all the team members to work together to understand and solve problems. We put our heads together to learn what's in the customers' best interests."

Another SVP adds, "A difference in the culture now is that we look at things end-to-end [in their full context, from start to finish]. We document solutions. We have group learning in which we include different points of view."

The Heart

As we have discovered, unless the emotions are engaged in a change effort—and engaged in a positive way—deep change cannot happen. Downplaying the role of the heart in organizational change has been the rule, but since many of us derive a good deal of our identity and sense of self-worth from our work, it isn't surprising that changes at work, and in our relationship to it, carry tremendous emotion. Some changes seem to beckon to us, and others seem to loom over us like impending doom. In either case, our emotional reaction holds a charge.

Traditionally, emotion has been an off-limits topic in the workplace. Although a limited set of emotions may be sanctioned (for example, showing enthusiasm or mild frustration), for the most part, showing an emotional reaction in the workplace is deemed unprofessional and/or inappropriate. There are good reasons for this; not all emotions are appropriate to express in a work setting. However, it is important to set up forums in which it is safe for people to express emotions related to the change effort.

Most of us are uncomfortable dealing with emotions—both our own and others'. To some extent, we are uncomfortable because we're unskilled at dealing with emotional expressions. Often we squelch them. Then the emotions go underground and show up in distorted and sometimes destructive ways. To successfully implement change, and especially to sustain it, will require that you learn some of the techniques described in this book for working in the heart arena and apply them. The tremendous upside of attending to the arena of the heart is that you can release energy into making the change succeed.

The make-or-break nature of a turnaround effort brings with it a special intensity. It may not be possible to continue to work at that level of intensity when everything is going well, but the fact that such intensity exists at times shows the power of the heart, of engaging the emotions in a way that carries true meaning for people. On the other hand, organizations are dynamic, always changing, and (we hope) learning in the process. The need for continuing feedback to fuel the learning and change doesn't go away, even in the good times.

Make no mistake about it: working through change in the arena of the heart is tough, and the challenges associated with it should not be minimized. A regional manager, evaluating his team's work, said,

"We did well on the head, but we had a harder time with the heart. It took more time and was more challenging. But it's how you create intensity and focus—by getting heart."

The Hands

In all three arenas, change is about learning something new and usually unlearning something old. In the arena of the hands, change means learning new skills and habits. Fortunately, we know a lot about how people learn and develop new skills and how to help people break old habits and establish new ones. Often the barrier to effective change in the hands arena is that we simply forget that new behaviors don't just appear. New behaviors must be defined, learned, developed, and practiced, with relevant feedback and coaching.

Often in the work setting, people feel they should be able to do something perfectly (or at least do it really well) the first time they try it. Frequently they are trying to produce some ideal pattern of behavior they might not have seen before. People around them usually have different, often unexpressed, ideas about what the ideal behavior is— what "good" looks like. But when and where is it appropriate to practice new behaviors and hone new skills? Who provides accurate, timely feedback?

A member of the CIT explained how the team and organization came to see the need to modify behavior to promote effective learning.

> The team and the retail organization created (behavioral) tools to use in their work. Explaining the gap between understanding and doing, and how to close the gap, is key. The first part of this was related to being in a position to notice. This was then followed up with coaching, feedback, recognition, teamwork, synergy, and accountability. But you can't close the gap unless you're in a position to notice first.
>
> We needed to assess the gap between expected and actual execution, and where and how it was breaking down. The new Change Scorecard and accompanying tools allowed us to take the leaders along to see and learn (1) if/how it was working and (2) how to accurately diagnose *why* it was or wasn't working. The old culture would have just rushed to fix it and move on.

The other thing we learned with "position to notice" was to not jump into coaching right away. Instead, we had to try to understand what was happening and *why* it was happening. This meant we had to teach the managers about the head and the heart.

A member of the CIT, Melanie, summed it up beautifully: "For an entire generation of store managers, the SOP and the efforts of the DMs, RMs, and the CIT helped take the mystery out of success."

CHANGING AND LEARNING

Changing and learning are two sides of the same coin. When you learn something well enough to take effective action using it, you are changed. And usually when you change, you learn something new. To be proficient at changing and adapting, an individual, team, or organization needs to incorporate learning as a part of everyday life, on a continuing basis.

What does the Best Buy constituency have to say about the changes brought about via the SOP change implementation process and organizational learning?

- **One retail executive:** "What SOP did on a deep level was that it instilled the notions of discipline and process into the fabric of the culture. And we learned *how* to learn."

- **Another retail executive:** "What is important is changing the culture to recognize that *how* we do something is as important as getting results—and getting people to feel like they're part of something big, which is making a contribution to society that they can be proud of."

- **A CIT member:** "Organizational learning is key. We learned about creating an environment where there is less fear of criticism or retaliation. This creates emphasis on finding ways to get better results."

- **One RM:** "I needed to recommit to principles centered around learning. As I did, my group meetings became more self-directed than directed by me. I learned to put less emphasis on my personal focus as the leader and driver and to blend in more. Team learning is very important."

- **A VP:** "I saw the tone of the organization shift from being about power to being more about learning."

STAYING THE COURSE

At any point in the change process, the temptation exists to proclaim that the change is "done," or at least your part in it is done. It is easy to slip into a narrow perspective and to believe that the change is complete when you can see obvious changes in your immediate environment. There are many factors, however, within each organization that can make it difficult to gain a perspective that is broad and deep enough to get an accurate read of the overall progress of a change effort. To assess the degree and momentum of change on the larger scale, you need to have reliable, accurate ways of monitoring all reaches of the changing system. Also, just because you've made headway in any or all of these arenas doesn't mean that another person has.

In the early part of a change process, when the larger constituency is beginning to come to grips with the problem, the sponsors of the change usually have had months (or even years) to work through their own doubts and questions. These people, who are typically at the executive level, can be frustrated that others in their organization don't immediately grasp the need to change, with all its attendant implications. However, the sponsors will need to rein in their impatience and allow others the opportunity to come to their own understanding of the need to change. Throughout the process, the continuing, visible sponsorship of the change effort by the top leaders is absolutely a requirement for a successful, sustained change.

Working through the change means continuing to explore, explain, and understand what the change means, how it's received, and how it applies to each person's work life. It is important to try to neutralize organizational politics and power struggles, which can obscure or put a spin on how the progress of change is assessed and interpreted, in either a positive or negative way. And denial is an ever-present danger. Working through a change implies that the organization is willing to tolerate the challenges of learning on a large scale.

To make new ways of thinking, feeling, and behaving stick requires a consistent, sustained effort to consolidate and to extend the lessons learned to new situations. It may take a conscious effort to maintain the forward momentum of the change effort when the organization has made some gains and started realizing some successes. Signs of success can result in either a renewing of enthusiasm and effort or a slacking off. Those invested in making the change effort successful must consciously watch for this turning point, both in themselves and throughout the organization, and recommit to the change.

A CIT member describes what transpired at Best Buy: "The changes have persisted for a long time. We are running a marathon and not a sprint. We keep moving up our goals, using a stair-step model of growth. When we do get to a plateau, we avoid falling all the way back. No longer do GMs and DMs who have losing profit-and-loss centers get bonuses. Initially this was a shock to them." This elimination of bonuses for managers who don't show a profit is an example of a systemic alignment to reinforce the new behaviors the change requires. Obviously, the consistent support of the senior executives for the sustained focus on the change, alignment of reward systems, and required emphasis on learning is a key component.

Table 50, Three Elements of Staying the Course, summarizes the essentials that resonate throughout the stages of organizational change.

THE SOP CHANGE IMPLEMENTATION AT BEST BUY

What are some of the other factors that led to effective and sustained change at Best Buy? Two things stand out. The first key was the partnership between the experts on changing human and organizational behavior and the internal change agents, and second was Best Buy's ownership for the success or failure of the change effort.

Table 50

Three Elements of Staying the Course

1. Perspective: Do you have the complete picture?
2. Knowing that people will process the change at different rates.
3. Continuing, visible support from the executive sponsors of the change is essential to the success of the change process.

Partnerships

Partnering is an easy term to bandy about in business, but what does it really mean? One working definition is, "When I care as much about your success as I do my own." It's a two-way street. Both partners have to trust that they have each other's best interests at heart. This kind of relationship does not happen overnight; nor does it happen because of effective marketing and sales tactics. It happens when the partners work side by side and have the opportunity to observe one another's behavior in challenging situations. The trust must be deep and shared.

Another component of effective partnerships is respect for one another and respect for one another's areas of expertise. Part of why the Best Buy SOP change implementation was successful is that the experts in changing human behavior didn't try to be experts in retail operations. And the experts in retail operations didn't pretend to be experts in changing human behavior. We had a lot to learn from one another, and we respected one another's expertise. The blending of the two areas of expertise, with no hoarding of knowledge and know-how, produced a coalition with an amazing power to transform the company.

Ownership

Successful, sustained organizational change is not something that someone can come in and "do to you." From the very beginning, one of the retail SVPs insisted, "This needs to be—and to be seen as—a Best Buy 'thing,' not a consultant 'thing.'" He was right. The responsibility and ownership cannot lie with either internal or external "experts"—be they consultants, human resource people, or organization development groups.

The people who work "where the rubber meets the road" and know what it is to have to deliver results are your most effective agents of change. To sustain a change effort requires that these people develop the skills it takes to successfully implement change. Transferring and developing know-how requires learning the essential principles for all three arenas—head, heart, and hands—to be able to take effective action in applying the principles learned.

WHERE IS THE CIT NOW?

The Change Implementation Team has become an important entity at Best Buy, and the membership turns over regularly, in a planned way. The Best Buy CIT proved to be an excellent vehicle for developing high-potential managers and leaders. The abilities to think analytically and systemically, to influence without authority, and to grasp the importance of attending to all three arenas of human change are now essential elements of effective leadership at Best Buy.

One of the Best Buy CIT leaders, who has continued to advance within the organization and is an officer of the company, reflects: "I wonder if I were in the CIT member role today, facing the challenges that we did, if I could do it. I didn't realize the risks we were taking—all of the political land mines. To be a successful change agent, *you have to behave like you don't have a lot to lose.* Being a change agent seems simple when what you're doing is full-time change management. When you have to do another job in which you're also expected to get results, it's much harder to effect change."

Another leader acknowledged the value (and the difficulty) of continuing to preserve the autonomy and objectivity of the CIT: "The CIT member should be the person with the mirror. A key competency for being a member of the CIT is telling the truth, and in a way that the other person can hear it."

This is how one of the Best Buy leaders perceives the current role of the CIT: "In a sense, the CIT members are now functioning as leadership coaches for their regions. They're like unbiased advisers to the other leaders they work with, who are discipline-specific, technical experts. While the other leaders are in the heat of the battle, the CIT member is thinking and advising them strategically. It's hard to think with bullets whizzing by your head. The CIT members can, in a sense, stop time and help a leader make an effective decision or remind her of a tool she's overlooking. The CIT members are still implementing new initiatives, but their responsibilities have evolved into much more."

One of the lessons demonstrated again and again by the CIT is that one of the best ways to really learn something is to teach it to someone else. We recommend that you replace the old, derogatory saying "Those who can, do; those who cannot, teach" with the realities of the knowledge era: "Those who can, do; those who *understand*, teach."

As we mentioned, the CIT, with regular, planned turnover of its members, lives on at Best Buy. Many of the original CIT members have moved on (and up) to assume significant leadership positions at Best Buy. These people have been instrumental in keeping alive the learnings from the SOP change implementation and in extending the know-how of change to meet other organizational challenges.

WHAT HAPPENED TO THE SOP?

The SOP is in effect today, although, as you can imagine, substantially modified, as the company modified its store formats, which required changing aspects of how the stores operate. Other changes have also occurred, as a member of the first-year CIT explains.

> We still work on the SOP every day. It's part of our four key practices. When these practices are in place, store results are very positive, and customers and employees have a very positive experience. People understand the practices and know the practices. We have people learn the key practices when they come in, and then sustain them. We no longer depend on having individual heroes to make a store succeed.

Recently [in 2001] I looked at what the CIT had as tools. The current CIT still uses scorecards. We're still new in the self-assessment process, but managers at every level are doing it on a regular basis, and we're trying to get the district staff to use the self-assessments in coaching. We're asking, Do the scorecard results match the business results? We check this constantly.

We've learned about change. It isn't fast, it isn't easy, and you have to plan for it. You need to sit and talk in advance about what the roadblocks are likely to be. We are much more proactive. Culture has changed here.

So what happened with the next big change in the company?

THE NEXT BIG CHANGE

A new set of changes was needed in another part of Best Buy. Best Buy stores offer proprietary warranties on products that are sold in its stores and on-line. The warranties are fulfilled by the service centers that Best Buy operates throughout the country. After the retail SOP implementation was well under way, the service centers were faced with at least two major changes: the introduction of a services SOP and an elimination of commission-based compensation for the technicians. While the change implementation at the service centers has had its own challenges (like any change effort) it *has* been a success. The implementation of the service changes required an internal Change Implementation Team, which was mentored by the retail CIT, and eventually the two teams were combined.

An RM gives his perception of this change: "The next big change was the service centers change initiative. We took a lot of the learning from the SOP change effort and applied it. The score on the first services Change Scorecard was 1.7 [using a 5-point scale]. The managers in the service centers were really upset. We had to actively manage their expectations and communicate more. The service centers change effort moved much faster. We brought in GMs from retail to run several of the service centers, too."

The latest challenges taken on by the team have been to work with the leaders responsible for integrating several other companies that Best Buy has acquired in the past few years. The CIT has played a pivotal role in the successful integration of these other organizations.

THE PRICE OF CHANGE IS CONSTANT VIGILANCE

Today, there are mixed opinions on how well the lessons of the experience of the SOP change implementation "took." Here's an opinion from one of the veterans of the first-year CIT: "Our culture is both different and still the same in many ways. We're still very scorecard driven—we have scorecards to keep track of our scorecards. We measure everything. However, in the past we only scorecarded the results. Now we scorecard our ability to adapt our behaviors and our processes, as well as our results. We've grown. But, of course, we still want to be the best." While acknowledging the changes within Best Buy, one executive emphasizes the need for constant attention to sustain important practices: "The elements of the old culture are still around today and are gaining ground again."

Several veterans of the first-year CIT offered their perspectives on how the SOP change effort has had an impact on the company.

> Young people, eighteen to twenty, are given scope to take on major responsibilities and perform at high levels. The company has invested in the relationships with their managers and developing people. People have guidelines and tools to run the business with clear direction. We have an increased ability to be more profitable.

> We're more methodical but still move fast. Our downside is that we still think we know the answers.

> How is it the same? We haven't lost our entrepreneurial spirit and can exert the heroic efforts when needed.

What do we make of these differing opinions? That the dialogue continues and that people are honestly reflecting on and discussing what they perceive. And Best Buy continues to change.

USING THE MAP TO EXPLORE NEW TERRITORY

Is it possible to generalize the map or framework described in this book to other types of organizations? If we keep in mind that the map is not the territory, the answer is yes. The framework—consisting of the head, heart, and hands, as well as the stages of change—was defined and used with other organizations before and after the Best Buy SOP change implementation, but on smaller scales. How to tailor the approach depends on the culture of the organization, the type of business, and the types of change involved. The idea that behavioral change requires an approach that integrates the head, heart, and hands is not new to education and counseling; we certainly cannot claim to have invented it. We *can* claim to have applied it in a different way than we'd seen it applied before.

Would it work with a very different kind of change? We've mentioned that Best Buy is applying the framework to integrate a number of companies that they have acquired, and we've worked in merger/ acquisitions with other clients. But, to consider applying the framework even more generally, we can ask, What elements of the framework and program are universal? A Change Scorecard might not be appropriate to use in some types of organizations or cultures; it might need to be modified, or the organization might require a measuring tool tailored to its own needs. But the need for a quantifiable means of monitoring the progress of the change effort and the need for feedback to assess your progress are universal. These are intrinsic aspects of learning and changing behavior.

In any organization that requires its people to think, problem-solve, and develop good judgment, you will want people who use their heads—people who try to understand why something is important and what, exactly, it consists of. To teach these people and to convince them of the need to change something, you will need to explain to them the "why and what" of the change in ways that can be applied to their own work. Anyone who is committed to her work at all has an emotional investment in her role, job, or career. And when that role, job, or career changes, the person will react emotionally. The heart will be affected. For that reason, any successful change effort needs to engage people's hearts. And, no matter what the work of the organization is—from financial analysis to manufacturing—if people's behaviors need to change, they will need to use their hands. They will need models of what "good" looks like. They will need practice with feedback and coaching, as well as an appropriate alignment of rewards to reinforce their new behaviors.

What about using a Change Implementation Team? Does every change effort require a fully dedicated team of change agents? Maybe not, but any change effort must be led by people who have established credibility with their colleagues in the organization—credibility that includes a proven track record of success and an understanding of the challenges everyone faces. And they will need some degree of autonomy and immunity. (Remember, "To be a successful change agent, you have to act like you have nothing to lose.") Executive sponsorship on a continuing, visible basis will always be important. Change needs leaders—all the way to the top—who are willing to engage in the change process and model openness to feedback and change for their constituencies.

EPILOGUE

No doubt about it, Best Buy has done well as a business. During 2001, in a weak economy struggling to pull out of a recession, earnings jumped more than 40 percent and sales increased 28 percent, to $19.6 billion. Best Buy achieved these results despite the bursting of the inflated technology and dot-com bubbles. And while these results were down from those of the previous year (the final year of one of the longest expansion periods in history), Best Buy clearly outpaced its competitors.

In 2002, Best Buy was named to Business Week's top fifty best-performing S&P 500 companies. However, beginning in July of that year, the company began to face some challenges—from falling short of earnings expectations in the second quarter, to layoffs at corporate headquarters, to negotiations over the renewal of the MSN contract with Microsoft and a decline in the stock price. In September 2002, Best Buy decided to put off for eighteen months any international expansion or acquisition, to cut costs amid weak consumer spending. It also froze corporate hiring and delayed other initiatives. In October, CEO and Co-Chairman Brad Anderson described this turn of events: "Best Buy has enjoyed an uninterrupted series of enormous successes in the past five to six years. The company has warned Wall Street that the next six months will continue to be very difficult. And it is expecting the next fiscal year also to prove challenging."

Daunting? Not really. Historically, Best Buy has come through the toughest times to emerge stronger than before. "I'd much rather come into an environment in challenge," said Brad Anderson. "As a leader, it is going to be much easier to move the bar farther when we know we need to move the bar." It's at times like these that the unquenchable can-do essence of Best Buy shines the brightest.

APPENDIX A
An Excerpt from *A Field Guide to Implementing the SOP*

When faced with implementing the SOP, many people had the natural response, "Why change?" Although the new processes and expected behaviors were described in precise detail, the underlying rationale and incentive to change were not as clear. We sought to bridge this gap by creating *A Field Guide to Implementing the SOP*, which identified and discussed the important implications of the changes—both for the company and for the individual employee.

In this excerpt from the *Field Guide*, we provide the following information for each discipline (inventory, operations, merchandising and media, and sales).

1. Why we have the operating platform
2. What's important about it
3. What it can do for me, the employee

INVENTORY
Why the SOP: The Big Picture

- We get a lot of merchandise, in different size loads, in different forms, and at different times of the day.

- We need to know what we've received and what we have on hand. Why?

- To get merchandise to customers who want to buy it.
- To track merchandise and to reduce or eliminate missing merchandise.
- To know when to order more merchandise.

- We want to prevent accidents involving employees, customers, or both.
- We want to help new or transferring employees come up to speed quickly and efficiently.
- We want to be productive and efficient.

What's Important About It

- To receive and unload according to a schedule and a routine.
  - People know what's expected of them and in what time frame.
  - People learn their jobs and can concentrate on the task at hand without distraction.
- To sort and stage merchandise in a way that makes it easy and efficient to get it onto the floor; for safety's sake, take merchandise out only when store is closed.
- To focus someone on tracking merchandise and controlling missing merchandise.
  - To get merchandise to customers who want to buy it.
  - To track merchandise and to reduce/eliminate missing merchandise.
  - To know when to order more merchandise.

What It Can Do for Me

- Make my job safer.
- Make my job easier to learn and easier to teach.
- Save effort and avoid wasting my time and energy.
- Reduce searching for merchandise and/or finger pointing.

OPERATIONS

Why the SOP: The Big Picture

- What goes on at the front of the store makes a big impression on our customers, and there is a *lot* going on there.
- Customers get confused about what lines to stand in and frustrated that they have to be in line.
- We handle a lot of complex business when we're providing customer service by arranging for financing or returns/exchanges/repairs.
- Making "saves" makes us or saves us a lot of money—money that can go into upgrading employee skills, expanding into new stores that create job and promotion opportunities, etc.
- Generally, when people are at the front of the store and dealing with operations, they are already Best Buy customers. It is important to keep them as customers and not turn them off.

What's Important About It

- Seeing things from the customer's perspective.
  - Organized: Is it clear or confusing for them to navigate the lines and find the right one for them?
  - Efficient: Does it look like employees are taking customers seriously and paying attention to their needs?
  - Professional: Or, does it look like people are standing around behind the counter talking or doing non-customer-directed tasks? Does the phone keep ringing and ringing?
- Doing what it takes to make all possible saves: refer all customers to either the in-store tech or PC tech.
- Splitting the specialist roles so that all functions are covered competently.
  - Financing: People haven't bought the merchandise yet. Long lines or the perception that employees don't care or don't know how to do the job can send customers right out the door without buying.

– Returns: These are disappointed customers who are spending time doing something that's an extra chore. Some of them may find it hard to return things.

- We want to keep them as customers over the long haul.
- They would like to leave with whatever they bought actually working.

What It Can Do for Me

- Reduce the amount of conflict I have to deal with—conflict with either customers or co-workers; reduce finger pointing.
- Make my job less confusing; make it easier to focus on what I need to do.
- Help me to grow my skills and confidence.
- Make my job easier to learn and easier to teach.
- Save effort and avoid wasting my time and energy.

SALES

Why the SOP: The Big Picture

- Customers come into our stores looking for a wide variety of merchandise. Most need some assistance; many need a lot.
- We stock a huge assortment of merchandise. Much of it is technically sophisticated.
- We need to "sort" customers according to their needs and then get them the right kind of assistance.
- To do this, we need to know where to quickly find the salespeople who can
  - Answer the customers' questions.
  - Help them make the best buying decision to meet their needs.
- Get to the customer.
- Reduce missing merchandise by using zoning.

What's Important About It

- Talking to customers to get a picture of what they're looking for.
- Translating what customers say into who would be the best salesperson to work with them.
  - "Quick-serve" and "full-serve" are ways of translating the customers' needs into who can best help them.
  - Taking it a step further: knowing what salespeople are experts in what merchandise and getting the customers to them.
- To connect the customer with the right salesperson for him or her, you need to know where to find that salesperson.
  - This is why *zones* are important.
  - To work, the zones need to be defined and used consistently.
- When the floor get busy, zoning becomes even more important. To learn zoning, and make it a habit, we need to use it at all times, not just when it's really busy.
- Teamwork.
  - Hand-offs between salespeople need to be smooth and professional.
  - Coordination and cooperation with other departments (disciplines) are essential to stocking the right merchandise, keeping it organized and neat, and completing the sale.
- Performance SKUs: Some of our merchandise is very high value to the customer and makes a higher profit for us. When the customer asks for our recommendation, we should recommend the Performance SKUs.
- Accessories: Customers often don't know what accessories to buy. Educate the customer as to what accessories will add to the functionality, ease of use, or fun factor of their purchase.
- Warranties: Customers win and so do we.
- Know what your personal sales goals are for each day: warranties, accessories, etc.
- Schedule experienced, senior salespeople at peak times: nights and weekends.

- Gardening: We all need to take responsibility for how our departments look and know where merchandise is located.

What It Can Do for Me

- Increase my sales and technical skills by learning from other salespeople who may be more experienced than I am in some areas.
- Help me focus on interacting with and selling to the customer.
- Make and keep our customers satisfied, so they're more pleasant to deal with.
- Increase my sense of competence and self-confidence.
- Make my job easier to learn and easier to teach.
- Save effort and avoid wasting my time and energy, especially that spent hunting down other salespeople when I need them.
- Help me learn from other people who may have experience that I don't have.
- Allow me to take pride in a good-looking department. Help me stay in touch with the products in my department. If I do my part to help merchandising, they can do their part to help me.

MERCHANDISING AND MEDIA

Why the SOP: The Big Picture

- The job of merchandising in our stores has grown increasingly difficult; it requires really good merchandising skills and focused concentration.
  - People need time to learn how to do their jobs.
  - People need to be able to complete their tasks.
  - Consistency and accuracy in signage are necessary for sales and legal reasons.
  - Being able to plan the days or week ahead on a regular basis allows us to manage our business efficiently and make the best use of our resources.

- Maintaining a safe workplace in the midst of the pressures of running an intense business is crucial.

What's Important About It

- Scheduling the work on a daily and weekly basis to make the best use of time and resources.
- Sticking to the priorities set for the day.
- Taking responsibility for your area or department: pricing, planograms, etc.
- Keeping the overall store needs constantly in mind: coordinating and cooperating with other disciplines so the entire store wins.
- Organizing and sorting media and other types of merchandise efficiently.

What It Can Do for Me

- Get my job done without stopping and starting.
- Grow skills as a merchandiser.
- Increase my sense of competency and of making a real contribution.
- Help increase my and others' efficiency.
- Give me a picture of how each week will unfold, allowing me to plan ahead.
- Give me most Saturdays off.

INTERDISCIPLINARY WORK

Why the SOP: The Big Picture

- We work together and help each other; because that's the only way we can succeed in implementing the operating platform and winning in our stores.
- It's not enough just to play your own instrument well; you have to get the whole band playing together well.

- You actually make work for other departments when you don't support them. On the other hand, your jobs will be easier if you support each other.

What's Important About It

- Hand-offs of activity between disciplines. Find out how to make this work well for the disciplines you interact with.

- Teamwork in merchandising and sales. The boundaries may never be totally clear, because your responsibilities overlap.

What It Can Do for Me

- I will have more fun working on a team that is pulling together.

- My job will be easier when I have the support of others and give it.

APPENDIX B
Embedding Knowledge and Know-How in a Change Scorecard

ORGANIZATIONAL CULTURE: BEHAVIORS, VALUES, AND ASSUMPTIONS

An extensive array of behaviors, beliefs, values, and assumptions make up what is called corporate culture. Figure 16 shows one way of conceptualizing organizational culture and its tacit elements. Challenging out-of-date assumptions, reinforcing core values, bringing unconscious behaviors to a conscious level, and so on, are all ingredients that can be incorporated into a Change Scorecard.

ORGANIZATION AND CULTURE-SPECIFIC KNOWLEDGE

The Best Buy culture needed to evolve from "making it up as you go" to a more disciplined and systematic way of working. But management clearly did not want and had not hired people who would be content to blindly follow orders. They wanted and needed to keep on board and engaged those people who were curious, quick, and able to think on their feet. How do you convey that balance between discipline and what was called "being a cowboy" in the Best Buy lingo?

Figure 16

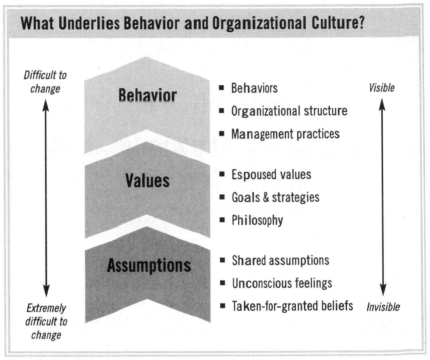

How do you move the organization toward greater discipline while keeping alive what had been at the heart of Best Buy's success— the can-do spirit and innovation of its people? And, how do you get that across in a set of questions you ask as part of a scorecard? This is just one example of the subtle challenges you face when consciously embedding tacit messages and lessons in a Change Scorecard. Following is one of the early scorecard items for the Best Buy merchandising team that makes the distinction between exercising good judgment and "cowboying it." The question is targeted at someone in store manage-

Example of Scorecard Item

Merchandising questions

"How closely do you follow the (merchandising) planner?"

Listen for: Critical thinking in applying the spirit of the platform vs. cowboyism. May vary with the size of store.

ment who is responsible for following the guides issued by corporate headquarters that describe how to arrange merchandise in the store.

Here is another scorecard item that conveys the sense that it's okay to adapt the specifics of the operational change to fit a particular situation, but it should be done mindfully.

Example of Scorecard Item

> In talking to other people, we have found that some stores have adapted the SOP slightly to fit their needs. How have you adapted the platform to fit your needs in this store?
>
> *I listen for the following:*
>
> *– Have they adapted it at all?*
>
> *– Do they understand the implications of any adaptation?*
>
> *– Are they implementing the spirit of the platform?*

Another challenge may be to address some of the identified development needs of the organization as a whole. One example would be "Learning and using the thinking skills needed for effective problem solving and for making the most of opportunities." Such thinking skills include the following.

- How to recognize and analyze situations and opportunities.
- How to think more systemically. For example, when making a decision ask yourself, How would that action affect the rest of the store or the company? Making that action work well would require collaboration from another function. How would I gain their support? What might be some delayed consequences or side effects of that action?

Next is an example question intended for Best Buy store managers that emphasizes using analytical thinking in problem solving. Just below the scorecard item are some probing questions that the rater can use to help the person think through her answer, without giving the answers away.

Example of Scorecard Item

Problem solving

1. You learn that your warranty numbers are the lowest in the region. What do you do?

Listen for the following:

— Do they mention warranty training?

— Do they mention quick-serve and full-serve?

— Do they review their zoning?

— Do they mention head count/staffing?

— Is other management involved?.

— Do they mention communication and coaching for supervisors and employees?

— Are other teams besides sales involved?

Probing questions:

- In thinking through your answer, what did you take into account? Or, What can you tell me about your thinking on this?

- Anything else you'd like to add?

INDUSTRY-SPECIFIC KNOWLEDGE

The two examples on the following page are quite technical and specific to best practices. Both questions are specialized for people working in retail operations. These are people you might encounter if you were returning an item to the store.

Both of these examples are derived from the nitty-gritty of the change at Best Buy. At one level, the change—introducing the SOP to the stores—was about introducing standardized, good retailing practices. So the questions are grounded in the concrete operational processes that people should be using under the SOP. However, the questions are also designed to emphasize analytical thinking and problem-solving skills.

Example of Scorecard Item

Operations questions

1. What are three reasons you should find a technician when customers bring back problem products?

Listen for the following:

− Do they understand the purpose behind the principle?

2. Why are "saves" important? How do they have on impact on the store?

Can ask this question of an in-store tech, a PC tech, and a service counter representative to assess each persopn's knowledge and how they work as a team.

ORGANIZATIONAL STRUCTURE: LEVELS AND FUNCTIONS

Do different levels within the company have different roles to play? Are those roles going to change? If so, in the Change Scorecard you need to address why they are changing and how they will be changing. For example, within Best Buy, the SOP Change Scorecard had components that were applicable only to store management. These components brought the managers' attention to the key issues they needed to be focusing on to make the change successful. Did they understand the why and what of the change well enough to explain it to someone else? Did they grasp what it takes to be a leader of change?

What about functions? Do you develop different components of the scorecard for different functions? Usually, the answer is yes, but it depends on the type of change involved. Within Best Buy, there were employees from four different store functions who needed to learn new and different ways to do their job: sales, merchandising, operations, and inventory. The SOP Change Scorecard therefore was designed with different sections that were to be applied in the appropriate function. There were also some things that everyone in these functions needed to learn, such as getting the big picture of the overall functioning of the store. The items that pertained to issues (such as teamwork) that applied to everyone in the store were asked of all people, regardless of function or level.

CHANGE MANAGEMENT KNOW-HOW

Following are some questions that are designed to tap into a person's capacity to effectively lead and manage change.

Example of Scorecard Item

Change leadership

1. Describe the ups and downs of how the change has had an impact on you.

Look for the following:

– *Can this person manage him/herself—first—through the change process and deal honestly with the impact of the change on him/herself?*

2. Give an example of a discussion you've had with an employee to help him/her deal with the change.

Look for the following:

– *Can this person help others as they deal with the change?*

– *Does this person discuss pluses and minuses, allow objections and work through them?*

ADDRESSING CHANGE-SPECIFIC ISSUES

When the SOP was first introduced to the stores, people were assigned to one of four broad functions, or disciplines: sales, merchandising, operations, and inventory. We heard rumblings of a breakdown in teamwork in the stores and increasing friction between the sales and merchandising teams for a few months before we got involved with the change effort. As we explored what was happening, we found that the clear demarcations between disciplines, as well as some perceived inequities in status and pay (remember the heart) were causing problems in operations and procedures that required people to think in terms of the whole store system. Tasks were not being done because of the attitude, "It's not in my job description," and things were falling through the cracks.

This is an example of an organizational metaphor taken too far. The notion of an organization as a machine is the basis of concepts such as organizational structure, function, roles, and so on. These are important concepts that should not be ignored, but they are not sufficient to understand or change an organization. People are not parts of a machine, and when they work together, they do not work as a machine. To start addressing the issue of bickering teams within the store, we introduced the following scorecard items on the first iteration of the Change Scorecard.

Example of Scorecard Item

Interactions & Teamwork

1. Describe the key points of interaction between and/or teamwork among the four major departments.

2. What are the most common roadblocks to effective, efficient interaction between departments?

3. How are these roadblocks best overcome?

Since we know that measuring something sends a message and is an intervention itself, simply bringing these issues to the attention of the people in the stores and expecting them to be able to answer the questions was an intervention.

BEHAVIORAL ANCHORS

Scorecard examples 9 through 20 show some behavioral anchors that were used in the SOP Change Scorecard.

Scorecard Example 9

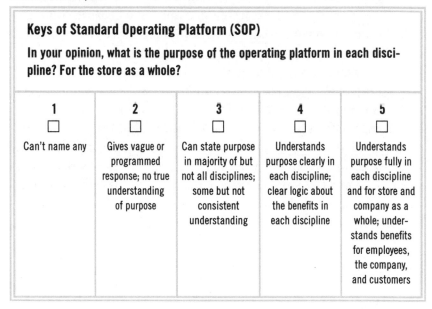

Scorecard Example 10

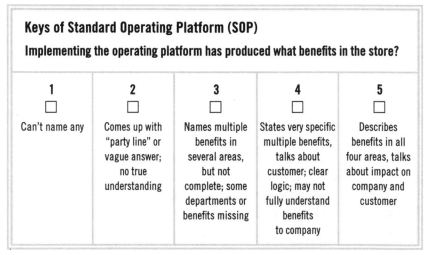

Scorecard Example 11

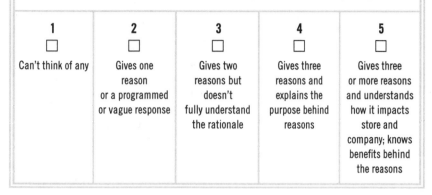

Operations questions

What are three reasons why you should find a technician when customers bring back problem products?

Listen for the following: Do they understand the purpose behind the principle?

1	2	3	4	5
☐	☐	☐	☐	☐
Can't think of any	Gives one reason or a programmed or vague response	Gives two reasons but doesn't fully understand the rationale	Gives three reasons and explains the purpose behind reasons	Gives three or more reasons and understands how it impacts store and company; knows benefits behind the reasons

Scorecard Example 12

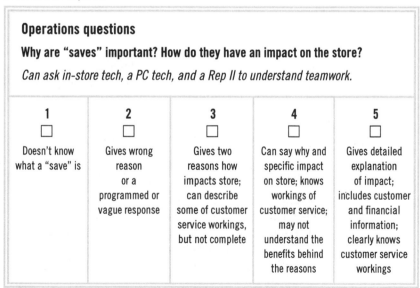

Operations questions

Why are "saves" important? How do they have an impact on the store?

Can ask in-store tech, a PC tech, and a Rep II to understand teamwork.

1	2	3	4	5
☐	☐	☐	☐	☐
Doesn't know what a "save" is	Gives wrong reason or a programmed or vague response	Gives two reasons how impacts store; can describe some of customer service workings, but not complete	Can say why and specific impact on store; knows workings of customer service; may not understand the benefits behind the reasons	Gives detailed explanation of impact; includes customer and financial information; clearly knows customer service workings

Scorecard Example 13

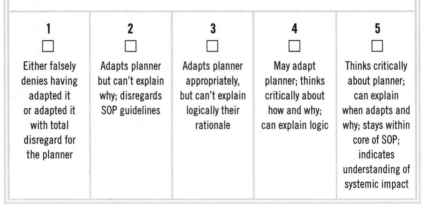

Merchandising questions

How closely do you follow the (merchandising) planner?

Listen for: Critical thinking in applying the spirit of the platform vs. cowboyism. May vary with the size of store.

1	2	3	4	5
☐	☐	☐	☐	☐
Either falsely denies having adapted it or adapted it with total disregard for the planner	Adapts planner but can't explain why; disregards SOP guidelines	Adapts planner appropriately, but can't explain logically their rationale	May adapt planner; thinks critically about how and why; can explain logic	Thinks critically about planner; can explain when adapts and why; stays within core of SOP; indicates understanding of systemic impact

Scorecard Example 14

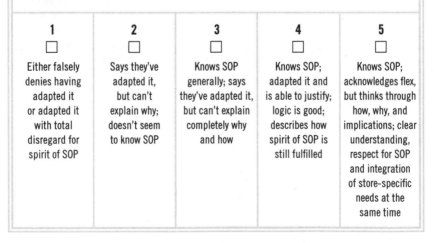

Operations questions

In talking to other people, we have found that some stores have adapted the SOP slightly to fit their needs. How have you adapted the platform to fit your needs in this store?

Listen for the following: Have they adapted it at all? Do they understand the implications of any adaptation? Are they implementing the spirit of the platform?

1	2	3	4	5
☐	☐	☐	☐	☐
Either falsely denies having adapted it or adapted it with total disregard for spirit of SOP	Says they've adapted it, but can't explain why; doesn't seem to know SOP	Knows SOP generally; says they've adapted it, but can't explain completely why and how	Knows SOP; adapted it and is able to justify; logic is good; describes how spirit of SOP is still fulfilled	Knows SOP; acknowledges flex, but thinks through how, why, and implications; clear understanding, respect for SOP and integration of store-specific needs at the same time

Scorecard Example 15

Problem solving

You learn that your warranty numbers are the lowest in the region. What do you do?

Listen for the following:

— Do they mention warranty training?

— Do they mention quick-serve and full-serve?

— Do they review their zoning?

— Do they mention head count/staffing?

— Is other management invovled?

— Do they mention communication and coaching for supervisors and employees?

— Are other teams besides sales involved?

1	2	3	4	5
☐	☐	☐	☐	☐
Can't answer question	Gives a superficial answer, reference to one or no elements, or mentions one of them; programmed responses	Answer indicates they've thought it through, mentions at least three of above elements; some of rationale may be incomplete	Answer indicates they've thought it through, mentions at least four of above elements; logic is clear, including one of the following: zoning or quick-serve and full-serve	Incorporates all elements listed above and puts them together; explains own "rules of thumb" for when it's OK to adjust and how to teach this to employees; systemic under-standing clear; works proactively to prevent this from being a challenge for floor

Probing questions:
In thinking through your answer, what did you take into account? Or, What can you tell me about your thinking on this? Anything else you'd like to add?

Scorecard Example 16

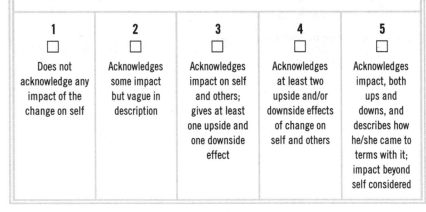

Change leadership

Describe the ups and downs of how the change has had an impact on you.

Look for the following: Can this person manage him/herself—first—through the change process and deal honestly with the impact of change on him/herself?

1	2	3	4	5
☐	☐	☐	☐	☐
Does not acknowledge any impact of the change on self	Acknowledges some impact but vague in description	Acknowledges impact on self and others; gives at least one upside and one downside effect	Acknowledges at least two upside and/or downside effects of change on self and others	Acknowledges impact, both ups and downs, and describes how he/she came to terms with it; impact beyond self considered

Scorecard Example 17

Change leadership

Give an example of a discussion you've had with an employee to help him/her deal with the change.

Look for the following: Can this person help others as they deal with the change? Does this person discuss pluses and minuses, allow objections and work through them?

1	2	3	4	5
☐	☐	☐	☐	☐
Cannot give example of discussing gain/loss or impact of change with subordinate	Gives example of a one-way discussion with employee	Can give example; limited to either upside or downside, or limited depth; allows limited input from employee	Gives in-depth example of either upside or downside; allows employee to air objections; two-way communication is noted	Gives one in-depth example where both ups and downs were discussed; allows employees to air objections and helps work through them

Scorecard Example 18

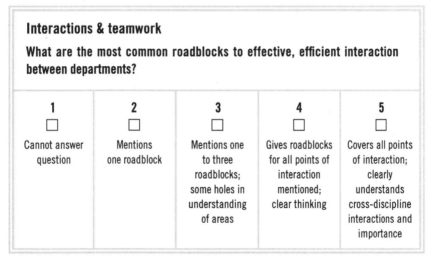

Interactions & teamwork

Describe the key points of interaction between and/or teamwork among the four major departments.

1 ☐	2 ☐	3 ☐	4 ☐	5 ☐
Can't answer question at all	Describes one point of interaction or teamwork, but has a vague or programmed response	Describes at least two points of interaction or teamwork; understanding of some disciplines incomplete	Describes four points of interaction or teamwork with specific examples	Describes points of interaction between all areas; gives specific examples of clear understanding of whole store flow

Scorecard Example 19

Interactions & teamwork

What are the most common roadblocks to effective, efficient interaction between departments?

1 ☐	2 ☐	3 ☐	4 ☐	5 ☐
Cannot answer question	Mentions one roadblock	Mentions one to three roadblocks; some holes in understanding of areas	Gives roadblocks for all points of interaction mentioned; clear thinking	Covers all points of interaction; clearly understands cross-discipline interactions and importance

Scorecard Example 20

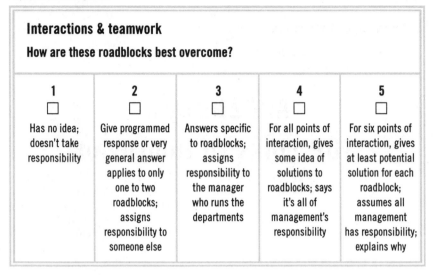

Interactions & teamwork

How are these roadblocks best overcome?

1	2	3	4	5
☐	☐	☐	☐	☐
Has no idea; doesn't take responsibility	Give programmed response or very general answer applies to only one to two roadblocks; assigns responsibility to someone else	Answers specific to roadblocks; assigns responsibility to the manager who runs the departments	For all points of interaction, gives some idea of solutions to roadblocks; says it's all of management's responsibility	For six points of interaction, gives at least potential solution for each roadblock; assumes all management has responsibility; explains why

APPENDIX C
SOP Links to Improved Business Results

OUR APPROACH

We evaluated the relationship between SOP scorecard results for each store and the business results of those stores. The results were evaluated nine times over a four-year period from April 1997 to February 2001. We calculated Pearson correlations between scorecard results and the following set of business outcomes.

1. Revenue and net operating profit by store.

2. Employee survey results for each store over three time periods, 1998, 1999, and 2000. An overall favorable response variable summarized how positively the employees viewed the store.

3. Annual employee turnover by store for exempt, non-exempt, full-time, and part-time employees. Turnover is the ratio of the average terminations divided by average head count.

4. Stock price for the month in which the scorecard data was collected.

The scores from the SOP scorecard were converted to z-scores. The average SOP scorecard was calculated by taking the average of the z-score of the overall store averages from 1997 to 2001. Conversion to z-scores allowed the combination of pre-1998 data with later data since the metric was different while the later instrument was scored on a

Table 51

Correlations of Scorecards with Business Results

Criteria	Dimensions				
	Sales	Operations	Inventory	Merchan-dising	Leader-ship
Overall operating profit	.019	.138[3]	.157[3]	.203[3]	.215[3]
Overall turnover[1] (all employees)	-.291[3]	-.243[3]	-.138[2]	-.195[3]	-.189[3]
Overall turnover[1] (all employees)	-.291[3]	-.243[3]	-.138[2]	-.195[3]	-.189[3]
Overall exempt turnover	-.298[3]	-.323[3]	-.058	-.281[3]	-.234[3]
Overall non-exempt turnover	-.193[2]	-.290[3]	-.128	-.210[3]	-.157[2]
Overall part-time turnover	-.331[3]	-.186[3]	-.107	-.165[2]	-.151[2]

[1]Turnover is the ratio of the average terminations divided by average head count
[2] $p < .05$
[3] $p < .01$

100-point scale. Additionally, the dimensions rated were different between the two instruments.

SCORECARD AND BUSINESS RESULTS

Table 51, above, lists correlations of scorecards with business results.

Scorecard results correlate with store profitability and turnover. Further support for the validity of the scorecards comes from the fact that, as expected, they did not predict the total revenues of the stores. Store revenues are more a function of the store's size (square footage), location (more or less competition), and use of advertising (which affects all stores in a geographic area, regardless of their individual effectiveness).

EMPLOYEE TURNOVER: SCORECARDS VERSUS EMPLOYEE SURVEY

Table 52 lists correlations of scorecards and employee survey data with business results.

Table 52

Correlations of Scorecards and Employee Survey Data

Criteria	Dimensions	
	Average Scorecard	Average Survey
Overall turnover (all employees)	-.312	-.057
Overall exempt turnover	-.353	-.128
Overall non-exempt turnover	-.273	-.145
Overall part-time turnover	-.283	.003

[1]Significant correlations ($p < .05$)

A regression analysis was conducted predicting overall turnover from SOP scorecard and Viewpoint data. The model was significant ($R^2 = .124$, $F = 14.629$, $p < .000$). Only SOP scorecard was a significant predictor of overall turnover ($t = -5.338$, $p < .000$). The results of the employee survey did not add to the prediction in this model.

SCORECARD AND STOCK PRICE

Additional analyses were performed to compare the average SOP scorecard with the stock price over the seven observation periods. The stock price at the end of the month in which the scorecard was measured was correlated with the average SOP scorecard. As we have noted before, correlations are not statistically definitive proof of causality. However, the resulting correlation was surprisingly strong ($r = .884$, $p < .000$) and in the expected direction. That is, the stock price moved up and down with the average of the SOP scorecards. Table 53 shows the results of the correlations.

Table 53

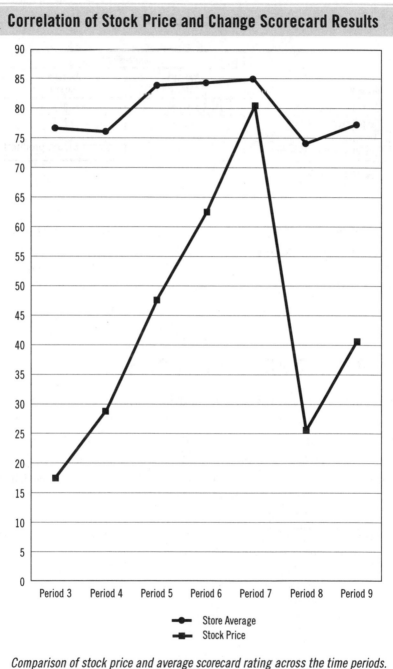

Comparison of stock price and average scorecard rating across the time periods.

INDEX